Critical
Childhood
Studies

ALSO AVAILABLE FROM BLOOMSBURY

Early Childhood Theories and Contemporary Issues, Mine Conkbayir and
Christine Pascal
Reflective Teaching in Early Education, 2nd edition, Jennifer Colwell
and Amanda Ince with Helen Bradford, Helen Edwards, Julian Grenier,
Eleanor Kitto, Eunice Lumsden, Catriona McDonald, Juliet Mickelburgh,
Mary Moloney, Sheila Nutkins, Ioanna Palaiologou, Deborah Price and
Rebecca Swindells
Why Do Teachers Need to Know About Diverse Learning Needs?,
edited by Sue Soan
Why Do Teachers Need to Know About Child Development?, edited by
Daryl Maisey and Verity Campbell-Barr
Reimagining Childhood Studies, edited by Spyros Spyrou, Rachel Rosen and
Daniel Thomas Cook
Historical Perspectives on Infant Care and Development, Amanda Norman
Observing Children From Birth to 6, 5th edition, Carole Sharman,
Wendy Cross and Diana Vennis

Critical
Childhood
Studies

Global Perspectives

**E. Kay M. Tisdall,
John M. Davis, Deborah Fry,
Kristina Konstantoni,
Marlies Kustatscher,
M. Catherine Maternowska
and Laura Weiner**

BLOOMSBURY ACADEMIC
NEW YORK • LONDON • OXFORD • NEW DELHI • SYDNEY

BLOOMSBURY ACADEMIC
Bloomsbury Publishing Plc
50 Bedford Square, London, WC1B 3DP, UK
1385 Broadway, New York, NY 10018, USA
29 Earlsfort Terrace, Dublin 2, Ireland

BLOOMSBURY, BLOOMSBURY ACADEMIC and the Diana logo are trademarks of
Bloomsbury Publishing Plc

First published in Great Britain 2023

Cover design by Holly Capper
Cover image © Stephen Simpson / Getty Images

A catalogue record for this book is available from the British Library.

A catalog record for this book is available from the Library of Congress.

ISBN: HB: 978-1-3501-6321-8
PB: 978-1-3501-6320-1
ePDF: 978-1-3501-6322-5
eBook: 978-1-3501-6323-2

Typeset by Deanta Global Publishing Services, Chennai, India
Printed and bound in Great Britain

To find out more about our authors and books visit www.bloomsbury.com and
sign up for our newsletters.

Contents

Figures

Tables

Acknowledgements

This book draws on our many collaborations and interactions with children, young people and adult professionals across numerous continents and in a variety of settings. We are indebted to them for the learning and inspiration that these projects have generated and have done our best to reflect this rich content in the chapters of this book.

We are grateful to all the students, practitioners and researchers who have taken part in our childhood studies programmes and courses over the past decades and whose critical engagement and reflections have shaped our own understanding and development of childhood studies.

We started off this book journey by considering a critical reader. We subsequently decided it was more practical to write our own. We want to acknowledge all those colleagues who kindly responded in 2016 to our initial invite to know what key texts they used in their own teaching.

We would like to thank all those colleagues who have generously contributed to this book by sharing quotations and insights from their work or by providing critical feedback on drafts: Mohammed Alruzzi, Liliana Arias-Urueña, Usang Marian Assim, Ruth Barnes, Simon Bateson, Caralyn Blaisdell, Erica Burman, Parise Carmichael-Murphy, Loritta Chan, Ruth Davidson, Mariel Deluna, Chandrika Devarakonda, Ruth Edmonds, Akwugo Emejulu, Laura Hill, Charlotte Leonard-Wakefield, Fiona Morrison, Harla Octarra, Karina Padilla, Kirrily Pells, Alina Potts, Samantha Punch, Kirsten Sandberg, Pavithra Sarma, Morgan Tudor and Yan Zhu.

Our contacts at Bloomsbury Academic have provided continuous support for this book, and we are thankful to the reviewers for their invaluable feedback.

Contributors

Sarada Balagopalan is an associate professor at Rutgers University in the Department of Childhood Studies. Her research broadly focuses on postcolonial childhoods and often combines archival and ethnographic research. She has published on child labour, children's rights and schooling in India. She is the author of *Inhabiting 'Childhood': Children, Labour and Schooling in Postcolonial India* (2014).

Erica Burman (University of Manchester, UK) is well known as a critical developmental psychologist and methodologist specializing in innovative and activist qualitative research. Her research has focused on critical developmental and educational psychology, feminist and postcolonial theory, childhood studies, and critical mental health practice (particularly around gender and cultural issues). Her recent work addresses the connections between emotions, mental health and social (as well as individual) change, in particular as anchored by representations of, and appeals to, childhood. She has co-led transnational research projects on conceptualizing and challenging state and interpersonal violence in relation to minority women and children, on educational and mental health impacts of poverty and 'austerity', on superdiversity and 'traditional' Muslim healing practices, and she is a co-investigator on a cross-national project exploring post-socialist childhoods. She sees debates about children and childhood as central to current theories and practices around decolonization.

John M. Davis is Professor of Education at the University of Strathclyde. John was previously Professor of Childhood Inclusion at the University of Edinburgh. His research focuses on the areas of childhood, disability, inclusion and social justice. John's research has utilized participatory childhood research methods to support parents, children and young people to contribute to creative processes of change in education, early years, health and social services. He is adept at promoting innovative approaches in integrated and multi-professional children and family services.

Deborah Fry is Professor of International Child Protection Research at Moray House School of Education and Sport, Director of Data at Childlight – Global Child Safety Institute at the University of Edinburgh, and a child protection expert and social epidemiologist. Deborah Fry undertakes primary research to measure the magnitude, drivers and consequences of child sexual exploitation and abuse, barriers and enablers to appropriate responses and the effectiveness of existing interventions. Deborah is also the academic lead for the University's Long-Term Agreement with UNICEF on child protection research, administrative data, and data training.

Kristina Konstantoni is Senior Lecturer in Childhood Studies at Moray House School of Education and Sport at the University of Edinburgh. Kristina is a member of Childhood and Youth Studies, the co-founder and co-lead of the Early Years Research, Policy and Practice Group, the co-director and co-founder of the Anti-Racist Early Years Collective and a member of RACE. ED. Kristina's research interests include children's rights, childhoods and intersectionality; children's human rights in informal learning public play spaces like community and business play-cafés; and children and young people's human rights and participation in research, practice and policy-making. She works both in Scotland and with cross-national partners in such places as Greece, Brazil, Eswatini, South Africa, Palestine, and Germany.

Marlies Kustatscher is Senior Lecturer in Childhood Studies at Moray House School of Education and Sport at the University of Edinburgh. Marlies Kustatscher is a member of Childhood and Youth Studies and a co-convenor of the Race and Inclusivity in Global Education Network (RIGEN). Her research interests include childhood and intersectionality, children's rights and participation, and emotions. Her work draws on interdisciplinary, arts-based approaches to activism and change with children and young people. Marlies currently works on projects on these themes with colleagues in Brazil, Colombia, Eswatini, Palestine, Scotland and South Africa.

M. Catherine Maternowska is Professor of Violence Prevention for Young People at Moray House School of Education and Sport at the University of Edinburgh, UK. She is a medical anthropologist working in the field of public health. For the last three decades, she has focused on structural determinants of health and violence as well as violence prevention and response for both children and women, including how best to provide quality services where human and financial resources are scarce. Her experience with violence prevention survey work, programming and practice, evaluation and policymaking spans four continents (Americas, Africa, Asia and Europe).

Tendai Nhenga is the director of the Child Rights Research Centre and dean of the School of Law, Africa University, Zimbabwe. Her research interests focus on violence against children and child labour. She has published, among others, on the application of international law on child labour in an African context and provides an overview of the law informing the rights of children in Zimbabwe. Tendai has conducted several collaborative implementation child-related researches with UNICEF, University of Edinburgh, Porticus, London School of Hygiene and Tropical Medicine, Academic Research Centre; University of Zimbabwe, Women's University in Africa, Zimbabwe on, inter alia: the Social Determinants of Violence against Children; Prevalence of School-Based Violence in Zimbabwe; Exploring children's formal help-seeking behaviour for violence in Zimbabwe; an interrupted time-series analysis on the trends in help-seeking for violence against children in Zimbabwe during the COVID-19 lockdowns, Access to essential health care services in Zimbabwe during COVID-19.

Irene Rizzini is a professor at the Pontifical Catholic University of Rio de Janeiro, Brazil (PUC-Rio), and director of the International Center for Research and Policy on Childhood (CIESPI) at PUC-Rio. Professor Rizzini has been focusing on various issues of rights violations, particularly children living in situations of vulnerability such as poverty, violence, urban slums, children and youth in institutions and living or working on the streets. She has also conducted studies on family support structures, children with mental and developmental disabilities, children in the juvenile justice system, and children and young people´s activism and their right to participation. Her most recent books are *Entre a casa, as ruas e as instituições* (Between home, the streets and institutions for children and youth (2021) and *Crianças e adolescentes em conexão com a rua: pesquisas e políticas públicas* (Street connected children and youth: Research and public policies (2019)).

E. Kay M. Tisdall is Professor of Childhood Policy, Childhood and Youth Studies at Moray House School of Education and Sport at the University of Edinburgh. Kay Tisdall's policy, academic and teaching work is centred on childhood studies and children's human rights. She undertakes collaborative research with children, young people and adults on areas such as children affected by domestic abuse, family law, inclusive pedagogy for young children, young people's mental health, and children's participation and activism. She is involved in a number of partnership projects, with teams in countries ranging from Brazil, Canada, Eswatini, India, Palestine to South Africa.

Professor Amanda Third (PhD) is a professorial research fellow in the Institute for Culture and Society at Western Sydney University, co-director of the Young and Resilient Research Centre, research stream co-lead in the Centre for Resilient and Inclusive Societies (Victorian government), and faculty associate in the Berkman Klein Center for Internet and Society at Harvard. An international expert in child-centred, participatory research, her work investigates children's technology practices, focusing on marginalized groups and rights-based approaches. She has led child-centred projects to understand children's experiences of the digital age in over seventy countries, working with partners across corporate, government and not-for-profit sectors and children and young people themselves. Professor Third is the lead author of: *Young People in Digital Society: Control/Shift* (Palgrave, 2019); *Our Rights in the Digital World: A Report on the Children's Consultations to Inform UNCRC General Comment 25* (5Rights Foundation/WSU, 2021); *Young and Online: Children's Perspectives on Life in the Digital Age* (WSU/ UNICEF, 2017); and *Children's Rights in the Digital Age: A Download from Children around the World* (Young and Well CRC/UNICEF, 2014). She co-authored the *UNCRC General Comment 25 on Children's Rights in relation to the Digital Environment*.

Laura Weiner is a PhD candidate at Moray House School of Education and Sport at the University of Edinburgh. Her doctoral research explores how young activists construct skills, knowledge and values developed in youth activist group spaces. Her research interests include children and young people's activism and participation, civic and citizenship education, informal learning spaces and equity in education.

1

Introduction
Childhood Studies, a Welcoming Field

Laura Weiner and John M. Davis

Chapter Outline

Introduction

Childhood studies has always been an eclectic and welcoming field. The field's scholars and practitioners hail from a variety of **cultures**, countries, professional backgrounds and academic **disciplines** to form 'new' and 'improved' understandings of a very specific point of time during our lives (childhood). We wish to carry on that warm tradition and welcome you to this text. We hope it will be the start to a fascinating and liberating journey.

The **interdisciplinary** academic area of childhood studies is ever-expanding. With around 26 per cent of the world's population under the age of fifteen (and with some countries having nearly 50 per cent of their population under eighteen), **childhood** is not a minority concern for international, national and local governance and accompanying services and provision (Szmigiera 2021). There is a corresponding growth in research interest areas, assisted by the international focus on the different stages of childhood (e.g. early years – OECD 2015; childhood – UNICEF 2015; adolescence – UN Committee on the Rights of the Child 2016). This expanded interest and relevance have brought many new academics, practitioners and children to the field, and may be part of the reason you have chosen this book.

In keeping with this international growth, this book has four central aims:

1. Provide an 'advanced-level' text on critical childhood studies which explores contradictions, false **dichotomies** and 'old' theory in a new light.
2. Make transparent authors' and contributors' **positionalities**.
3. Support **decolonization** and **social justice** in childhood studies.
4. Ask readers to consider their relationship to **theory and practice**.

We are aware that you will have different reasons for engaging with this text. For example, you may be a student, a policymaker, a lecturer, a practitioner, a service manager or a combination of some or all of these things. Our goal is to demystify our subject area, bring it to life and engage with your aspirations, thoughts and quandaries concerning childhood and its fullest cross-national and **cross-disciplinary** nature. With combined decades of collective experience working with students, plus the experience of one of the co-authors currently undergoing the PhD process, we have constructed this book to have wide appeal. You may be seeking to understand your own childhood, to answer a professional conundrum, to begin a process of developing questions for your own project with children or to answer a question set in an assignment. This book is designed to assist you in making choices when approaching uncharted junctions, both personal and professional. This book is also for lecturers of childhood studies, providing potential to teach and learn together with students.

In this book we outline a journey towards advanced understandings of childhood and, in doing so, map the contested ideas that pepper our field. Similarly, while we acknowledge that the purview is too often dominated by **global North** scholars' views of childhood, we likewise seek to recognize the work needed to recalibrate and take decolonization seriously within the childhood studies field. We have purposely raised these issues in all of our Chapters.

Childhood, while unique everywhere, is equally defined by its context. The globalization of postgraduate studies and cross-national interests in the field reflect an increasingly diverse area of study. We honour this diversity by involving commentators and contributors from around the world and from people in the field who self-define as practitioners, policymakers, students, researchers, teachers and more.

These perspectives shed light on many of the book's cross-cutting themes while presenting notable examples from different corners of the globe and representing the **multiple childhoods** depicted in this book. We also include literature and other resources that encourage a cross-national breadth and critical analysis.

The resonance of childhood studies: Key terms, themes and quandaries in the field

In this book, we situate childhood studies as a complex field, full of tensions and contradictions that can help in understanding children's lives. This book does not provide the 'answers'; rather, it challenges the ideas around childhood that have emerged over time. By supporting you to develop a questioning approach, we hope you benefit from seeing the possible flexibility of established concepts and theory. Through this book, we encourage you to renegotiate our ideas (as authors) and consider how we (and you) can use nuanced understandings of childhood studies to develop more considered, sympathetic and sensitive policies and practices.

We believe that 'positionality' matters. We ask you to question how researchers and practitioners critically reflect on their subjectivities – called **reflexivity** – and your own positionality. What is it about your experiences and world views that may attract you to specific positions? How do your academic, geographical, **epistemological** and other identities frame how you negotiate and understand childhood studies (see Chapter 5 for discussion on positionality in relation to **intersectionality**)? Adults, like children, do not arrive in social worlds as empty vessels. In this book we invite you to view childhood studies as unbounded, without definitive theories and approaches, and to 'try out' different positions as you travel through the pages.

We ask you to embrace our field's dynamism and make choices about the information in this book based on wisdom rather than accepting it as truth. In the process, we hope that you articulate where you are most comfortably located in the field of childhood studies. We are aware that as you navigate your studies and ultimately your career, your personal, professional and/or political options will define your path forward. Our hope is that this book may influence your destination, and we (the authors) highlight our own positionalities later in this Chapter to transparently reflect this process.

When setting out on our journey to demystify childhood studies, we were reminded of occasions in the past where we struggled to engage with 'impenetrable' books on social theory. While some readers will have proceeded directly from their undergraduate degrees, others may have had some years away from academic study and bring a wealth of work and volunteer experience that provides a practical context from which to challenge the ideas in this book. Our book seeks to practice what it preaches regarding transformative **praxis** and assumes that you will bring your own previous experiences and learning to the cases and debates discussed.

However, do not worry if you are new to the field and/or have studied childhood from one specific disciplinary perspective (e.g. psychology, law, political studies). First, the range of concepts explored in childhood studies reflects the diversity of researchers who are connecting with this field. Second, we are keen to inspire you to engage with children's complex lives, identities and views in a way that eschews subject boundaries and robustly questions the concepts that underpin decision-making concerning childhood in the real world. Hence, this is a book about complex theory, but it is also a book that considers the tensions that occur when we put theory into practice.

Our students have come from varied backgrounds; former students that we have supported include heads of children's services, university lecturers, directors of professional organizations, government ministers, civil servants and graduate entrants to NGOs/international organizations such as Save the Children, UNICEF and UNESCO – and many have added their voices to this book through quotations throughout the Chapters. We also introduce our five critical commentators, a grouping of geographically and disciplinarily diverse authors who provide a critical context to our Chapters. The commentators sit at the very edge of the childhood studies timeline presented later in this Chapter and thus provide indications of what ideas the field is currently engaging and negotiating with, as well as where it might be headed, from the front lines of childhood studies scholarship.

In this introduction we begin to map the terms, thinkers, themes and events of childhood studies. In doing so, we create a resource for advanced explorations of childhood and its foundational roots, inherent ambiguities, practical applications and related constructs across a range of cultural, geographical and disciplinary backgrounds. By engendering a 'critical' childhood studies we have sought to both represent the heterogeneity of the field globally and identify what childhood studies is a reaction against. We recognize that there are limitations to our starting point: we are predominantly working in the English language, are authors based in the social sciences in Scottish universities and are writing from North American (United States/Canada) and Euro-centric (Greek/Italian/Scottish) rooted beginnings.

How concepts are used in this book, therefore, and more broadly in childhood studies, is important (see Glossary as an additional resource). Central to this book is how we understand children and childhood.

- Childhood: It can be generally defined, described and understood as a state of early life, which includes a variety of geographical, contextual, emotional, material, **embodied** and historical aspects. Tisdall (see Chapter 2) argues that 'conceptualizing childhoods' is one of the most complex contentions within our field – hence, there can be no one definitive concept for what childhood is or what it should be. A central theme that runs through our book is the tension between childhood as related to biological age and development (Piaget 1972) and **childhood as a social construction** reflected in the **'new' sociology of childhood** (James and Prout 1990).

- Children: Based in this understanding of childhood, we consider children as multifaceted and have sympathy for the argument that we should not overly focus on age (see Commentary Chapter 2). Most Chapters of this book predominantly follow the **UN Convention on the Rights of the Child (UNCRC)** to think of children as between the ages of 0–18. However, we are aware that some texts also include in the concept of childhood various ages of **young people**/adolescents (e.g. ages 16–21, 18–21 or 18–26) (Sawyer et al. 2018).

Other concepts play a reoccurring role in this book, based on their prominence in childhood studies theory.

- **Agency:** A key concept and highly contested term within childhood studies. Broadly, childhood studies asserts that children are not passive subjects but are **social actors** expressing agency, in their lives, in research and in practical/professional contexts. However, the exact role of agency, how we understand the concept and its portrayal in the field, is debated (see Chapter 2 for discussion).

- **Decolonization:** In childhood studies, this can refer to deconstructing and parsing out 'dominant models of childhood' that are often presented as 'natural' or 'universal'. Constructions of childhood and methods related to practice and research have historically been rooted in colonization. This book aims to address efforts to 'decolonize' scholarship using childhood studies, and some of the Chapters' accompanying Commentaries particularly explore the lasting legacy of **hegemonic** theories rooted in the global North and the necessity of looking to perspectives of the **global South**. Further, our field and this book promote the exploration of children's varied positionalities, the questioning of ethnocentric world views and the recognition of the ongoing influences of colonialism and racism (see Chapter 2 for discussion).

- **Intersectionality:** Rooted in **Black feminist thought**, intersectionality considers how the complex interweaving and synthesis of categories such as age, **race**, **gender**, class, sexuality, disability and religion can create systemic forms of oppression and privilege (see Chapter 5 for discussion).

- Social justice: It can be defined as a person's right to be treated with regard/care, to be entitled to **legal rights** and to be recognized as having attributes and strengths (Davis et al. 2014; Fraser 2003; Honneth 2000; Young 1999). This concept argues for equity by material redistribution but also the redistribution of recognition, entitlement (e.g. to the law, services and democratic processes) and respect.

- False dichotomies: These are generally accepted divisions which may rely on 'taken-for-granted' binaries. For example, the child/adult dichotomy demarcates childhood from adulthood (see Chapter 2). Gender as a binary, or the idea that there are two genders (and often the notion that these genders correspond to sex), impacts how we understand the identities of children (see Chapters 5 and 6). Similarly, global perspectives of childhood studies question global North/ global South stereotypes that group together countries and children in terms of their socio-economic and political histories and that privilege conceptualizations of childhood from the global North while excluding or marginalizing those of the global South (e.g. Tisdall and

Punch 2012; Twum-Danso Imoh 2016). Yet, it should be noted that when 'breaking down' dichotomies and examining identity as socially constructed, we do not completely ignore the biological/embodied nature of childhood (see Chapters 6 and 7).

As you read this book, we ask you to grapple with these concepts and identify what you wish to 'take away'. We encourage you to question our frameworks and to think about how such theories have implications in practice. Contemporary social theorists often unintentionally fall into the trap of replicating the very categorical stances they set out to critique. For example, we see this in the case of the shift to the use of global North/global South terminology, which seeks to point to the effects of the colonialist legacy on childhood studies today, and, yet, the term is criticized itself for being euphemistic for other value-laden and binary language (e.g. developed/developing countries) and homogenizing experiences of childhood (see Commentary Chapter 4).

Additionally, this book at times discusses research, theory and practice as siloed areas. However, our aim is for you to gain an understanding of how to connect these three areas to create a more robust form of childhood studies. Praxis, variably described in this book, is the bridge between theory and practice – reflexivity and transformation (Cologon et al. 2019). **Counter-hegemonic praxis** is seen as a practice that involves identifying, addressing and opposing power imbalances (e.g. **hegemonic whiteness**'s role in political and social spheres, as well as within **knowledge production** traditions) through collective action. By drawing together your positionality, engaging in reflexivity and applying criticality towards 'fixed' concepts and 'natural' or 'universal' dichotomies, you should be able to transform your personal and professional understandings of childhood, family and society.

A critical childhood studies timeline

Childhood studies parameters are not fixed, which reflects the field's beginnings. Early writing and research on childhood tended to suggest that both women and children needed to be taught how to behave because their brains were not sufficiently developed (Bales and Parsons 1956). Drawing from developmental psychology, Piaget introduced an 'age and stage-based' way of thinking about childhood which set out the **'normative'** stages of cognitive development (Piaget 1972). Piaget's theory aligned biological age with four stages that were seen as universal and inherently obtained. Piaget and related theories were later critiqued in childhood studies for inherent assumptions that **universalized** or colonized particular constructions of childhood (see Chapter 2).

Vygotsky's sociocultural theory stood in contrast to Piaget in its attention to the role of social interactions in **child development** (Vygotsky and Cole 1978). Vygotsky's theory further emphasized the zone of proximal development, in which children could learn with the support of a knowing adult (or peer). As a result, Vygotsky's theory did not ascribe the same notions of universality as Piaget's theory, since development was locally based on a child's social interactions and thus could differ between children. However, a critique of this approach is it minimizes the role of the individual.

Bronfenbrenner drew on Vygotsky's approach to sociocultural elements that impact individual development but sought to address how the individual related to their environment. **Bronfenbrenner's ecological systems theory** draws on the premise that an individual's social environment influences their development (Bronfenbrenner 1979). **Socio-ecological frameworks** that draw on Bronfenbrenner's theories, however, are criticized in sociology for needing to go beyond the understanding of social systems as neat layers and attend to the local power politics between the social and ecological levels (see Chapters 3 and 6).

An important critique of developmental psychology theories is that the discipline was dominated by male psychologists such as Vygotsky, Bronfenbrenner and Piaget; early psychology is consequently associated with the persecution of those who did not fit with white male patriarchal norms (e.g. disabled people, Black, minority ethnic, LGBTQ+ people). However, feminist writers counteracted these 'deterministic' and discriminatory attitudes (see Bradburn 1989; Bruce 2004). Anthropologists proposed that such approaches were sexist and that treating women and children differently from men resulted in a 'pathetic and pitiful' representation of both that downplayed their complexity, abilities and ideas (Hardman 1973). This challenge was adopted by some psychologists (e.g. Burman 1994, 1996; Corsaro 1997; Stainton-Rogers and Stainton Rogers 2001; Woodhead and Faulkner 2000), who began to view children as subjective and intersubjective beings and criticized those who represented children as passive objects who could not think for themselves. New approaches emerged which focused on the importance of learning with and from peers (Opie and Opie 1959), the impact of age, class, disability, gender, religion or **ethnicity** on learning (Corker and Shakespeare 2002; Crenshaw 1989; Young

1990) and children's abilities to make reflexive (thought and change) choices (Corsaro 1996; James and Prout 1990). These new approaches created a context in which childhood studies was ripe to develop.

Contemporary childhood studies origins are, therefore, evolved from the notion that childhood is socially constructed, which was established in the 1980s and 1990s in the new sociology of childhood (later to become 'new social studies'). This term was developed by specific writers (James et al. 1998; Mayall 2012; Qvortrup et al. 2009; Spyrou et al. 2019; Wyness 2015). Such writers reacted 'against' existing depictions of childhood (e.g. child development, functional sociology) and different trajectories of the new sociology of childhood developed in different parts of the world (e.g. United States, Denmark, Norway, Germany, Brazil). We go further, in using 'childhood studies' to respect disciplines beyond the social sciences who are engaging with our field (see Chapter 3).

We present a childhood studies timeline documenting the major events, ideas and debates discussed in this book. If you are new to childhood studies, the timeline illustrated here provides our partial and subjective overview of the field. If you already bring a particular specialty to this book and are looking to place these ideas in a broader context, this timeline may also help (Table 1.1).

Table 1.1: A Select Childhood Studies Timeline

1924	Geneva Declaration of the Rights of the Child adopted by the League of Nations
1928	*A Child's Rights to Respect* published (by Goldszmit, pen name Janusz Korczak)
1936	*The Origins of Intelligence in Children* published (by Piaget, text on cognitive development)
1948	Universal Declaration of Human Rights adopted by the UN General Assembly
1959	Declaration on the Rights of the Child adopted by the UN General Assembly
1960	*L'Enfant et La Vie Familiale Sous L'Ancien Régime* published (by Ariès, translated title *Centuries of Childhood*)

1974	*Escape from Childhood* published (by Holt, an example of the 'kiddy libbers')
1978	*Mind in Society: The Development of Higher Psychological Processes* published (by Vygtosky)
1979	*The Ecology of Human Development* published (by Bronfenbrenner, on social-ecological theory)
1989	'Convention on the Rights of the Child' adopted by the UN General Assembly
1989	*Demarginalizing the Intersection of Race and Sex* published (by Crenshaw, significant for bringing ideas about intersectionality into wider academic circles)
1990	World Summit for Children held at the UN
1990	*Constructing and Reconstructing Childhood: Contemporary Issues in the Sociological Study of Childhood* published (by Prout and James, set out the paradigm for the 'new sociology of childhood')
1998	*Theorizing Childhood* published (by James, Jenks and Prout, set out the pre-sociological and sociological approach to childhood)
1999	'African Charter on the Rights and Welfare of the Child' entered into force (adopted by the Organisation of African Unity in 1990. The OAU is now called the African Union)
2000	Two optional protocols to the UNCRC adopted by the UN General Assembly: On the Involvement of Children in Armed Conflicts and On the Sale of Children, Child Prostitution and Child Pornography
2014	Third optional protocol to the UNCRC adopted by the UN General Assembly, enabling communications to the UN Committee to the Rights of the Child regarding violations of children's rights
2016	'INSPIRE: seven strategies for ending violence against children' framework is published (by World Health Organization)
2020	'Child as method' analytical approach proposed (by Burman)

The timeline draws a historical line from childhood studies foundations (theoretical, policy-based, disciplinary and intersectional) to its use in practice, policy and research today. This timeline is meant to provide readers with a broad context of critical events and when/how ideas developed in childhood studies. However, the timeline should not be taken as a definitive **genealogy**. Rather, it is a tool to help connect ideas between the Chapters. We ask you to use this resource merely as a starting line for further exploration.

Engaging with *Critical Childhood Studies*

The book is primarily aimed at the 'advanced level', in the sense that it seeks to make a virtue out of the many complexities childhood studies entails. Our book builds upon work in the field which provides strong introductory resources on theoretical conceptualizations (e.g. Kehily 2013; Mayall 1996; McNamee 2016; Robinson and Jones Diaz 2005; Wells 2017), law, guidance and policy (Percy-Smith and Thomas 2009), practice (Broadhead et al. 2010; Clark 2013; Dahlberg et al. 1999, Davis and Smith 2012; Foley and Rixon 2014; Jones and Walker 2011) and methods (e.g. Christensen and James 2000; Fraser et al. 2004; Morrow and Alderson 2020; Mukherji and Albon 2014). This book hopes to provide an additional resource for advanced-level readers, particularly for honours level and postgraduate students, and enable you to draw connections between theoretical, practice and policy literature.

You can engage with individual Chapters or the text as a whole. However, the book addresses topics and contentions within childhood studies, as well as more broadly in academic scholarship, that stretch across the individual Chapters, and the conclusion hopes to draw these themes together. We signpost these areas within the Chapters to help you identify how key concepts align – or deviate – between authors, lenses and topics. Additionally, the Chapters range in their writing and depth as they serve different purposes for this book and for you (the reader). Our positionality has impacted how we authored this book – reflected in a variety of approaches – from the historical to the theoretical to the applied. You will also see different writing styles, disciplinary roots and foci portrayed in the Chapters. Chapters 2 and 4 encompass abundant literature and discussion of key terms and policy to help ground you in the field. Chapter 3 applies a broader lens to help you see how childhood studies connects with other disciplines and suggests reading if you would like to engage in a more in-depth exploration. Chapters 5 and 6 draw you into the narrative around intersectionality and theory into practice, respectively, to provide some guidance for your path down these roads.

As writers, we introduce ourselves – our positions, our backgrounds and our subjectivities – to situate where we (and as a result, this book) have come from.

John M. Davis: Chapters 1 and 7

I am a professor of education at the University of Strathclyde and a Disabled man. I have worked with children in a variety of **multidisciplinary** health, education and community practice environments and have qualifications in sports coaching and early years. I studied sociology and social anthropology at the University of Ulster during 'the Troubles' and completed a PhD at the University of Edinburgh on inequality in play and sports education. I was born in Fife in Scotland in the late 1960s, and my early life involved a poverty of emotional and material resources, including being in the 'special needs' class at my local primary school and experiencing violent and detached parenting. These early experiences enshrined in my 'DNA' a keen eye for children's rights, empathy, fairness, generosity, **inclusion**, warmth and acceptance of people's differences – themes that I have brought to my writing on childhood, disability, early years and family studies. Throughout my life I have sought to talk truth to power – no matter the consequences and this has enabled me to challenge toxic academic and practice environments that are so very often focused on output, promote elitism and engender cultures of overwork. 'Fighting the good fight' comes with consequences and in 2019, I was hospitalized while travelling in Phoenix, Arizona. I owe the fact that I have been able to contribute to this book to the skill, care and professionalism of the surgeons and medical staff at John C. Lincoln Hospital.

Deborah Fry: Chapters 3 and 6

I grew up in the Pacific Northwest of the United States and was always very interested in traveling to and learning about different contexts. This led me to initially undertaking a degree in international relations. What I discovered just at the end of that degree, when I was doing an internship with a women's health organization in Zimbabwe, was that I was really drawn to adolescent and women's health after hearing women's stories about lack of access to care. I then undertook another degree in public health focusing on maternal mortality prevention. I really wanted the research work I did to have real-world impact. Through this work, I became more exposed to the issue of violence against women during pregnancy and set on what would become a lifelong path to better understand the scope, nature and **drivers of violence** against women and children. I started my research career through a master's level practicum as a researcher in an NGO focused on sexual violence prevention in New York City and then moved to join a **child protection** research team in the UK. I came to academia later in life, after already leading research teams in the NGO sector, and did my PhD by Research Publications and am still driven by using data to **safeguard** and prevent **violence against children**.

Kristina Konstantoni: Chapters 4 and 5

As a child I spent my life in two countries, Greece and the UK, as my mother was English and my father was Greek. Early experiences of discrimination that I faced due to my dual identity led to a deep personal interest in childhoods, rights and inequalities. I have worked in various early learning and childcare settings in both Greece and Scotland and in children's rights organizations. I completed a degree in sociology in Greece (University of Crete) and then went on to complete an MSc in childhood studies and a PhD in education (both at the University of Edinburgh). Throughout my life and work, I came to realize the importance of the links between research, policy, teaching and practice for sustained change in making children's rights real in homes, communities and institutions. I am also a mother of two young children (5.5 years old and 1 year old) who continue to inspire me and guide my learning in the areas of **early childhood**, play, rights and social justice. My children played an important role in my decision to study further about early childhood through the Froebel in Childhood Practice course (University of Edinburgh) and focus on new fields of interest linked to early childhood, children's rights, play and public life.

Marlies Kustatscher: Chapters 3 and 5

I grew up in a multilingual and multicultural region in Italy, which shaped my interest in issues around identities and diversity from an early age. I knew I wanted to pursue a profession that connects with people and enables everyone to experience the same opportunities, so I studied to become a social worker. During my studies, I was exposed to ideas from sociology, social policy, counselling and other disciplines, and this opened up a whole new world for me in terms of framing and theorizing some of my beliefs and ideas. Through various placements and research assistant jobs, I developed an interest in how children are positioned in our societies and particularly how they experience and challenge social inequalities. I was lucky to pursue this further through my PhD research and then through my research and teaching positions at the University of Edinburgh.

M. Catherine Maternowska: Chapter 6

When I was about two years old, in sync with healthy child development, I started asking 'why'. Psychologists say it is a sign of curiosity and a toddler's desire to understand the big and often daunting world around them. I have never really stopped asking 'why' (and I still find the world big and daunting); it ensures that I push to uncover challenges and find ways to generate solutions. I first studied social geography and economics, then I learned the beauty of applying science in the field of public health. My PhD in medical anthropology pulled all these disciplines together with a good dose of political economy framing my 'but, why?' questions. My life as a research practitioner has been a beautiful string of adventures – living in the Americas, Africa, Asia and Europe. I have moved in and out of the civil society/non-governmental world, academics and even the UN, where I worked for UNICEF for a decade. I am currently a professor at the University of Edinburgh and now, as I move back into applied research, I really want to understand why child sexual abuse ever happens in the first place.

Kay Tisdall: Chapters 2 and 4

While I have lived in Scotland for over thirty years, I grew up in Canada. I worked my summers in my teens at various summer camps in North America and frequently with disabled children. This led to my interest in social policy (in my mind, that means how policy impacts on people) and eventually a PhD in social policy at the University of Edinburgh. I went from there to work at a non-governmental organization, Children in Scotland, mostly trying to improve policy itself. As I worked a lot with law, I decided to credentialize and get a law degree too. I currently work in childhood and youth studies, University of Edinburgh, and primarily concentrate on children's **human rights** in teaching, policy and research.

Laura Weiner: Chapters 1 and 7

Growing up in New Jersey, United States, I began working as a youth worker in afterschool programmes and summer camps throughout high school and university. I increasingly became interested in informal education spaces, and how children and young people use these spaces to fit their needs and build safe communities. My interests coalesced with my sociology degree and different educational advocacy and non-profit roles, and I increasingly focused on educational resource inequities and access to different kinds of experiences and childhoods. My current PhD research expands on my work, focusing on 'youth development' discourse in informal learning in youth activist groups. In this book, I bring both my personal and professional experiences entering the field of childhood and youth studies and navigating the history, theory and practice in relation to my PhD and wider research.

Accompanying the Chapters, we have created pedagogical (learning and reflection) tools to aid you in engaging with, and pushing beyond, the literature (whether student, practitioner or teacher). These reflective and practical exercises invite you to challenge your thinking and to grapple with the complexities of childhood studies in theory and practice. Provided pedagogical tools include *critical challenges* (i.e. discussion and reflection questions), *exploring concepts further* excerpts, individual and group *activities, quotations* from childhood studies students and practitioners, and a *glossary*. In each Chapter, we have put a glossary word or phrase in bold the first time it is used. The book is intended to be interactive and will ask you to surpass mere knowledge acquisition in favour of embracing the theories, ideas and cases explored in the Chapters and their impact on practices or research of interest to you.

Our book explains, interrogates and clarifies the contested contemporary landscape of our field while encouraging you to think about how contradictions have implications for practical contexts. By revisiting key theoretical concepts and engaging with their complexities, you can turn to contemporary issues with a new lens. Over the course of the book, we discuss resources using flexible theory and multiple **knowledges** which can be used in forthcoming crises and pressures, some of which we can anticipate – like climate change – and others which are still yet unknown. In discussing some of these current crises, such as the COVID-19 pandemic and violence against children, our Chapters hope to demonstrate how core childhood studies concepts can shed light on these matters and reciprocally how these current topics shed new light on 'old' theory. We invite readers to think robustly about these ideas, as a means of seeing advanced childhood studies as a continuously expanding and complex entity, and to disagree with what is put forward. The Commentaries accompanying each Chapter provide models to extend and debate ideas set forth in this book.

In Chapter 2, 'Foundations of Childhood Studies', Tisdall offers an initial entry to key concepts and unpacks debates, meanings and contestations concerning agency/structure, **adultism/childism**, **generational orders**, **materialism** and decolonization. Tisdall invites you to immerse yourself in the childhood studies historical, theoretical and geographical developments. From these foundations, we ask you to consider how childhood studies is used today and what conceptual resources in childhood studies can usefully provide for your own disciplinary area, policy context and/or practice setting.

In Chapter 3, 'Childhood Studies Meets Other Disciplines', Kustatscher and Fry examine childhood studies relationship with varied disciplines, exploring contributions, for example, from geographies, psychology and critical child development, history, social anthropology, economic studies, philosophy, public health, race and ethnicity studies, gender studies and educational studies. This Chapter asks you to consider childhood studies as a field defined by its interdisciplinarity and to question the boundaries between disciplines, fields and paradigms when framing your own topics of study. For example, you are asked to consider what an interdisciplinary, multidisciplinary or **transdisciplinary** approach may offer for your own work/research and question the ways in which disciplinary boundaries are constructed (and deconstructed), as well as the importance of thinking beyond such clearly delineated silos. This Chapter is particularly useful if you are working within and across disciplines and within and beyond childhood studies disciplinary affinities, or if you wish to better understand how disciplinary concepts may overlap or come in conflict in your workplace.

These ideas are further picked up in Tisdall and Konstantoni's in-depth exploration of how 'children's rights' scholarship, childhood studies, social policy and the political interact (Chapter 4). The Chapter highlights disciplinary tensions with legal studies (e.g. on the role of international law), **children's participation** in decision-making (e.g. in practice settings) and the universality – or not – of childhood across the world. Engaging with this Chapter you can consider arguments for (and against) children's human rights, think about the challenges of putting concepts such as best interests into practice and interrogate alternatives to children's human rights (such as children's **wellbeing** and **vulnerability**).

In Chapter 5, 'Intersectional Perspectives on Childhood', Kustatscher and Konstantoni analyse what is meant by an intersectional childhood studies field. It depicts how childhood studies often neglects the 'intersectional' theories derived from Black feminist writers, such as Crenshaw (1989), that seek to investigate the interconnected contexts of our lives and to explore the connections between equity issues such as race, disability, gender, religion, sexuality, class and ethnicity. Intersectional writers argue, in relation to family and childhood, that discrimination and injustice are related to a complex interplay of factors and that no single issue can fully explain our lived experiences, perspectives and life stories of discrimination, silencing and oppression. The Chapter asks you where you stand on this issue and how you will avoid replicating past mistakes in your own work.

In Chapter 6, 'Childhood Studies in Practice', Maternowska and Fry bring theory into the practice realm and draw from a multi-country study to ask how childhood studies can benefit practice contexts and, in turn, practice can help develop more robust theory. This Chapter teases out a context in which understanding and representing the multiple identities of children is core for understanding violence against children. By examining research concerning violence against children in Vietnam and Peru, you are asked to explore how theory is negotiated through a child-centred age, gender and power **integrated framework** and consider how you might place children, their views and perspectives at the heart of your practice and/or research.

Davis and Weiner, 'Conclusion: Using Childhood Studies Concepts to Further Emancipatory Praxis', conclude the book by employing examples from contemporary crises and disability, early years and youth studies to draw together the learning from Chapters 2 to 6. We ask you to explore how you, as an advanced reader, can use the concepts, theories and debates introduced and explored in this book for emancipatory praxis. The Chapter extracts the key threads stitched across the book to answer the question: What does childhood studies provide for the student, the researcher, the practitioner in today's context and into the future?

As you read, consider the concepts you find useful, areas that you see rife with contention and how to push beyond accepted false dichotomies, neutralities and barriers. Own your journey and use it to make a positive impact.

References

Bales, R. F. and Parsons, T. (1956), *Family: Socialization and Interaction Process*, 1st edn, London: Routledge.

Bradburn, E. (1989), *Margaret McMillan: Portrait of a Pioneer*, London: Routledge.

Broadhead, P., Howard, J., and Wood, E. (eds) (2010), *Play and Learning in the Early Years: From Research to Practice*, London: Sage.

Bronfenbrenner, U. (1979), *The Ecology of Human Development: Experiments by Nature and Design*, Cambridge, MA: Harvard University Press.

Bruce, T. (2004), *Developing Learning in Early Childhood*, London: Sage Publications.

Burman, E. (1994), 'Innocents Abroad: Western Fantasies of Childhood and the Iconography of Emergencies', *Disasters*, 18 (3): 238–53.

Burman, E. (1996), 'Local, Global or Globalized? Child Development and International Child Rights Legislation', *Childhood*, 3 (1): 45–66.

Christensen, P. and James, A. (2000), 'Research with Children: Perspectives and Practices', *British Journal of Educational Studies*, 48 (3): 344–5.

Clark, A. (2013), *Childhoods in Contexts*, Bristol: Policy Press.

Cologon, K., Cologon, T., Mevawalla, Z., and Niland, A. (2019), 'Generative Listening: Using Arts-based Inquiry to Investigate Young Children's Perspectives of Inclusion, Exclusion and Disability', *Journal of Early Childhood Research*, 17 (1): 54–69.

Corker, M. and Shakespeare, T. (eds) (2002), *Disability/Postmodernity: Embodying Disability Theory*, London: Continuum.

Corsaro, W. A. (1996), 'Transitions in Early Childhood: The Promise of Comparative, Longitudinal', in R. Jessor, A. Colby, and R. A. Scweder (eds), *Ethnography and Human Development: Context and Meaning in Social Inquiry*, 419–58, Chicago: University of Chicago Press.

Corsaro, W. A. (1997), *The Sociology of Childhood*, Thousand Oaks, CA: Pine Forge Press/Sage Publications Co.

Crenshaw, K. (1989), 'Demarginalizing the Intersection of Race and Sex: A Black Feminist Critique of Antidiscrimination Doctrine, Feminist Theory and Antiracist Politics', *University of Chicago Legal Forum*, 1989 (1): Article 8.

Dahlberg, G., Moss, P., and Pence, A. (1999), *Beyond Quality in Early Childhood Education and Care: Languages of Evaluation*, London: Routledge.

Davis, J., Hill, L., Tisdall, K., Cairns, L., and McCausland, S. (2014), 'Social Justice, the Common Weal and Children and Young People in Scotland', *The Jimmy Reid Foundation*. Available online: http://reidfoundation. org/wpcont ent/uploads/2014/03/Childhood1. pdf (accessed 15 May 2017).

Davis, J. M. and Smith, M. (2012), *Working in Multi-professional Contexts: A Practical Guide for Professionals in Children's Services*, London: Sage.

Foley, P. and Rixon, A. (eds) (2014), *Changing Children's Services: Working and Learning Together*, Bristol: Policy Press.

Fraser, N. (2003), 'Social Justice in the Age of Identity Politics: Redistribution, Recognition and Participation', in N. Fraser and A. Honneth (eds), *Redistribution or Recognition? A Political-philosophical Exchange*, 7–109, New York: Verso.

Fraser, S., Lewis, V., Ding, S., Kellett, M., and Robinson, C. (eds) (2004), *Doing Research with Children and Young People*, London: Sage.

Hardman, C. (1973), 'Can There be an Anthropology of Children?', *Journal of the Anthropological Society of Oxford*, 4 (2): 85–99.

Honneth, A. (2000), 'The Possibility of a Disclosing Critique of Society: The Dialectic of Enlightenment in Light of Current Debates in Social Criticism', *Constellations*, 7 (1): 116–27.

James, A., Jenks, C., and Prout, A. (1998), *Theorizing Childhood*, Cambridge: Polity Press.

James, A. and Prout, A. (1990), *Constructing and Reconstructing Childhood: Contemporary Issues in the Sociological Study of Childhood*, London: Falmer Press.

Jones, P. and Walker, G. (2011), *Children's Rights in Practice*, London: Sage.

Kehily, M. (ed.) (2013), *Understanding Childhood: A Cross-Disciplinary Approach*, 2nd edn, Bristol: Policy Press.

Mayall, B. (1996), *Children, Health and the Social Order*, Buckingham: Open University Press.

Mayall, B. (2012), 'An Afterword: Some Reflections on a Seminar Series', *Children's Geographies*, 10 (3): 347–55.

Morrow, V. and Alderson, P. (2020), *The Ethics of Research with Children and Young People: A Practical Handbook*, New York: Sage.

Mukherji, P. and Albon, D. (2014), *Research Methods in Early Childhood: An Introductory Guide*, London: Sage.

McNamee, S. (2016), *The Social Study of Childhood*, Basingstoke: Palgrave.

OECD (2015), 'Starting Strong IV, Monitoring Quality in Early Childhood Education and Care', 28 October. Available online: https://www.oecd.org/public-ations/starting-strong-iv-9789264233515-en.htm (accessed 11 June 2022).

Opie, I. and Opie, P. (1959), *The Language and Lore of Schoolchildren*, Oxford: Clarendon Press.

Percy-Smith, B. and Thomas, N. P. (eds) (2009), *A Handbook of Children and Young People's Participation: Perspectives from Theory and Practice*, London and New York: Routledge.

Piaget, J. (1972), *The Psychology of Intelligence*, Totowa, NJ: Littlefield, Adams.

Qvortrup, J., Corsaro, W., and Michael-Sebastine, H. (eds) (2009), *The Palgrave Handbook of Childhood Studies*, London: Palgrave Macmillan.

Robinson, K. and Jones Diaz, C. (2005), *Diversity and Difference in Early Childhood Education: Issues for Theory and Practice*, Maidenhead: McGraw-Hill Education.

Sawyer, S. M., Azzopardi, P. S., Wickremarathne, D., and Patton, G. C. (2018), 'The Age of Adolescence', *The Lancet Child & Adolescent Health*, 2 (3): 223–8.

Spyrou, S., Rosen, R., and Cook, D. T. (2019), *Reimagining Childhood Studies*, London: Bloomsbury Academic.

Stainton Rogers, W. and Stainton Rogers, R. (2001), *The Psychology of Gender and Sexuality: An Introduction*, Maidenhead: McGraw-Hill Education.

Szmigiera, M. (2021), 'Proportion of Selected Age Groups of World Population in 2021, by Region', *Statista*, 13 August. Available online: https://www .statista.com/statistics/265759/world-population-by-age-and-region/#:~:text =As%20of%20mid%2D2020%2C%20about,were%20under%2015%20years %20old.&text=Globally%2C%20about%2026%20percent%20of,over%2065 %20years%20of%20age (accessed 11 June 2022).

Tisdall, E. K. M. and Punch, S. (2012), 'Not So "New"? Looking Critically at Childhood Studies', *Children's Geographies*, 10 (3): 249–64.

Twum-Danso Imoh, A. (2016), 'From the Singular to the Plural: Exploring Diversities in Contemporary Childhoods in sub-Saharan Africa', *Childhood*, 23 (3): 455–68.

UN Committee on the Rights of the Child (2016), 'General Comment No. 20 (2016) on the Implementation of the Rights of the Child during Adolescence', *Committee on the Rights of the Child*, 6 December. Available online: https://tbinternet.ohchr.org/_layouts/treatybodyexternal/Download .aspx?symbolno=CRC%2fC%2fGC%2f20&Lang=en (accessed 11 June 2022).

UNICEF (2015), *A Post-2015 World Fit for Children*, January. Available online: https://www.unicef.org/turkiye/media/3381/file/AN%20AGENDA%20FOR %20 (accessed 11 June 2022).

VygotskyL. S. and Cole, M. (1978), *Mind in Society: The Development of Higher Psychological Processes*, Cambridge, MA: Harvard University Press.

Wells, K. (2017), *Childhood Studies: Making Young Subjects*, London: Wiley.

Woodhead, M. and Faulkner, D. (2000), 'Subjects, Objects or Participants? Dilemmas of Psychological Research with Children', in P. Christiansen and A. James (eds), *Research with Children: Perspectives and Practices*, 10–39, London: Falmer Press / Routledge.

Wyness, M. (2015), *Childhood*, Cambridge: Polity Press.

Young, I. M. (1990), *Throwing Like a Girl and Other Essays in Feminist Philosophy and Social Theory*, Bloomington: Indiana University Press.

Young, I. M. (1999), 'Justice, Inclusion, and Deliberative Democracy', in Stephen Macedo (ed.), *Deliberative Politics: Essays on Democracy and Disagreement*, 151–8, New York: Oxford University Press.

2

Foundations of Childhood Studies

E. Kay M. Tisdall

Introduction

What is childhood? This is a seemingly easy question to ask but, according to **childhood studies**, a fascinating and complex one to answer. Alderson provides us with a start by explaining '"Childhood" variously refers to the *status* of being a minor, the early-life *state* of immaturity whether actual or ascribed, and the *process* of growing towards adulthood' (2013: 4, italics in original). The complexity can go further in recognizing that these three aspects are themselves geographically, contextually or historically specific (Lancy 2022). To pick one example, the 'status of being a minor' has a history in Roman law, which brings with it particular legal connotations as well as social ones in places such as Brazil (Rizzini 2011) or Scotland (Marshall 1997). Such understandings are of great interest to childhood studies, not only to track their meanings and particularities but also because they have practical implications for children's lives and their communities.

This Chapter starts with this fundamental idea within childhood studies – that **childhood** is socially constructed. This idea was central to the **'new' sociology of childhood** that took hold in the 1990s in the UK and continues into what is now called childhood studies. The Chapter goes on to consider key concepts and ongoing debates. The Chapter seeks to provide a foundation of key ideas within childhood studies – past and present – which can inform other fields as well as encourage new research, conceptual and policy agendas of their own. It draws particularly on the literature written in English, recognizing our **positionality** as authors in Europe, North America and the UK, while seeking to learn from other literatures from other parts of the world.

Childhood is socially constructed

Activity: Considering proverbs

Different ways of constructing childhood are reflected in proverbs. Consider this selection, attributed to various countries:

1. Children are an investment in the future (South Africa).
2. Children should be seen and not heard (UK).
3. You don't have to be old to be wise (Nigeria).
4. The egg should not be smarter than the duck (Vietnam).

- What ideas about childhood does each proverb express?
- What ideas about adulthood does each proverb express?
- What are the implications of such ideas for adult–child relations?
- Can you think of another proverb, from where you lived as a child? What are its implications?

If you are working as a group, discuss these additional proverbs from group members. What is similar or different about the **social constructions of childhood**?

(This activity was inspired by Kirby and Woodhead (2003). We intend it as a provocation, but we recognize that proverbs do not necessarily represent current societal thinking in their contexts.)

In 1990, Prout and James articulate this **paradigm** for the new sociology of childhood:

1. Childhood is understood as a social construction.
2. Childhood is a variable of social analysis.
3. Children's social relationships and **cultures** are worthy of study in their own right.
4. Children are and must be seen as active in the construction and determination of their own social lives, the lives of those around them and of the society in which they live.
5. Ethnography is a particularly useful methodology for the study of childhood.
6. Proclaiming a new paradigm of childhood is also part of reconstructing childhood in society (summary of points, from 1990: 8).

Prout and James capture the essence of the **social construction of childhood** in this quotation:

> A child's immaturity is a biological fact: but how this immaturity is understood and how it is made meaningful is a fact of culture . . . (1990: 7)

This form of social construction emphasizes that childhood and children are thought of in particular ways, that certain aspects of that group of people are considered important – immaturity, for example – and that these create particular understandings of children and childhood.

I first heard about social construction of childhood when undertaking my MA childhood studies courses. Although my sociology background gave me insight into the importance of locating people's views of children and childhood in sociocultural, political, economic and historical contexts, I still found this concept abstract because at that time I took my own views of childhood for granted and couldn't look beyond them. This concept made more sense to me when we were invited by the tutor to use a couple of words to describe children and childhood. Since I was in an international class with classmates from all around the world, I surprisingly heard numerous views of children and childhoods from peers. These vivid examples perfectly helped me to understand that children and childhood could be constructed in very different ways.

Yan Zhu, Lecturer in Education Studies, University College London, UK

Exploring concepts further: Social construction and social constructivism

Leeds-Hurwitz provides a succinct definition of **social construction**:

> social construction (SC) assumes that people *construct* (i.e., create, make, invent) their understandings of the world and the meanings they give to encounters with others, or various products they or others create; SC also assumes that they do this *jointly*, in coordination with others, rather than individually. (2016: no page, italics in original)

The emphasis on the joint, or social, aspects of social construction is worth noting, as this distinguishes it from **constructivism**. As Guterman writes:

> although both constructivism and social constructionism each endorses a subjectivist view of knowledge, the former emphasizes individuals' biological and cognitive processes, whereas the latter places knowledge in the domain of social interchange. (2013: 20)

Thus, constructivism believes reality and knowledge are constructed within individuals, so the focus is on individuals' learning and minds, whereas social constructionism considers how reality and knowledge are constructed through **discourse**, so the focus is on what happens between people as they come together to create realities.

Ariès famously wrote about how childhood was constructed historically in his much-cited book *Centuries of Childhood*. The book was first published in 1960 in French and then widely translated. Ariès puts forward that European medieval society did not have the idea (or *sentiment*, in French) of childhood. He does not deny that people in the past may well have had affection for children, but he argues that the awareness of children as being different from adults was lacking in medieval times. The *sentiment* of childhood emerged, according to Ariès, in the Renaissance (fourteenth to seventeenth centuries) and particularly the Reformation (sixteenth century), and was associated with childhood innocence and weakness. Children thus required discipline. Ariès continues his historical review to consider how childhood became further distinguished from adulthood as children were removed from the labour market into compulsory education and from public life into private family households. While his historical sources, techniques and findings have been much challenged subsequently for being inadequate and at times incorrect (see Cunningham 1995; Pollock 1983), his work remains a key building block to the new sociology of childhood's social construction of childhood.

Different social constructions of childhood

Ariès' work covers what James and colleagues (1998) refer to as 'pre-sociological' discourses of childhood. In their seminal book, James and colleagues suggest a taxonomy of such pre-sociological approaches, which are summarized in Table 2.1.

Table 2.1 Taxonomy of Pre-sociological Approaches to Childhood

Approach	Explanatory Description from the 1998 Book	(Historical) Authors Who Exemplify This Approach
The evil child	'children are demonic, harbourers of potentially dark forces which risk being mobilized if, by dereliction or inattention, the adult world allows them to veer away from the "straight and narrow" path the civilization has bequeathed to them.' (10)	Hobbes
The innocent child	'Essentially pure in heart, these infants are angelic and uncorrupted by the world they have entered.' (13)	Rousseau
The immanent child	'Locke's child is *immanent* in that it has mental processes and perception and, if we provide the appropriate environment, we can elicit the reason from it.' (16)	Locke
The naturally developing child	'Piaget's child, poor biological creature that it is, is imbued therefore with a grand potential to become not anything, but quite specifically something. It is predicted, and in his work on the development of thought and bodily skills – the path to intelligence – Piaget lays out for us some inevitable and clearly defined stages of growth which are well sign-posted.' (18–19)	Piaget
The unconscious child	'childhood became the province of retrospectives . . . Freud opened up a concern with children as adult pasts.' (20)	Freud

Summarized from James, Jenks and Prout (1998)

The pre-sociological constructions have been predominant in particular times and places but still can be found today. For example, 'the evil child' can be found in public outcries and media depictions when children commit particular crimes. The 'innocent child' is evident in calls for the return to childhood or the crisis of childhood, which are concerned with children being unduly exposed to the dangers of the adult world and should instead be contained within places of protection and play. Locke's idea of an immanent child appears in ideas of schooling and education, which seek to develop children into **autonomous**, rational adults. The naturally developing child is prevalent across many domains, rooted within current **global North** ideas of education, fixations on children's competence and capacity, and developmental milestones. The unconscious child is associated with Freud, as a device to illuminate adult concerns. While such pre-sociological constructions may be prevalent, James and colleagues find this set of constructions problematic, conceptually and practically.

The problems of the 'naturally developing child' are picked up by Qvortrup and colleagues in their cross-European project. Qvortrup reflects on children being constructed as **'human becomings'** rather than **'human beings'**:

> adulthood is regarded as the goal and end-point of individual development or perhaps even the very meaning of a person's childhood. They are however revealing for the maybe unintended message, which seems to indicate that children are not members or at least not integrated members of society. This attitude, while perceiving childhood as a moratorium and a preparatory phase, thus confirms postulates about children as 'naturally' incompetent and incapable. (1994: 2)

Constructing children as **human becomings** focuses on children as future adults. The focus then is on children achieving adulthood and, further, to becoming contributing members to society.

My first degree was in psychology, which has given me great knowledge about **child development**. When I then came to childhood studies, it helped me question my adult-centrism and my notions about childhood. I understood that children are experts in their lives – I can only prevent violence if I learn about their perspectives and experiences.

Karina Padilla, Psychologist, Peru

In contrast, children can be socially constructed as human beings, valuing children as **social actors** in the present, expressing **agency** and competence (e.g. see Bühler-Niederberger 2010). Childhood and the experiences of it are worthy of attention in their own right. This requires attention to children, and not only to families, and the importance of childhood studies and not only family studies. While families are typically very important to children, and a key societal structure across most contexts for children's survival and upbringing, children are often submerged conceptually (and in practice) in the category of families, with the experiences of parents privileged over children. This is sharply evident in social statistics, which are often gathered at the level of family households, occluding information specifically about children and childhood (e.g. see Alderson 2013; Qvortrup 1997). Childhood is a permanent structural feature of society (Qvortrup 2011); thus children might transition through childhood and age into adulthood but childhood remains a permanent category. Childhood, therefore, becomes worthy of research attention.

Following their pre-sociological approaches, James and colleagues (1998) run through a list of sociological approaches to which they give more credence but also critique (see Table 2.2 for summary). Some forms of social constructionism go further than Prout and James' quotation earlier: that there is no reality. In such forms, childhood is *solely* a social construction (see Stainton-Rogers and Stainton-Rogers 1992), the first row on the table. James and colleagues query whether this form of social constructionism loses the importance of children's bodies and the broader material world (see later for further discussion). For the 'tribal child', James and colleagues group together studies of childhood and childhood culture in their own right, which are depicted as different and distinct from adults. Opie and Opie's work (1969) exemplifies this, where they concentrate on the historical continuity of playground games and songs. Treating childhood as a world apart, however, can ignore the interactions children have with adults (see **generational orders**). The minority group child is associated with children's **human rights**, which considers childhood as a minority group alongside other minority groups who risk oppression (such as women, Indigenous people or persons with disabilities). However, this can unduly treat children as if they are all the same whereas they differ vastly (see Chapter 4). Finally, the social structural child is exemplified by Qvortrup and colleagues' work (see earlier discussion). It is useful in terms of carving out attention to childhood and respecting it as a social category. Its attention to macro-level concerns, however, can problematically universalize childhood and lose the

Table 2.2 Taxonomy of Sociological Approaches to Childhood

Approach	Explanatory Description from the 1998 Book	Authors Who Exemplify This Approach	Potential Critique of This Approach
The socially constructed child	'Childhood does not exist in a finite and identifiable form.' (27)	Stainton-Rogers and Stainton-Rogers (1992)	Does the socially constructed child risk losing the embodied material child?
The tribal child	'It sets out from a commitment to children's social worlds as real places and provinces of meaning in their own right and not as fantasies, games, poor imitations or inadequate precursors of the adult status of being.' (28)	Opie and Opie (1969)	Does the tribal child lead to whimsical tales and quaint fables? Does a child-only culture exist?
The minority group child	'its politicization of childhood in line with previously established agendas concerning an unequal and structurally discriminatory society. . . . Through ascribing to children the status of a minority group this approach seeks, therefore, to challenge rather than confirm an existing set of power relations between adults and children.' (30)	Oakley (1994)	Does the minority group child treat all children as the same?
The social structural child	'The "social structural child", then, has certain universal characteristics which are specifically related to the institutional structure of societies in general and are not simply subject to the changing natures of discourses about children or the radical contingencies of the historical process.' (33)	Qvortrup (1994)	Does the social structural child unduly *universalize* childhood and can it sufficiently consider local differences?

Summarized from James, Jenks and Prout (1998)

diversity of local differences. In the end, James and colleagues argue for attention across several dimensions: from the local to the global and from agency to structure.

James and colleagues' taxonomy is not the only range of social constructions discussed within the literature. For example, Jenks (2005) separately develops his **dichotomy** between the Dionysian view of childhood (the child being innately evil or corrupt) and the Apollonian one (the child having natural goodness and being innocent). Zelizer (1994) puts forward the construction of the 'priceless child'. She argues that children in the global North have been increasingly removed from paid labour and the labour market. Thus, economically children no longer have a 'price', but childhood becomes symbolically of great importance and emotionally 'priceless'. More recently, commentators such as Kjørholt (2013) note the social construction of childhood as an 'investment'. Exemplified by the economic case put forward for investing in **early childhood** (e.g. Heckman et al. 2013), this construction values childhood but primarily in terms of what benefits childhood will bring society in the longer term. Moran-Ellis and Tisdall (2019) consider the construction of the 'competent child' within childhood studies literature itself. They encourage more interrogation of this social construction for its unintended negative consequences. It risks perceiving competency as a characteristic of a child, rather than something that can be enhanced by support, information and experience and is expressed in context and relationally. Competency is often used as threshold concept, so that if a child is considered competent they will be included in decision-making and society more generally but if they are considered to fall below that threshold they can be excluded. These writers are taking that key idea forward, as articulated by Prout and James, that childhood is socially constructed and that there are considerable implications for both individual children and society.

Wyness (2012) provides an overview of the implications of the common construction of childhood, in the global North, as a transitional phase. This excludes children from a status or position in society, in comparison to adults, across three realms. In the political realm, they have less political rights, limited access to legal redress and are subject to more regulation such as mass compulsory schooling (Wyness points out that while children are required to go to school, adults can still choose not to work (2012)). Adult norms and informal rules dominate the cultural realm, leading to children being excluded from or controlled in relation to spaces, times and their own bodies. Finally, children are largely excluded from the economic realm, with little direct recourse to the state, and children's poverty is often hidden and unaddressed within families and households. Wyness points out that these realms interact, leading to the subordinate status of children and childhood in relation to adults and adulthood.

Activity: Childhood constructions in the media

Have a look at media articles you can find online or in print that refer to children.

- How do the media articles construct childhood?
- Do these constructions fit with the categories presented by James and colleagues (Tables 2.1 and 2.2)? Would you suggest another category?
- What are the implications of how the media articles construct childhood for policy and practice?

UNICEF (n.d.) has produced guidelines for journalists reporting on children: https://www.unicef.org/eca/media/ethical-guidelines.

As the new sociology of childhood has aged, so criticisms have grown about social constructionism and other aspects of the paradigm. Social constructionism is accused of being unreflective and unreflexive, becoming a 'theoretical orthodoxy' (Wyness 2015: 19). Social constructionism, as used within the new sociology of childhood, has itself become unduly structured, failing to recognize relationality, **materiality**, fluidity and complexity – ideas that have become commonplace in other sociological debates. Alanen criticizes social construction as a slogan without definition, leading to 'evidence-free assertions' (2015: 151) of these social constructions and their conceptual and methodological implications remaining unexplored. Hammersley (2015) suggests that the underlying political agenda means that important issues – like children lacking some capabilities that most adults have – are not examined nor evidenced. Both Alanen and Hammersley argue that childhood studies version of social constructionism is inherently problematic because it does not apply the same attention to its own social construction. Spyrou (2018) puts forward his answer, advising childhood researchers to recognize that knowledge is perennially mediated through concepts and theories. Researchers, he argues, thus must be mindful and reflexive about how they produce knowledge. Rather than denying ethical and political commitments, Spyrou states that researchers should be committed to disclosing knowledge 'which matters', which is 'knowledge with preferred material consequences on children's lives' (2018: 9). Alderson (2013) provides another answer, in applying **critical realism** to childhood studies. Here, there is an acceptance of **ontological** reality, but also that representing this social world will always be situated within and limited by specific historical, cultural and social frameworks. These more recent critiques are picked up in areas of theoretical development in what is now more commonly called childhood studies.

Critical challenge: What do you think of the social construction of childhood?

- Do you agree with the new sociology of childhood that childhood is a social construction? Why or why not?
- Look at the list of points of the new sociology of childhood paradigm on pages 23. What are the implications of these points for how childhood and children are constructed in policy and practice? Can you think of particular examples?
- Consider your own ethical and political commitments. How might these impact on how you understand **knowledge production** and the construction of childhood?

Key concepts and ongoing debates

The new sociology of childhood is no longer so new: it gained prominence from the 1990s onwards and, at the time of writing this book, is decades old. This has led to a gathering of critiques. Most are encouraged by cross-fertilization from theoretical debates outwith the field, which then challenge some of the precepts of the 1990s' paradigm. These have been enhanced by the increasing **cross-disciplinary** nature of the field, which now is more inclusive of the range of social sciences, human geography, arts and humanities and aspects of the other sciences (see Chapter 3). This has led to the term 'childhood studies', which is used generally throughout this book.

This section rehearses five debates that address key concepts within childhood studies. Generally, there has been a move away from binary categories – dichotomies – that are unhelpfully juxtaposed against each other. An early one that received criticism is the dichotomy between human beings and human becomings, as arguably people are always human becomings whatever their age. A second dichotomy is between humans and the material world: social constructionism is criticized for unduly ignoring bodies, the environment and other aspects of the non-human world. A third and substantial critique is how children's agency was reified in childhood studies research, with substantial reconsiderations now widely accepted in the field. The fourth debate concerns generational ordering, which certain writers have sought to rehabilitate, considering the relations between children and adults. Lastly, there is a growing demand to address the challenge of **decolonization** theories, to decentre global North dominance and to recognize the historical and current repercussions of colonialism. These debates are considered further.

False dichotomies

Early developments of the new sociology of childhood were highly dependent on distinctions between childhood and adulthood. It was these categories that were being socially constructed; it was adults and adulthood that were being held up as the 'golden norm' of rationality and autonomy leading to the subjugation and disregard of children and childhood. The ringing distinction used by Qvortrup (1994) – of whether children were perceived as human beings or human becomings – encapsulates this binary. With the predominant view of children as human becomings, there are practical implications as described by Shamgar-Handelman: 'childhood, whatever form it may take in any given society, always determines children's dependency on adults for supplying their needs and protecting their interests' (1994: 251). The distinction between human being and human becoming has been picked up widely, typically used to advocate for valuing children and childhood in their own right as human beings and not only human becomings.

The dichotomy between human beings and human becomings, however, itself came in for critical attention. Lee (2001) makes a persuasive argument that adulthood itself is not a finished outcome. He documents the increased uncertainties for adults in their identities, careers, relationships and other trajectories, so that adults are also, continually, becomings. The dichotomy of children as human becomings and adults as human beings thus becomes unsettled, if '[t]he condition of human becoming is spreading through the life-course' (Lee 2001: 85). Uprichard also undermines the dichotomy in a different way. She argues against its reliance on the 'arrow of time' and temporality. Drawing on empirical work with children, she underlines how

> 'Looking forward' to what a child 'becomes' is arguably an important part of 'being' a child. By ignoring the future, we are prevented from exploring the ways in which this may itself shape experiences of being children. (2008: 306)

Uprichard hints in her conclusion to the need to also consider the past, which is picked up by Hanson (2017) to explore the past's influence in human rights law and (de)colonization (see discussion on decolonization).

In these ways, dichotomies from the early days of the new sociology of childhood – and particularly childhood versus adulthood and human beings versus human becomings – have become unsettled within childhood studies. Such unsettling was soon applied to other elements, as detailed later.

Critical challenge: Thinking about dichotomies

While these dichotomies are unsettled within childhood studies, can you think of practices or other fields in which the dichotomies are still dominant?

Bringing back the material world?

The quotation from Prout and James (see page 23) is not an extreme form of social constructionism: it does not deny there is a materiality to children's immaturity but rather focuses on how such immaturity is understood in particular contexts. Materiality was picked up within childhood studies writings on the importance of the body and bodies for childhood (e.g. Alderson 2013; Christensen 2000; Coffey et al. 2016). But childhood studies literature increasingly encouraged theorizations to go further, drawing on broader philosophical and sociological trends associated with **posthumanism** and **materialism**.

These concepts challenge global North preoccupations with humans as the central defining category, hierarchically superior to other species and perceiving the non-human as inanimate material to be exploited (see Ritchie 2012; Skott-Myhre 2020; Taylor and Giugni 2012). Instead, humans are de-centred, bringing in other aspects – such as the physical environment, animals and technology – to how the social world is constituted and knowledge is produced (Spyrou et al. 2018). Myers builds on such theorizations to provide an explanatory overview:

> That is, humans alone do not create the world or the relationships and meanings therein; space is opened for matter in different and often confounding ways. All material bodies – human and more-than-human-alike – are phenomena in relation emerging through a kind of intra-action that is both *material* and *discursive* in nature. . . . There is no longer a hierarchy between the meaning-making subject and the passive object, as all being and knowing are *entangled*. (2019: 8, italics in original)

Such understandings are thus highly relational, spatial and temporal, unsettling the privileging of individuals, humans and knowledge acquisition.

> Relational materialism helped me think differently about children's agency, in terms of how agency comes about through social interactions. Reading about relational materialism helped me analyse how agency was expressed in relationship not only with other people but also with different kinds of non-human actors as well. Hillevi Lenz Taguchi's work with young children was especially helpful for me as she gives practical examples (and photos!) of material relations.
>
> *Caralyn Blaisdell, Lecturer in Initial Teacher Education,*
> *Queen Margaret University, UK*

This unsettling connects within Indigenous thought. Ritchie, for example, writes about Māori understandings about human and non-human relations:

> For Māori, the Earth Mother Papatūanuku and the Sky Father Ranginui are the original ancestors not only of people but also of fellow descendants – the trees, animals, birds and insects. All living creatures are related through this **genealogy**. This is a form of relationality that differs from the binary dynamic of human dominance over nature, in that this view of relationality positions humans as cohabitants of a shared realm, reflecting an ethic of care and respect for the more-than-human world as something to which humans are privileged to be in relation with. (2012: 86, bold not in the original)

Taylor and Giugni (2012) combine such Māori understandings with the ideas of human geographer Massey on place. Massey notes the importance of landscapes for a sense of place. While often described as 'natural' and treated as stable (see Massey 2006), landscapes themselves are 'continuously changing, folding, rupturing and being reshaped' (Taylor and Guigni 2012: 114). Such change can be over immense amounts of time – like geological shifts of land from the equator to other parts of the world – or more sudden changes like volcanoes or earthquakes. Thus, both human and non-human elements are 'on the move', albeit not necessarily at the same time, and belonging needs to recognize migration, openness and the possibilities of living together (see Massey 2005).

The rise of such **post-humanist** theories, however, risks another colonization of Indigenous thought. Famously, Todd writes of Euro-Western academic appropriation of these ideas in post-humanism, which ignores the heritage and continuity in Indigenous thought:

> When anthropologists and other assembled social scientists sashay in and start cherry-picking parts of Indigenous thought that appeal to them *without engaging directly in (or unambiguously acknowledging) the political situation, agency, legal orders and relationality of both Indigenous people and scholars,* we immediately become complicit in colonial violence. (2016: 18, italics in original)

She suggests practical tools to consider Indigenous ontologies with care and respect, through accounting for location and Indigenous Place-Thought and recognizing the continuing colonial imperatives within academia (Todd 2016; see also Rosiek et al. 2020). Nxumalo and Cedillo (2017) apply such tools to place-based early childhood education, for example, to focus politicized attention to place, to question what counts as 'nature' and which children are seen as belonging or not to such places of nature. These connections between the social and the material, the human and the non-human, across time and space, are not a recent innovation but rather a new challenge to global North constructs of humans and society.

Exploring concepts further: Assemblages

You may see in the childhood studies literature reference to **'assemblages'**. This idea comes from Deleuze and Guattari's work (e.g. see 2003). Anderson explains:

> Assemblage theory offers a challenge to conventional configurations of the relations between parts and wholes. In a challenge to the

concept of organic and seamless entities, assemblage theory argues that wholes . . . are constructed by the coming together of separate and individual parts. From the perspective of assemblage theory, parts can function autonomously, yet they can also become part of assembled wholes, be removed from them, and then become part of further yet-to-be-assembled 'coming togethers'. (2021: no page)

Questioning agency?

If social constructionism has been described as a theoretical orthodoxy for the new sociology of childhood, children's **agency** has been considered one of its mantras (Gallagher 2019). The popularity of children's agency grew from the critiques of child development, sociology and anthropology when children were treated and perceived as passive subjects. In response, childhood studies asserted that children are and can be social actors – a key principle within the paradigm (see earlier discussion). From there grew a crescendo of interest in children's agency, underpinned by a host of qualitative research studies showing how children are in fact agents across settings and contexts (for critique, see Hammersley 2017; James 2010). Several authors reflect that this likely arises from the researchers' ethical and political agendas, to support the visibility of children, the value of children and childhood in their own right, and children's rights (e.g. Spyrou 2018; Tisdall and Punch 2012). Showing that 'children are agents' is part of reconstructing childhood.

Agency was thus often mentioned within childhood studies literature but rarely defined and conceptually discussed. It has been much discussed in sociology. Giddens (1984) provides a seminal definition, often cited: 'An agent ceases to be such if he or she loses the capability to "make a difference", that is, to exercise some sort of power' (14). This definition is part of Gidden's structuration theory – which he does not develop in light of children and childhood – where he is concerned about the relationships between structure, systems, agency and power. As James and James (2008) explain, according to Giddens, '[p]eople can and do have the power, through their actions, to change the very social structures and institutions through which they live and work' (10). When applied to children, then, they too can exercise some power and make a difference. Mayall (2002) discusses how agency relates to the term 'social actor' central to the new sociology of childhood paradigm (see page 23, 27). She makes this distinction:

> A social *actor* does something, perhaps something arising from a subjective wish. The term *agent* suggests a further dimension: negotiation with others, with the effect that the interaction makes a difference – to a relationship or to a decision, to the workings of a set of social assumptions or constraints. (2002: 21, italics in original)

Mayall thus requires an agent to be more than a social actor: that person must have a social connection (i.e. negotiation with others) and makes an impact (i.e. make a difference).

The mantra of children's agency has since come under much scrutiny. This asks whether agency's application has always been helpful to analysis and practice, and debates its theoretical content. Children's agency, as it has been used, has been problematic in several ways. First, childhood studies emancipatory agenda meant that children's agency tended to be presented as innately and inevitably positive, thus leading to problems if children's agency seemed questionable. For example, Bordonaro and Payne (2012; see also Edmonds 2019) write about the 'ambiguous agency' of children, when children's agency threatens or goes against existing moral and social orders. Children who go against social norms can have their agency taken away, problematized or ignored, such as when children undertake paid work, are soldiers or engage in sex work (e.g. see Liebel 2020; Montgomery 2007; Rosen 2007). Second, children can be blamed if they are perceived as not expressing their agency (LaFrancois 2008) or made more **vulnerable** by insensitive insistence that they are agents (Tisdall and Punch 2012). Third, inadequate consideration can be given to context and other circumstances. Klocker develops the concepts of 'thin' and 'thick' agency to reflect this:

> 'thin' agency refers to decisions and everyday actions that are carried out within highly restrictive contexts, characterized by few viable alternatives. 'Thick' agency is having the latitude to act within a broad range of options. It is possible for a person's agency to be 'thickened' or 'thinned' over time and space, and across their various relationships . . . Structures, contexts, and relationships can act as 'thinners' or 'thickeners' of individuals' agency, by constraining or expanding their range of viable choices. (2007: 85)

Structures can limit children's expressions of agency in particular circumstances and, according to this critique, need to be taken into account when considering children as social actors (see Chapter 6).

With such criticisms, the mantra of children's agency is increasingly questioned, as described by Huijsmans:

> a counter-movement is emerging which does not reject the importance of studying children as social actors who are exercising agency but which is critical of the tendency in childhood studies to treat children's agency in a celebratory, uncritical, a-theoretical, non-relational, locally-bound and nonreflective manner. (2011: 1308)[1]

The counter-movement moves away from conceptualizing agency as a characteristic of an individual child or something that they possess. In other words, a child is not an agent and a child does not have agency. Instead, agency is something that is expressed relationally and in context. This can be seen in the traditions of the new sociology of childhood, such as Corsaro's research with young children in Italy. He developed the concept of interpretive reproduction, where children are contributing to cultural production and change while also being constrained by their societies and cultures (Corsaro 2017). A child thus might express agency in a particular context, with the questions turning to when, where and how children's agency happens (Oswell 2013; Spyrou 2018) – and perhaps why as well.

Relational agency has also gone beyond considerations of the social and the human to the material and the non-human (see previous discussion). Myers, for example, summarizes how a post-human perspective understands agency:

> not as something to be *possessed*, but as something that *arises* from the intra-connections between bodies as they make themselves known to each other. Agency is an action, or the collectivity of actions, rather than a characteristic of any one human, being, or thing. (2019: 231, italics in original)

Gallagher (2019) discusses possibilities for reconsidering agency as a result. For example, agency does not have intrinsic ethical value (it is not inevitably a 'good thing') so its ethics can only be determined by examining specific instances. It could be helpful to think of different types of agency, from the more routine to the more inventive. In comparison to routine agency, inventive agency is more unexpected, but neither is intrinsically superior. Agency is best analysed within its wider interactions, moving beyond humanistic accounts to include the material.

Agency is often discussed through a lens of individualism and notions of 'the self' – like concepts of autonomy, self-efficacy and self-confidence. But, in some parts of the world, notions of identity are inherently relational and not individualistic – they are deeply connected with family and community positions, roles and responsibilities – and thus 'agency' is exercised in ways which reflect this relationality in everyday life. Taking a more culturally informed view of 'agency' means recognizing how it is exercised and what is meaningful about the ways it is exercised from a local perspective, rather than imposing ideas from elsewhere.

Ruth Edmonds, Cultural and Ethnographic Researcher, Keep Your Shoes Dirty (research consultancy) and Centre for Research on Families and Relationships, University of Edinburgh, UK

Gidden's theorization of agency emphasizes individual knowledge and **reflexivity**, and the power of the individual to act and make a difference. This associates agency with individuals, choice, rationality and autonomy. Thus, discussions of children's agency can slip into discussions of children's choice and autonomy without due consideration. However, such concepts can be critically considered. Mühlbacher and Sutterlüty (2019), for example, argue against an understanding of autonomy as solely individualistic and for one that is developed relationally with others. Oswell (2013) provides a powerful critique that Giddens' insistence on reflexive rationality and autonomous action can be inapplicable to children, particularly children who are very young. Esser and colleagues (2016) discuss how agency's association with the autonomous individual has been inappropriately applied to more communal contexts in the **global South**, which value the social and the relational. Wyness returns to agency's relationship with autonomy, to conclude:

> Children as agents are immersed within the social world and thus embedded in relations within which they have a formative influence. The child agent is not only capable but also fully social. Agency cannot simply be equated with individual choice or individual autonomy . . . it needs to be viewed as a relational concept, an effect of complex shifting social arrangements. (2015: 13)

The debates on children's agency continue within childhood studies. The predominant turn, at the time of writing, is to consider agency as relational and contextual, rather than a fixed characteristic of a child. There are growing calls to go beyond agency as a human expression, recognizing the relationships between the human and the material.

Activity: Thinking about agency

Select a theorization of agency, either discussed in this Chapter or by another author. Based on this, try writing your own 'children's agency' definition.

- How might this definition reflect your and/or the author's perspective?
- Do you think 'agency' is useful in childhood studies or is it too problematic to be of use?

Considering generational order?

The structural approach of Qvortrup and others (see previous discussion) was picked up and developed by authors such as Alanen, Leonard, Mayall and Punch to present ideas of **generation**, generational orders and **generationing**. These developments perceive the binary distinction between childhood and adulthood as conceptually and practically important while bringing in more explicit children's agency within these social structures of generations. Mayall (2001) provides a clear description of how childhood is distinguished from adulthood, by adults, through three sets of relationships:

> [Firstly] . . . Children are identified by adults as non-adults, so the social world that adults construct consists of two groups with somewhat separate interests and relationships to the social order. Secondly, children's lives are structured by adults – by their interests, understandings and goals; the social condition of childhood is defined through adult-child relations mediated through these interests, understandings and goals. Thirdly, the family and to a lesser extent the school operates on the basis of personal including affective relationships between adults and children. Thus, the permanent social category childhood can be seen as structured in relation to adulthood. (114)

Mayall's Chapter goes on to discuss her research findings, from a study in London with nine- to ten- and twelve- to thirteen-year-olds, on children's own understandings of being a child or being called a child. This exemplifies how conceptualizations of generational orders can incorporate children's expressions of agency. Leonard coins the term '**intergeneragency**' to capture this, emphasizing both the generational and agency aspects of her framework:

> The 'gener' aspect of the concept involves acknowledging the ongoing relevance of generation for understanding the location of childhood and adulthood and the implications of this positioning for both parties. Both children and adults are part of a wider social order based on generation that permeates and demarcates everyday life. The 'agency' aspect of the concept recognises children as agents who actively construct their own everyday lives and the everyday lives of those around them, while emphasising the importance of locating children's agency within the positioning of childhood relative to adulthood. Hence, the term encapsulates the structural positioning of childhood while simultaneously acknowledging children's active agency in generational relationships. (2015: 132)

Leonard recognizes the interplay within generations, for example across peers and in schools, so she contributes the term '**intra-generagency**' to frame such relations. As Leonard writes, concepts based on generations show the power and durability of **inter-** and **intra-generational relationships** and children express their agency within these.

Exploring concepts further: Generational order

Alanen (2011) explains the concept of **generational order**:

> The core idea in the notion of a generational order is that there exists in modern societies a system of social ordering that specifically pertains to children as a social category, and circumscribes for them particular social locations from which they act and thereby participate in ongoing social life. Children are thus involved in the daily 'construction' of their own and other people's everyday relationships and life trajectories. (2011: 161)

If childhood and adulthood are distinguished primarily by age, in the global North, then age becomes an explanatory social category alongside other characteristics such as **gender, ethnicity**, disability, social class and sexual orientation. This recognition has practical implications. Just as social research routinely considers characteristics like gender or ethnicity when developing a survey sample or to ensure sufficient diversity across case studies, age should be considered routinely as a potentially relevant social category. Service or development projects would have to pay due attention to age, just as they are required by funders (and sometimes law) to consider characteristics such as gender. Recognizing the salience of age does not need to homogenize children, presuming that all within the category are the same. Children can differ as do other populations by all the characteristics listed above and more: for example, by whether they live in rural or urban settings (Rees et al. 2017), their access to digital technology (OECD 2020) or the holdover of the caste system in India (Vart et al. 2015). But the argument is that age is also a characteristic to consider and a pervasive and important one to do so.

In the two decades since ideas of generational orders and generationing were put forward, the concepts have not pervaded childhood studies to the same extent as agency or the social construction of childhood. Punch reflects upon this in her 2020 article, suggesting three reasons. First, early critiques argued against the dichotomy between children and adults, childhood and adulthood (see earlier discussion). Their critiques spread onto generational orders because of their use of the binary between childhood and adulthood. Second, other aspects of social life than age can be perceived as more important. This led to less empirical investigations of generational order within childhood studies and thus the empirical basis is thin on them. Third, Punch notes that intra-generational relations – that is, across a generation – need to be considered alongside intergenerational relations – that is, between children and adults. Punch, for example, has undertaken research on sibling relations in Bolivia, pointing out that age and birth order can be more salient for children's work roles than gender (see also Punch 2001; 2016). Punch argues that further development of generational orders would greatly enhance childhood studies itself and would provide an important influence more generally on the social sciences.

The ordering between adults and children is also important for those who develop the concepts of **childism** or **adultism**. As Wall (2019) writes, childism extends such intergenerational considerations to even broader critiques of social norms, systems and indeed scholarship. Childism recognizes that embedded power relations privilege adult norms:

> adulthood becomes naturalized and at the same time age becomes a legitimate power order when it comes to the age categorization of children, since children's subordination is regarded as something natural and often desirable;

children are viewed as 'under development' and in need of adult protection and care. (Sundhall 2017: 165)

An example is excluding children's views in contested contact cases in family law, due to adults' concerns that children are too vulnerable or are incompetent to express their views, rather than perceiving children as actors within their families and their views relevant for the considerations (Morrison et al. 2020). Another example is children's own contributions within 'child-headed households' being insufficiently acknowledged, leaning to policy responses that fail to address their financial needs and undermine their functioning (e.g. Payne 2012; van Dijk and van Driel 2009). Both examples demonstrate that the attitudes, systems and institutions may not be maliciously intended and, instead, people involved may have the best of intentions. However, the results may be systematic discrimination against or disadvantages for children that bring age into assessments of **intersectional** oppression (see Chapter 5).

The respective definitions and conceptualisms of childism and adultism are, at the time of writing, in dispute. Young-Bruehl (2012) powerfully writes about childism in the United States, defining it as societal prejudice against children, akin to racism, sexism and anti-Semitism. Adultism, in contrast, is prejudice in favour of adults (Young-Bruehl 2012). But Young-Bruehl is roundly criticized by Wall for only offering 'a negative, deficit-oriented lens for studying childhoods, and not a positive, agentic one' (2019: 263). Childism, in contrast, deconstructs adultism and reconstructs social norms (Wall 2019). A way forward could be to associate adultism more sharply with negative prejudice (akin to sexism) and childism with the reconstructive potential (akin to feminism).[2] Both are powerful concepts for analysis and reformulation, gathering increasing interest in childhood studies and, aspirationally, potentially a wider contribution to other fields.

Discussions of generational ordering, on the one hand, and of childism or adultism, on the other hand, are not commonly found in the same writings. The first is more sociological, observing the creation, challenge and reformulation of generational ordering, while the second is more directional in challenging and decentring the predominancy of adult norms. But they have similarities in observing the relations between childhood and adulthood, and the power imbued within those relations. Ordering by age and stage is pervasive.

Activity: Critical thinking about Mosquito devices

Mosquito devices are machines that produce a sound, which most adults cannot hear. Children though can typically hear the sound and the sound can be distressing. The devices have been used in Scotland and elsewhere to make older children leave public spaces such as train stations.

- Pick one of the authors on generational orders mentioned earlier, and apply their concepts to this practical example of the Mosquito devices. What is your critical analysis as a result?
- Pick one of the authors on childism or adultism mentioned earlier, and apply their concepts to this practical example of the Mosquito devices. What is your critical analysis as a result?

(**Young people** in Scotland were so concerned about these devices that they petitioned the Scottish Parliament. For more information on their views and the ensuing policy discussions, see the website for Commissioner for Children and Young People Scotland.[3])

The challenge of decolonization

Decolonization requires more than an unsettling of certain ideas in childhood studies: decolonization requires change in the world order (Tuck and Yang 2012: 31). It draws attention to the entwined forces of colonialism, empire and racism shaping the contemporary world. It is sharply critical of academic knowledge creation and promulgation: Smith (2021) highlights how accepted research concepts (such as 'discovery' or 'truth') are rooted in colonial histories and facilitate Indigenous people's exploitation. It requires alternative ways of thinking about the world, disrupting dominant, established ways of knowing, decentering the dominance of Euro-Western concepts, norms and objectives. Kurtiş and Adams (2017) put this in another way: the first strategy is to normalize patterns in diverse **Majority World** settings and the second is to denaturalize patterns in **Minority World** settings. As Mignolo (2008) writes, this need not erase the Euro-Western-centred narrative but rather recognize it does not have the right to be the narrative for the rest of the world. Tuck and Yang (2012), drawing on earlier work by Fanon and Césaire, famously argue that decolonization needs to go beyond developing critical consciousness: it has practical ramifications in repatriation of land to Indigenous People.

Decolonization theory highlights the historical ubiquity of imperial colonization since at least the fifteenth century. As of the start of the World War I, nine-tenths of the world were controlled or occupied by imperialist powers (Cannella and Viruru 2004; Young 2016). Imperialism was facilitated and justified by ideas of racial superiority, with European cultural values around rationality, individuality and autonomy seen as better than those subjected to imperial powers, allowing for the 'civilizing mission' of imperialism to progress and oppress (Nieuwenhuys 2013). Imperialism inspired particular ways of organizing, imposing administrative structures that categorized people in certain ways and geographical boundaries that led into (often disputed) nation states (Liebel 2020; Ndlovu-Gatsheni 2013). While imperialist powers largely were unable to sustain their empires politically after the World War II, the argument is that colonialism is still current today. Kurtiş and Adams put this succinctly and powerfully:

> Standard narratives in intellectual and everyday social discourse represent everyday realities of the modern global order as the benign product of a steady march of human cultural progress. In stark contrast, decolonial theorists use the term *coloniality* to emphasize the extent to which everyday realities of the modern global order are the harmful legacy of the **racialized** colonial violence that enabled Euro-American global domination. (2017: 47, italics in the original, bold not in the original)

Thus, colonization continues to have ongoing impact, politically, economically and culturally.

Decolonization then has considerable implications for childhood studies (e.g. see Cheney 2018; Liebel 2020; Nieuwenhuys 2013). Balagopalan (2018) challenges childhood studies to go further than its ethnographic studies undertaken in the global South, used to discuss '**multiple childhoods**', to address underlying questions of power due to colonization. She critiques many of these studies for failing to challenge more fundamentally the conceptual categories drawn from the Euro-American contexts. This requires historicizing the particular contexts for children. She draws on post-colonial and decolonization theories to argue that colonial contexts are not just in the past but continue to have pervasive influence on current childhoods (see Commentary Chapter 2).

Writers about childhoods, using decolonizing theory, provide a particular critique about imposing developmentalism on children. De Castro (2020a), for example, writes about how developmental psychology took hold from the nineteenth century onwards, creating the scientific study of childhood that understands human development as a biographical trajectory leading from the inferior child to the superior adult (see also Burman 2019; Cannella and Viruru 2004). Thus, the familiar critique from the early new sociology of childhood is linked with decolonization theory, to question the dominance of developmentalism and particularly the ways in which it universalized white, global North and middle-class childhoods. Certain ideas claimed to be European (such as individualization, rationality and autonomy) were and are used to demean ways of thinking in settings of the global South, as being pre-modern and uncivilized. Children are thus a prime focus for colonization, symbolically important not only for childhood but for societal development (see Commentary Chapter 5).

Activity: Applying decolonial theory to practices

Read some examples of applying decolonial theory to particular practices. Two studies you may appreciate are:

Basu (2019) writes about the contemporary juvenile justice system in India.

She discusses how the imposition of Euro-centred models of childhood and development led to marginalized children (e.g. from lower castes) being perceived as deviant and subject to state surveillance and intervention.

Pace-Crosschild (2018) writes about an Indigenous child and family centre (Opokaa'sin) located in traditional Blackfoot country in present-day Western Canada.

She explains the approach taken by Opokaa'sin to reject imposed colonial values (such as patriarchy, women's labour, the nuclear family and capitalist ideas about children) and to culturally reconnect with traditional Blackfoot language instruction, storytelling, music and elders' teaching.

Consider an area of practice you are interested in for your own research or based on your lived experience. What needs to be in place to develop ways of doing and being outside an Euro-centric model?

When I undertook fieldwork with waste picker families in India, I began to question Euro-centric discourses on eradicating child labour and the 'normal' protected spaces of childhood. I found that while there are undoubtedly risks of violence and exploitation, some children and young people find that the streets, and the informal work they engage in, bring value and opportunities to their own lives and identities.

Loritta Chan, Postdoctoral Research Assistant, School of Geosciences, University of Edinburgh, UK

Religion, schooling and more widely education are powerful instruments to mould particular constructions of childhood. Colonization is used to oppress and suppress Indigenous knowledge and ways of being (see also Dei and Asgharzadeh 2001; Gerlach 2018). Decolonization theories thus provide potential for transformative ways of learning, understanding and practice, providing a fundamental challenge to childhood studies.

Decolonization makes sharp critiques of certain elements well-discussed in childhood studies: namely in regard to the 'global child', to children's agency and to human rights (see also Chapter 4). In the 1990s, globalization became a popular theoretical concept, as a way for social sciences to grapple with spreading capitalism, the increased connectivity provided by the internet and how to understand the connections between local communities and global networks and influences (e.g. Held et al. 2000; Scholte 2000). Childhood studies picked up this concept as well to consider global childhoods. It was used, for example, to discuss consumerism and how global consumer culture was creating the 'consuming child'. Children are increasingly constituted by international markets' demands, which treat them as consumers and thus actors across the world (e.g. Buckingham 2011; Cook 2004). De Castro (2020b), though, questions this global child, as a continuation of colonization as it accepts the (neo)imperial project of capitalism. He argues that it perceives a universal trajectory for colonized nations, as well as for children. Once again, the dichotomy is made between the global South and the global North, he argues, where the template is the individualized, competent, agentic consuming child.

Decolonization theory, which originated from outwith childhood studies, thus challenges childhood studies. Some of these challenges buttress other trends, such as the questioning of developmentalism, universal norms and constructions of childhood, and false binaries. Other challenges more fundamentally question Euro-centric norms, to provide spaces for other ways of understanding and being, and particularly to reconsider childhood studies own tenets around children as social actors and children's human rights arguments (see Chapter 4).

Conclusion

This Chapter outlines the foundations of childhood studies, as it has developed particularly in the global North and in the English language. In the 1990s, the new sociology of childhood gained increasing attention in suggesting that childhood is socially constructed, that childhood is worth studying, that children are social actors in their own right – and that these elements have practical and political implications. Since then, the field has expanded to a wider range of **disciplines**, with contestation over several key concepts. How childhood studies has used agency, for example, has been much debated. Currently, most argue for agency to be understood as something expressed relationally and in context, rather than an inherent characteristic or possession. Further, the field has been challenged to go beyond agency as an individualistic, human concern to consider context and the material world. The value of considering age as a social category is having a renaissance in the revised ideas about generationing and adultism/childism. Decades on from the new sociology of the childhood from the 1990s, these and other productive developments are taken forward in later Chapters of this book.

Childhood studies has the potential to challenge 'mainstream' disciplines that can continue to ignore children and childhood, age and generationing, as characteristics of potential relevance alongside other dimensions more regularly considered such as ethnicity or gender. Childhood studies equally has been challenged to consider its own 'blinkers'. For example, it has empirically been influenced by studies in the global South as well as the global North, but its own social constructions have not necessarily taken on concepts, ideas and research developed *within* the global South and particularly those written in languages other than English. Thus, ideas of decolonization provide important challenges to unsettling childhood studies own narrative in productive ways.

Activity: Debates in the childhood studies literature on theory and research

Consider the arguments between Hammersley, Kim and Thomas about childhood studies theory and research. This includes debates about the social construction of childhood, children's rights and **children's participation** in research. Do you agree or disagree – and why?

The first set of articles:

Hammersley, M. (2015), 'Research Ethics and the Concept of Children's Rights', *Children & Society,* 29 (6): 569–82.

Hammersley, M. (2017), 'Childhood Studies: A Sustainable Paradigm?', *Childhood,* 24 (1): 113–27.

Kim, C.-Y. (2016), 'Why Research "by" Children? Rethinking the Assumptions Underlying the Facilitation of Children as Researchers', *Children & Society,* 30 (3): 230–40.

The response:

Thomas, N. P. (2021), 'Child-led Research, Children's Rights and Childhood Studies: A Defence', *Childhood,* 28 (2): 186–99.

The response to the response:

Hammersley, M. and Kim, C.-Y. (2021), 'Child-led Research, Children's Rights and Childhood Studies – A Reply to Thomas', *Childhood,* 28 (2): 200–2.

Notes

1. To note, my attention to this quotation and article came through Gallagher's (2019) article.
2. A similar suggestion is attributed to Wall, on the kindred media website, https://www.kindredmedia.org/glossary/childism/ (accessed 4 March 2023).
3. https://www.cypcs.org.uk/positions/mosquito-devices/#:~:text=Mosquito%20devices%20are%20machines%20that,of%20international%20human%20rights%20law (accessed 4 March 2023).

References

Alanen, L. (2011), 'Generational Order', in J. Qvortrup, W. A. Corsaro, M. Honig, and G. Valentine (eds), *The Palgrave Handbook of Childhood Studies*, 159–74, London: Palgrave Macmillan.

Alanen, L. (2015), 'Are We All Constructionists Now?', *Childhood*, 22 (2): 149–53.

Alderson, P. (2013), *Childhoods Real and Imagined*, Abingdon: Routledge.

Anderson, J. (2021), 'Assemblage', *Oxford Bibliographies*, 15 April. Available online: https://www.oxfordbibliographies.com/view/document/obo-9780199874002/obo-9780199874002-0114.xml (accessed 30 June 2022).

Ariès, P. (1962), *Centuries of Childhood*. Translated. (first published 1960), Harmondsworth: Penguin.

Balagopalan, S. (2018), 'Children, Culture, History', in S. Spyrou, R. Rosen, and D. T. Cook (eds), *Reimagining Childhood Studies*, 23–39, London: Bloomsbury Academic.

Basu, C. (2019), '"Ours" or "Theirs": Locating the "Criminal Child" in Relation to Education in the Postcolonial Context of India', in A. Twum-Danso Imoh, M. Bourdillon, and S. Meicsner (eds), *Global Childhoods Beyond the North-South Divide*, 57–79, Basingstoke: Palgrave Macmillan.

Bordonaro, L. I. and Payne, R. (2012), 'Ambiguous Agency', *Children's Geographies*, 10 (4): 365–72.

Buckingham, D. (2011), *The Material Child*, Cambridge: Polity Press.

Bühler-Niederberger, D. (2010), 'Introduction: Childhood Sociology — Defining the State of the Art and Ensuring Reflection', *Current Sociology*, 58 (2): 155–64.

Burman, E. (2019), 'Child as Method: Implications for Decolonising Educational Research', *International Studies in Sociology of Education*, 28 (1): 4–26.

Cannella, G. S. and Viruru, R. (2004), *Childhood and Postcolonization*, London: Routledge.

Cheney, K. (2018), 'Decolonizing Childhood Studies', in S. Spyrou, R. Rosen, and D. T. Cook (eds), *Reimagining Childhood Studies*, 91–104, London: Bloomsbury Academic.

Christensen, P. (2000), 'Childhood and the Cultural Construction of Vulnerable Bodies', in A. Prout (ed.), *The Body, Childhood and Society*, 38–59, Basingstoke: Macmillan.

Coffey, J., Budgeon, S., and Cahill, H. (eds) (2016), 'The Body in Youth and Childhood Studies', in *Learning Bodies*, Singapore: Springer Singapore

Cook, D. (2004), *The Commodification of Childhood*, Durham, NC: Duke University Press.

Corsaro, W. (2017), *The Sociology of Childhood*, 5th edn, London: Sage.

Cunningham, H. (1995), *Children and Childhood in Western Society Since 1500*, London: Routledge.

de Castro, L. R. (2020a), 'Decolonising Child Studies: Development and Globalism as Orientalist Perspectives', *Third World Quarterly*, 42 (11): 2487–504.

de Castro, L. R. (2020b), 'Why Global? Children and Childhood From a Decolonial Perspective', *Childhood*, 27 (1): 48–62.

Dei, G. J. S. and Asgharzadeh, A. (2001), 'The Power of Social Theory: The Anti-colonial Discursive Framework', *The Journal of Educational Thought*, 35 (3): 297–323.

Deleuze, G. and Guattari, F. (2003). *A Thousand Plateaus*, London: Continuum.

Edmonds, R. (2019), 'Making Children's "Agency" Visible: Towards the Localisation of a Concept in Theory and Practice', *Global Studies of Childhood*, 9 (3): 200–11.

Esser, F., Baader, M. S., Betz, T., and Hungerland, B. (2016), *Reconceptualising Agency and Childhood*, London: Routledge.

Gallagher, M. (2019) 'Rethinking Children's Agency: Power, Assemblages, Freedom and Materiality', *Global Studies of Childhood*, 9 (3): 188–99.

Gerlach, A. (2018), 'Thinking and Researching Relationally: Enacting Decolonizing Methodologies with an Indigenous Early Childhood Program in Canada', *International Journal of Qualitative Methods*, 17 (1): 1–8.

Giddens, A. (1984), *The Constitution of Society*, Berkeley and Los Angeles: University of California Press.

Guterman, J. T. (2013), *Mastering the Art of Solution-focused Counseling*, 2nd edn, Alexandria, VA: American Counseling Association.

Hammersley, M. (2015), 'Research Ethics and the Concept of Children's Rights', *Children & Society*, 29 (6): 569–82.

Hammersley, M. (2017), 'Childhood Studies: A Sustainable Paradigm?', *Childhood*, 24 (1): 113–27.

Hanson, K. (2017), 'Embracing the Past: "Been", "Being" and "Becoming" Children', *Childhood*, 24 (3): 281–5.

Heckman, J., Pinto, R., and Savelyev, P. (2013), 'Understanding the Mechanisms Through Which an Influential Early Childhood Program Boosted Adult Outcomes', *The American Economic Review*, 103 (6): 2052–86.

Held, D., McGrew, T., Goldblatt, D., and Perraton, J. (2000), 'Global Transformations, Politics, Economics and Culture', in C. Pierson and S. Tomey (eds), *Politics at the Edge*, 14–28, Stanford: Stanford University Press.

Huijsmans, R. (2011), 'Child Migration and Questions of Agency', *Development and Change*, 42 (95): 1307–21.

James, A. (2010), 'Competition or Integration? The Next Step in Childhood Studies?', *Childhood*, 17 (4), 485–99.

James, A. and James, A. (2008) *Key Concepts in Childhood Studies*, 1st edn, London: Sage.

James, A., Jenks, C., and Prout, A. (1998), *Theorizing Childhood*, Oxford: Blackwell.

Jenks, C. (2005), *Childhood*, 2nd edn, London: Routledge.

Kirby, P. and Woodhead, M. (2003) 'Children's Participation in Society', in H. Montgomery, R. Burr, and M. Woodhead (eds), *Changing Childhoods: Local and Global*, 233–84, Chichester: John Wiley & Sons and Open University.

Kjørholt, A.T, 2013. 'Childhood as Social Investment, Rights and the Valuing of Education', *Children & Society*, 27 (4): 245–57.

Klocker, N. (2007), 'An Example of "Thin" Agency: Child Domestic Workers in Tanzania', in R. Panelli, S. Punch, and E. Robson (eds), *Global Perspectives on Rural Childhood and Youth*, 83–94, New York: Routledge.

Kurtiş, T. and Adams, G. (2017), 'Decolonial Intersectionality: Implications for Theory, Research, and Pedagogy', in K. A. Case (ed.), *Intersectional Pedagogy: Complicating Identity and Social Justice*, 46–59, New York: Routledge.

LaFrancois, B. A., (2008), 'It's Like Mental Torture: Participation and Mental Health Services', *The International Journal of Children's Rights*, 16 (2): 211–27.

Lancy, D. (2022), *The Anthropology of Childhood: Cherubs, Chattel, Changelings*, 3rd edn, Cambridge: Cambridge University Press.

Lee, N. (2001), *Childhood and Society: Growing up in an Age of Uncertainty*, Buckingham: Open University Press.

Leeds-Hurwitz, W. (2016), 'Social Construction', *Oxford Bibliographies*. Available online: https://www.oxfordbibliographies.com/view/document/obo-9780199756841/obo-9780199756841-0106.xml (accessed 5 June 2022).

Leonard, M. (2015), *The Sociology of Children, Childhood and Generation*, London: Sage.

Liebel, M. (2020), *Decolonizing Childhoods: From Exclusion to Dignity*, Bristol: Policy Press.

Marshall, K. (1997), *Children's Rights in the Balance: The Participation-protection Debate*, Edinburgh: Stationery Office.

Massey, D. (2005), *For Space*, London: Sage.

Massey, D. (2006), 'Landscape as a Provocation: Reflections on Moving Mountains', *Journal of Material Culture*, 11 (1/2): 33–48.

Mayall, B. (2001), 'Understanding Childhoods: A London Study', in Alanen, L. and Mayall, B. (eds), *Conceptualising Child-Adult Relations*, 114–28, London: Routledge.

Mayall, B. (2002), *Towards a Sociology for Childhood: Thinking from Children's Lives*, Buckingham: Open University Press.

Mignolo, W. D. (2008), 'Preamble: The Historical Foundation of Modernity/ Coloniality and the Emergence of Decolonial Thinking', in S. Castro-Klaren (ed.), *A Companion to Latin American Literature and Culture*, 1–32, London: Wiley.

Montgomery, H. (2007), 'Working with Child Prostitutes in Thailand: Problems of Practice and Interpretation', *Childhood*, 14 (4): 415–30.

Moran-Ellis, J. and Tisdall, E. K. M. (2019), 'The Relevance of "Competence" for Enhancing or Limiting Children's Participation: Unpicking Conceptual Confusion', *Global Studies of Childhood*, 9 (3): 212–23.

Morrison, F., Callaghan, J., and Tisdall, E. K. M. (2020), 'Manipulation and Domestic Abuse in Contested Contact – Threats to Children's Participation Rights', *Family Court Review*, 58 (2): 403–16.

Mühlbacher, S. and Sutterlüty, F. (2019), 'The Principle of Child Autonomy: A Rationale for the Normative Agenda of Childhood Studies', *Global Studies of Childhood*, 9 (3): 249–60.

Myers, C. (2019), *Children and Materialities: The Force of the More-than-human in Children's Classroom Lives*, Singapore: Springer Verlag.

Ndlovu-Gatsheni, S. J. (2013), 'The Entrapment of Africa Within the Global Colonial Matrices of Power', *Journal of Developing Societies*, 29 (4): 331–53.

Nieuwenhuys, O. (2013), 'Theorizing Childhood(s): Why We Need Postcolonial Perspectives', *Childhood*, 20 (1): 3–8.

Nxumalo, F. and Cedillo, S. (2017), 'Decolonizing Place in Early Childhood Studies: Thinking with Indigenous Onto-epistemologies and Black Feminist Geographies', *Global Studies of Childhood*, 7 (2): 99–112.

Oakley, A. (1994), 'Women and Children First and Last', in B. Mayall (ed.), *Children's Childhoods*, 13–33, London: Routledge.

OECD (2020), 'Combatting COVID-19's Effect on Children', *Organisation for Economic Co-operation and Development*. Available online: http://www .oecd.org/coronavirus/policy-responses/combatting-covid-19-s-effect-on -children-2e1f3b2f/ (accessed 5 June 2022).

Opie, I. and Opie, P. (1969), *Children's Games in Street and Playground*, Oxford: Oxford University Press.

Oswell, D. (2013), *The Agency of Children*, Cambridge: Cambridge University Press.

Pace-Crosschild, T. (2018), 'Decolonising Childrearing and Challenging the Patriarchical Nuclear Family Through Indigenous Knowledges', in R. Rosen and K. Twamley (eds), *Feminism and the Politics of Childhood: Friends or Foes?*, 191–8, London: UCL Press.

Payne, R. (2012), 'Extraordinary Survivors' or 'Ordinary Lives'? Embracing 'Everyday Agency' in Social Interventions with Child-headed Households in Zambia', *Children's Geographies*, 10 (4): 399–411.

Pollock, L. H. (1983), *Forgotten Children: Parent–Child Relations from 1500 to 1900*, Cambridge: Cambridge University Press.

Prout, A. and James, A. (1990), 'A New Paradigm for the Sociology of Childhood? Provenance, Promise and Problems', in A. James and A. Prout (eds), *Constructing and Reconstructing Childhood: Contemporary Issues in the Sociological Study of Childhood*, 7–33, London: The Falmer Press.

Punch, S. (2001), 'Household Division of Labour: Generation, Gender, Age, Birth Order and Sibling Composition', *Work, Employment and Society*, 15 (4): 803–23.

Punch, S. (2016), 'Exploring Children's Agency Across Minority and Majority World Contexts', in F. Esser, M. S. Baader, T. Betz, and B. Hungerland (eds), *Reconceptualising Agency and Childhood*, 183–96, London: Routledge.

Punch, S. (2020), 'Why Have Generational Orderings Been Marginalised in the Social Sciences Including Childhood Studies?', *Children's Geographies*, 18 (2): 128–40.

Qvortrup, J. (1994), 'Introduction', in J. Qvortrup, M. Bardy, G. Sgritta, and H. Wintersberger (eds), *Childhood Matters*, 1–24, Aldershot: Avebury.

Qvortrup, J. (1997), 'A Voice for Children in Statistical and Social Accounting: A Plea for Children's Right to be Heard', in James, A. and Prout, A. (eds), *Constructing and Reconstructing Childhood*, 2nd edn, 83–104, London: Falmer.

Qvortrup, J. (2011), 'Childhood as a Structural Form', in Qvortrup, J., Corsaro, W. C., and Honig, M-S. (eds), *The Palgrave Handbook of Childhood Studies*, 21–33, Basingstoke: Palgrave.

Rees, G., Tonon, G., Mikkelsen, C., and Rodriguez de la Vega, L. (2017), 'Urban-Rural Variations in Children's Lives and Subjective Well-being: A Comparative Analysis of Four Countries,' *Children and Youth Services Review*, 80: 41–51.

Ritchie, J. (2012), 'Early Childhood Education as a Site of Ecocentric Counter-Colonial Endeavour in Aotearoa New Zealand', *Contemporary Issues in Early Childhood*, 13 (2): 86–98.

Rizzini, I. (2011), 'The Promise of Citizenship for Brazilian Children: What Has Changed?', *The Annals of the American Academy of Political and Social Science*, 633 (1): 66–79.

Rosen, D. M. (2007), 'Child Soldiers, International Humanitarian Law, and the Globalization of Childhood', *American Anthropologist*, 109 (2): 296–306.

Rosiek, J. K., Synder, J., and Pratt, S. L. (2020), 'The New Materialisms and Indigenous Theories of Non-Human Agency: Making the Case for Respectful Anti-colonial Engagement', *Qualitative Inquiry*, 26 (3–4): 331–46.

Scholte, J. A. (2000), *Globalization: A Critical Introduction*, London: Palgrave Macmillan.

Shamgar-Handelman, L. (1994), 'The Economic and Socio-Political Outlook', in J. Qvortrup, M. Bardy, G. Sgritta, and H. Wintersberger (eds), *Childhood Matters*, 249–66, Aldershot: Avebury.

Skott-Myhre, H. (2020), 'Posthumanism and Childhood', in D. T. Cook (ed.), *The SAGE Encyclopedia of Children and Childhood Studies*, 1287–8, London: Sage.

Smith, L. T. (2021), *Decolonizing Methodologies Research and Indigenous Peoples*, 3rd edn, London: Zed Books.

Spyrou, S. (2018), *Disclosing Childhoods*, Basingstoke: Palgrave Macmillan.

Spyrou, S., Rosen, R., and Cook, D. T. (eds) (2018), *Reimagining Childhood Studies*, London: Bloomsbury Publishing.

Stainton-Rogers, R. and Stainton-Rogers, W (1992), *Stories of Childhood*, New York and London: Harvester Wheatsheaf.

Sundhall, J. (2017), 'A Political Space for Children? The Age Order and Children's Right to Participation', *Social Inclusion*, 5 (2): 164–71.

Taylor, A. and Giugni, M. (2012), 'Common Worlds: Reconceptualising Inclusion in Early Childhood Communities', *Contemporary Issues in Early Childhood*, 13 (2): 108–19.

Tisdall, E. K. M. and Punch, S. (2012), 'Not So "New"? Looking Critically at Childhood Studies', *Children's Geographies*, 10 (3): 249–64.

Todd, Z. (2016), 'An Indigenous Feminist's Take on the Ontological Turn: "Ontology" Is Just Another Word for Colonialism', *Journal of Historical Sociology*, 29 (1): 4–22.

Tuck, E. and Yang, K. W. (2012), 'Decolonization Is Not a Metaphor, Decolonization: Indigeneity', *Education & Society*, 1 (1): 1–40.

UNICEF (n.d.), 'Guidelines for Journalists Reporting on Children'. Available online: https://www.unicef.org/eca/media/ethical-guidelines (accessed 4 February 2022).

Uprichard, E. (2008), 'Children as "Beings and Becomings"', *Children & Society*, 22 (4): 303–13.

van Dijk, D. and van Driel, F. (2009), 'Supporting Child-Headed Households in South Africa: Whose Best Interests?' *Journal of Southern African Studies*, 35 (4): 915–27.

Vart, P., Jaglan, A., and Shafique, K (2015), 'Caste-based Social Inequalities and Childhood Anemia in India: Results from the National Family Health Survey (NFHS) 2005–2006', *BMC Public Health*, 15: 537.

Wall, J. (2019), 'From Childhood Studies to Childism', *Children's Geographies*, 20 (3): 257–70.

Wyness, M. (2012), *Childhood and Society*, 2nd edn, Basingstoke: Palgrave, Macmillan.

Wyness, M. (2015) *Childhood: Key Concepts*, Cambridge: Polity Press.

Young, R. J. C. (2016), *Postcolonialism*, London: Wiley.

Young-Bruehl, E. (2012), *Childism*, New Haven, CT: Yale University Press.

Zelizer, V. A. R. (1994), *Pricing the Priceless Child: The Changing Social Value of Children*, Princeton, NJ: Princeton University Press.

Commentary on Foundations of Childhood Studies

Sarada Balagopalan

Over the past thirty years, scholars in **childhood studies** have productively worked at destabilizing a singular response to the question, 'What is a child?'. As part of her discussion on the foundations of childhood studies, Tisdall begins the Chapter with early efforts to answer this key question. Her subsequent mapping of shifts in the field helps foreground how a recognition of the exclusions that marked the initial framing of children as *particular* subjects helped engender the move away from an earlier preoccupation with centering children's **agency** and voice. The Chapter addresses several of these challenges through its focus on **materialities**, efforts to decolonize the field and attention to **generational orders**. In this commentary, I focus on 'the culturalization of **childhoods**' to elaborate some key challenges that relate to those that the Chapter discusses, thereby its analytic efforts in problematizing the fundamental question of 'what is a child?'.

The culturalization of childhood

A key point that the Chapter discusses is around **childhood as a social construction**. The primary idea that helps anchor this is the distinction being drawn between children's immaturity as a biological fact and how this gets understood and made meaningful as the work of **culture**. Given the role of the latter in influencing **socialization** practices, distinctions around these practices across different country contexts have been largely understood as cultural distinctions which need to be understood on their own terms. The cultural anthropologist and childhood studies scholar Stephens (1995) raised a couple of key questions fairly early on in the field's emergence which continue to remain significant. First, she wondered whether we were 'doing analytical violence to complex constellations of meanings and practices' when we used the terms 'childhood' and 'adulthood'. As 'terms (that) already presuppose a world of Western cultural assumptions' (1995: 5–6) she did not encourage cross-cultural comparisons like the '**multiple childhoods**' framing by James and Prout (1990) did. Rather, she was prescient in asking how children as symbols of the future figured in contestations around cultural identity and what role this particular modern construction of the child had played in structures of capital and the nation state.

Noting that research on children appeared to be centred on Western constructions of childhood (elaborated around **gender**, **race** and class differences) and compared with the childhoods of other cultures, Stephens argued that this framing often viewed 'childhood' within the realm of culture and therefore distinct from larger political economy considerations. Writing in the mid-1990s when the near-universal **ratification** of the UNCRC in 1989 had led to an explosion of **discourses** around children's rights around the world, Stephens urged childhood researchers to pay attention to larger social and historical macro-perspectives in order to better anticipate the new risks to children and childhood that this moment contained. Her research helped highlight how the 'child' figure was seldom separate from global processes that had transformed the world, including most significantly histories of colonialism. Stephens made a compelling case for the need to historicize how 'complex globalizations of once localized Western constructions of childhood' (1995: 8) had shaped histories of colonial and post-colonial modernity in the **global South** and the **global North**. In advocating for the importance of including a historical perspective in our culturalization of children's lives, Stephens added a much-needed critical perspective to emerging attempts to understand the differences that appeared to frame children's lives across the world and most significantly between the global North and the global South.

Stephens' critique, as well as efforts to move away from narrow attempts to 'culturalize' childhoods, resonates strongly in ongoing efforts to decolonize the field as well as related scholarship focused on the symbolic role that children and childhood play in projects aimed at stabilizing racial and civilizational differences (Balagopalan 2011; Ibrahim 2021; Sen 2005; Stoler 2006). In terms of decolonizing the field, as Tisdall discusses, it is an

epistemological challenge that post-colonialism and decolonialism pose to childhood studies. Not only do they compel us to recalibrate the hierarchies set in place by a **normative** childhood but they also make us recognize that the categories that the field employs have been predominantly drawn from frameworks that privilege liberal modernity. By purposefully moving us away from a simplistic, ahistorical framing of contemporary lives of marginal children in the global South as 'lacking' or not-yet modern, they also aid in decentring the moral self-evidence of children's rights discourses.

Rather, they remind us of the point Stephen makes when she discusses the symbolic role the culturalization of children and childhood historically played in setting in place and further sedimenting racial and civilizational hierarchies. Several more scholars have discussed how, across imperial contexts, childhood was used as a powerful metaphor to infantilize colonized populations. Nandy (1992) drew a parallel between childhood and the colonized stating that both were constructed as incomplete, irrational, lacking capacity and best 'saved' by white/liberal authoritative knowledge practices. In a different vein, George notes that 'Before the trade unionist, the wageworker, or the nationalist politician . . . the child was the first category of native to emerge as a universal subject in Africa' (2014: 6). But this was an imposition of the colonial state which was aimed less at recognizing Nigerian children's rights but more about using the figure of the child to contest native customs.

Even 'age', a category that we usually assume as both universal (because its unit of measure is a number or what is referred to as 'digits of age') and natural (linked to physical and psychological growth), though subject to cultural interpretations in terms of understandings of maturity and generational ordering as Tisdall discusses, has been similarly historicized. Scholars view its emergence as an exercise of power as discussed in the following quote,

> Age was inscribed into bodies through a range of bureaucratic procedures and investigative modalities as the colonial and national state came to 'manage their own denizens through an official time line, effectively shaping the contours of a meaningful life by registering some events like births, marriages, and deaths, and refusing to record others like initiations, friendships, and contact with the dead'. (Freeman, as cited in Pande 2020: 412)

Building on this, Pande (2020) asserts that the use of age as a measure to classify populations (adult/child, **youth**/adolescent/infant etc.) and enact justice (think about the different thresholds that countries have around criminalizing children who violate the law, for example) rests on an 'epistemic contract'. What this refers to is an implicit agreement that 'age is a universal and natural measure of human capacity, and hence of legal and political subjectivity' (Pande 2020: 415). This implicit and unspoken contract is what has helped us establish a 'child', but to Pande it is this very naturalness of age which obfuscates the fact that it is a form of knowledge derived from liberal juridical traditions and which was used to legitimize and shore up the colonial state's disciplinary and **racialized** rule.

In addition, as Tisdall discusses, the setting in place of 'multiple childhoods' as an interpretive lens to understand cultural differences in socialization practices has produced ethnographic research as a key methodology in childhood studies. Yet, the ways in which children's lives are ethnographically researched highlight the deeper effects of an a-historical 'cultural' framing, particularly when this is used to better contextualize the everyday lives of economically and socially marginalized children in the global South. This point is made clearer through drawing a contrast between ethnographic research on the gendered, classed and raced everyday worlds of children in the global North. In these ethnographies, 'culture' is understood to include the microphysics of subject-formation within domestic milieus, urban housing and public schools to name a few sites; that is, the cultural worlds of these children are seldom outside of the workings of the state and its institutions. Using Foucault (1995) we could say that in these ethnographies, the anatomic-physical register of the child's individuated body is intricately tied to a larger technico-political register of the workings of the capitalist state and its various institutions. It is the combination of both registers that allows these ethnographies to make intelligible the multiple processes of **discipline**, regulation, subjectification which are both shaped and transformed by children's agential actions while simultaneously shaping and transforming knowledge produced around the lives of children and youth. This textured framing that informs ethnographies on different populations of children in Euro-American contexts provides a robust epistemic framework that is descriptive yet critical, locally nuanced yet cognizant of structural and institutional workings of power and its everyday hierarchies. The best of these ethnographies combines a prescriptive or the disciplinary axis in terms of the racist, classist, gendered and **neoliberal** workings of the nation state and its institutions, along with analyzing the technico-political axis or the enormous pedagogic energy that bourgeois liberalism invests in creating the child into a moral citizen through the skills of self-discipline as a mode of self-governance. Even though these ethnographies may or may not explicitly invoke the state, the classed nature of the liberal state is continually referenced in the lives of children and their communities through a reflection on the racialized limits of its assurances and the regulatory nature of **inclusive** policies. In effect, it is the mapping of continued inequality against the formal assurance of equality or citizenship that allows 'culture' to attend to the micro-geographies of children's lives while incorporating the **biopolitics** of the state and its institutions. A good example of this is Annamma's ethnography titled *The Pedagogy of Pathologization* (2017) focused on the criminalization and exclusion of Black dis/abled girls. Her research focuses on the lived practices of these young girls in juvenile facilities and highlights how intersecting discourses of racism, abilism and carceral logics aid in pathologizing these girls through labeling and violence in school. By linking the multiple forms of marginality that these young women experience and explicating this in terms of how the school-to-prison pipeline works, Annamma not only offers us a structural analysis but also documents these women's resilience.

The temporal dimension in these ethnographies is not about the past of each individual child nor the histories of their community's identity-based struggles but more about the history of the liberal state and its assurance of formal equality for all of its citizens (Wells 2011). This historicity is starkly missing in our ethnographic research on children's lives in the global South, although several of these geographic contexts have similar liberal assurances of formal equality in their national constitutions and legal apparatus (Balagopalan 2019a). But we often tend to view these assurances as rhetorical and unwittingly invoke either a 'transition narrative' – in which countries in the global South are thought to be lagging/lacking and the global North is constructed as the ideal end point. Or we risk an overdetermined reading of subjectivity within a framework that takes the boundedness of these cultural practices as self-evident and non-pathological thereby effectively 'othering' these lives (Balagopalan 2019b).

Despite the richness of archival research on children's lives in these ex-colonies, we seldom factor these into our analysis: the ways in which the colonial state set in place **dichotomies** and distinctions whose exclusionary tactics not only attempted to culturally reproduce and preserve a racialized 'white' identity (Cooper and Stoler 1997) but also worked to justify the racism inherent in the 'civilizing mission' (Vallargada 2015) and accrue the gains made by colonial capitalism through the use of children's labour (Grier 2006). This body of research makes amply clear that the construction of colonized native children as the 'other' was seldom stable but instead worked as a difference that had to be always defined and maintained (Balagopalan 2014). So for example, continuing to read children's work in global South contexts as solely determined by their 'cultures' is evidence of a disconnect between the significant transformation in children's lives that colonial modernity set in place and our unwillingness or inability to factor this into our ethnographic research. Instead, we continue to read the work of the colonial state as a historical event rather than understand this in terms of its historicity or namely the continued effects of this colonial past on the present (Balagopalan 2011; Stephens 1995).

The 'culturalization of childhood' contains much more than a non-pathological assertion of cultural differences around children's socialization practices across the world. Our historicizing the role played by the 'child' in structures of modernity allows us to better understand and frame current global, national and local cultural transformations that continue to produce certain populations of children within shifting assertions around their being 'dangerous' or 'in danger'. Moreover, by illuminating the historical processes that helped sediment certain ideas that we now view as commonplace when it comes to children, like age, for example, we can begin to reframe 'foundations', as Tisdall does, less as canonical knowledge and more as that which also bears the traces of time and context in its production.

References

Annamma, S. (2017), *The Pedagogy of Pathologization: Dis/abled Girls of Color in the School-prison Nexus*, New York: Routledge.

Balagopalan, S. (2011), 'Introduction: Children's Lives and the Indian Context', *Childhood*, 18 (3): 291–7.

Balagopalan, S. (2014), *Inhabiting 'Childhood': Children, Labour and Schooling in Postcolonial India*, Basingstoke: Palgrave.

Balagopalan, S. (2019a), 'Why Historicize Rights Subjectivities? Children's Rights, Compulsory Schooling and the Deregulation of Child Labor in India', *Childhood*, 26(3): 304–20.

Balagopalan, S. (2019b), 'Childhood, Culture, History: Redeploying "Multiple Childhoods"', in S. Sprou, R Rosen., and D. Cook (eds), *Reimagining Childhood Studies*, 23–39, London: Bloomsbury.

Cooper, F. and StolerA. L., (1997), *Tensions of Empire: Colonial Cultures in a Bourgeois World*, Berkeley: University of California Press.

Foucault, M. (1995), *Discipline and Punish: The Birth of the Prison*. Translated by A. Sheridan, New York: Random House.

George, A. (2014), *Making Modern Girls: A History of Girlhood, Labor, and Social Development in Colonial Lagos*, Athens: Ohio University Press.

Grier, B. (2006), *Invisible Hands: Child Labor and the State in Colonial Zimbabwe*, Portsmouth, NH: Heinemann.

Ibrahim, H. (2021) *Black Age: Oceanic Lifespans and the Time of Black Life*, New York: New York University Press.

James, A. and Prout A., (ed.) (1990), *Constructing and Reconstructing Childhood*, 1st edn, London: Routledge Falmer.

Nandy, A. (1992), *Tradition, Tyranny and Utopias: Essays in the Politics of Awareness*, New Delhi: Oxford University Press.

Pande, I. (2020), *Sex, Law, and the Politics of Age: Child Marriage in India, 1891–1937*, Cambridge: Cambridge University Press.

Sen, S. (2005), *Colonial Childhoods: The Juvenile Periphery of India*, London: Anthem Press.

Stephens, S. (1995), *Children and the Politics of Culture*, Princeton, NJ: Princeton University Press.

Stoler, A. (eds) (2006), *Haunted by Empire: Geographies of Intimacy in North American History*, Durham, NC: Duke University Press.

Vallgarda, K. (2015), *Imperial Childhoods and the Christian Mission: Education and Emotions in South India and Denmark*, Basingstoke: Palgrave.

Wells, K. (2011), 'The Politics of Life: Governing Childhood', *Global Studies of Childhood*, 1 (1): 15–25.

3

Childhood Studies Meets Other Disciplines

Marlies Kustatscher and Deborah Fry

Chapter Outline

Introduction

Since its inception in the 1990s, **childhood studies** as a field has claimed to be **interdisciplinary** (e.g. James 2003; Prout and James 1990; Thorne 2007). Core **disciplines** drawn upon during the field's foundational years in the 1990s (that continue to feature strongly today) include anthropology, children's rights studies, cultural studies, history, human geography, sociology and philosophy (see Chapter 2). In recent years, additional disciplines have contributed to advances in childhood studies debates, for example, by utilizing **knowledges** from children's literature, critical **child development**, economics, educational studies, disability studies, media studies, philosophy, public health or **race** and **ethnicity** studies.

Indeed, it could be argued that the field's interdisciplinarity is an essential part of its identity, and the fact that childhood studies is framed in the plural form indicates its heterogeneity and diversity. Many of the questions that **childhood** scholars grapple with are inherently interdisciplinary: for example, the interplay of social and biological aspects in children's lives or the ways in which children's lives are shaped by their situated contexts – and the cultural, socio-economic, legal and environmental characteristics of these contexts. In addition, childhood studies, in part, owes its identity to delineating itself from disciplines with apparently opposing **ontological** and **epistemological** beliefs about childhood, such as developmental psychology (Woodhead 2015).

The first section of this Chapter discusses the interdisciplinary nature of childhood studies, including considerations on how disciplines can be defined in the first place and the ways in which disciplinary boundaries are constructed and deconstructed in this process. It highlights the importance of both being aware and mindful of how disciplinary perspectives may align or diverge while also stressing the need to think beyond disciplinary silos. The Chapter then delves into examples of how childhood studies has collaborated with other disciplines, from the more 'traditional' allies such as **children's geographies** to more recent and potentially contested collaborations such as with the medical sciences. The Chapter does not intend to provide an exhaustive list of disciplinary convergences but rather to illustrate some key examples which help to define complementarity as well as potential tensions. In doing so, the Chapter addresses the following overarching question: What are the opportunities and challenges of interdisciplinary approaches to studying children and childhoods?

(De)constructing disciplines

Before delving into interdisciplinary conversations that childhood studies is engaged in, this section reflects critically on what is meant by disciplines, fields or **paradigms** and calls for researchers' **reflexivity** in approaching these questions.

Childhood studies as inextricably interdisciplinary

Activity: What is a discipline? Boundary making and disciplinary identities

The term 'discipline' derives from the Latin *disciplina* and means teaching, training, method or study. In the English language today, the term holds multiple meanings: from a particular set of activities (e.g. within sports), to specific forms of instruction, to maintaining a certain order or even exercising punishment. In this Chapter, we are concerned with the broad meaning of discipline as 'a branch of learning or knowledge' or 'a field of study or expertise' (*Oxford English Dictionary*, no date).

Scholarly disciplines are usually united by an interest in a shared set of topics, a shared (and limited) set of methods and theories that are applied to these topics (with assumptions on *how* they should be applied) and often also shared ideological attitudes (Szostak 2012). Academic institutions, such as universities, tend to be organized around disciplinary groupings, conventions and hierarchies through colleges, institutes or departments. Similarly, research funding is often allocated through public or private bodies organized around disciplines, and disciplines can have powerful impacts on shaping **discourse** on particular topics by sharing and promoting epistemological beliefs about what constitutes valuable knowledge.

While many of us will have ideas and examples in mind when we think about what 'disciplines' are, in practice there is often no clear agreement. For example, people may debate whether 'genetics', 'ecology' and 'physiology' are independent disciplines or belong to the broader discipline of 'biology'. Thus, disciplines are constituted by ongoing processes of discourse and boundary making, driven by both those who see themselves as part of or outside particular disciplines.

- What does the word 'discipline' evoke in you?
- Thinking about any of your previous studies or experiences, do you feel that you have a 'disciplinary home'?
- If yes, what shapes this home?
- What scholarly disciplines have you encountered in your personal, professional and academic life? What has been your experiences of these encounters?

Many writers have explored the role of different disciplines for framing contemporary childhood studies: for example, Woodhead and Montgomery's (2003) *Understanding Childhood: An Interdisciplinary Approach* and Kehily's (2013) later edition of *Understanding Childhood: A **Cross-Disciplinary** Approach*. In order to provide a comprehensive understanding of children's contemporary lives and their complexities, these writers suggest that it is necessary to draw on knowledges and perspectives from different disciplines in order to reach answers that do justice to this complexity.

Such calls for combining disciplinary forces are not unique to childhood studies but are common across other areas of research. In a world shaped by complexity and problems that require multifaceted solutions (such as climate change or global health challenges presented by COVID-19), it makes sense to draw on all the knowledges that are available to address them.

However, despite these calls for interdisciplinarity, and their centrality to the field of childhood studies, there are no agreed definitions or procedures on what working across or between different disciplines entails. Woodhead (2015) proposes three metaphors which each go to different lengths in terms of 'genuinely' striving for interdisciplinarity:

> A 'clearing house model' would encompass all studies of children and childhood, all research questions, methodologies and disciplinary approaches.
> A 'pick 'n' mix model' would be more selective but still incorporates a wide range of approaches. The selection criteria might be about the specific topics studied or the orientation to the field.
> A 'rebranding model' might appear to have interdisciplinary aspirations but would mainly be about redefining a traditional field of inquiry while still adhering to conventional disciplinary boundaries. (27)

Thus, calls for interdisciplinarity in childhood studies can be realized to different extents, from encompassing any discipline to being more selective in terms of which disciplines are perceived to align productively.

Childhood studies is a **multidisciplinary** field where there had been a tendency towards working in sub-disciplinary silos. However, more recently, childhood studies has become more interdisciplinary with effective working integrated across disciplines.

Samantha Punch, Professor, University of Stirling, UK

Critical challenge: Multi-, inter- or transdisciplinarity?

There are different ways in which working with and across multiple disciplines can be conceptualized. Some common terms used are 'multidisciplinarity', 'interdisciplinarity' and 'transdisciplinarity'. While some people may use them interchangeably, others associate particular meanings to them.

For example, Choi and Pak (2006) suggest that **multidisciplinarity** refers to different disciplines working *alongside* each other on a particular issue.

Interdisciplinarity implies a more fertile interaction where the outcome may equal more than the sum of the individual parts.

Mitchell and Moore (2018), drawing on the work of Indigenous educator Christie (2006), put forward that **transdisciplinarity** suggests a move away from disciplines as understood in university environments and thus broadens understandings of what is included as knowledge in the first place. For example, Camponovo et al. (2021), in their study on co-producing knowledge with children by walking, propose that transdisciplinarity involves drawing on expertise not only from multiple relevant academic disciplines but also from non-academic stakeholders.

- Can you identify studies with children that claim to employ multi-, inter- or transdisciplinarity?
- How do they conceptualize the coming together of different disciplines?

Childhood studies: A paradigm, field or discipline?

The answer to this question is not settled – in part, because the definitions of these terms in themselves can vary widely. In their foundational text, Prout and James (1990) ask about the promises and problems of a new 'paradigm' for the sociology of childhood. Analysing advancement in the natural sciences, the philosopher Kuhn (1962) famously described a paradigm as a set of truths and practices which are accepted as 'normal' within a discipline and which tend to evolve in radical shifts or 'revolutions'. Thus, in the case of childhood studies (or the **new sociology of childhood,** as originally framed), the paradigm shift encapsulates a shift to new ideas around children's **agency** and competence, and the **social construction of childhood** (see Chapter 2 for details on what Prout and James' paradigm entails).

A discipline may be seen as encompassing different and opposing paradigms. A 'field' (of study or research), on the other hand, is a more loosely defined term which recognizes that there may be different components to it, with different expressions and gravitations to one another. As a *field*, childhood studies is connected through a shared focus on issues of childhood and this is how the term is used in this Chapter and throughout this book.

Some people suggest that childhood studies has become so diverse in recent decades that it may no longer be able to call itself a 'field' as there is a lack of common agendas and foci (James 2010). Questions have also been raised to what extent a self-proclaimed field of childhood studies risks reifying the category of childhood in particular ways (Cannella 2002).

Critical challenge: Rather than trying to settle the question of whether childhood studies is a paradigm, field or discipline, consider the following questions:

- What is to be gained or lost in the process of delineating particular areas in this way?
- What are the implications for finding community and moving forward understandings of childhood for the advancement of research, policy and practice?
- What is the appeal (or disinclination) of identifying with 'childhood studies' – whether seen as a paradigm, field or discipline – for you personally?

Disciplinary identities, values and reflexivity

The ways in which scholars perceive and relate across different disciplinary fields depend on their own disciplinary grounding and identity. While childhood studies scholars often call for engaging with 'other' disciplines (other than those already typically associated with the field, such as sociology, anthropology, human geography, history), there is at the same time a need to look inward too in terms of how 'our own' disciplinary lenses shape our understandings of childhood. James (2003: 25) suggests that 'what childhood is and who children are' depends not only on where one looks but also on the lens through which that gaze is directed (see also Spyrou 2018).

Different fields bring with them different conceptual and, importantly, methodological conventions. Common ontological and epistemological concerns of childhood studies include making children's views visible across all areas of life that affect them, highlighting age and generation as core categories of social stratification, recognizing children as competent **social actors** (James 2003; James et al. 1998; Prout and James 1990; Qvortrup et al. 1994) – and more recently, promoting children's rights. Childhood studies scholars have developed a wealth of methodological approaches to achieve this, and such practices of gathering and centring children's views are indeed a significant contribution that childhood studies has made to other disciplinary fields – particularly those where notions of children's lack of competence might prevail.

Ironically, calls for interdisciplinary approaches can sometimes reify these very disciplines in the process. There is a risk that, as disciplinary outsiders, scholars may rely on stereotypical or simplistic assumptions about ideas and practices in other disciplines. Inevitably, constructing disciplines as relatively homogeneous entities requires some simplification of what defines and unites a certain discipline. This has often been illustrated with the field of child psychology, which has played a strong role in the emergence of childhood studies. It exemplifies how constructing 'other' disciplines in certain ways can be a way to construct and delineate one's own disciplinary identity – sometimes at the risk of overexaggerating particular points of difference.

The following sections explore how different disciplines are converging with childhood studies and what some of the opportunities and challenges of these encounters are. Drawing on the broad disciplinary groupings of social sciences, arts and humanities and medical sciences, the Chapter sets out to explore what each of these areas can contribute to our understandings of childhood while highlighting examples of interdisciplinary research both within and across them.

Childhood studies has opened my eyes as a practitioner and early-career researcher to a vital array of interdisciplinary issues governing and intersecting with children's lives in Scotland and beyond. One of the most important aspects for me personally is a growing receptivity to the diverse means with which children challenge received childhoods and regulations in ways too often thought of as disruptive, which in fact offer us incredible clues about their worlds and the fundamental need for stronger democratic pedagogies.

Simon Bateson, Early Childhood Practitioner and Researcher, UK

Childhood in the social sciences

In terms of broader disciplinary context, childhood studies are most clearly situated within the social sciences. Social sciences include disciplines that are at the heart of childhood studies, such as sociology, social anthropology and human geography, and others which have converged with childhood studies to differing extents, such as 'development' studies, economics, education, environmental planning, law, linguistics, philosophy, politics and international relations, psychology, science and technology studies, social policy or social work. This section discusses some of the key disciplinary convergences and alliances within the social sciences and highlights others which have been in tension. While acknowledging that any such review is inevitably incomplete, it also highlights some emerging areas of fertile interdisciplinary crossover.

Children's geographies

The jury is still out on whether children's geographies are a part of childhood studies or a linked but independent disciplinary field. In any case, the synergies between the two are big. What distinguishes children's geographies is their focus on place and space in children's lives. Foundational texts in children's geographies (e.g. Aitken 1994; Holloway and Valentine 2000; Matthews and Limb 1999; Philo 1992) applied core ideas from human geographies within the study of childhood. This included a focus on how conceptualizations of childhood are spatially and temporally specific, on the linkages between local and global childhoods, as well as on how children's lives are heavily shaped by their access to and experiences of everyday spaces (Holloway and Valentine 2000). Particular attention has been paid to the institutionalization of childhoods, for example, through educational settings (e.g. Gallagher 2011; Holt 2003), as well as areas such as families and relationships, conflict or child labour (Skelton 2017).

Exploring concepts further: Space, place and time

Since their 'spatial turn' (Thrift 2006: 139), the social sciences have become increasingly concerned with the spatial dimension of social lives. For childhood studies, this has opened up opportunities to think about how children's spaces and places are constructed, how children themselves make sense of these and what spatial **dichotomies** might be created in these processes (e.g. child/adult spaces, **global South/global North**).

Such discussions build on (though not always explicitly) rich historical debates around the concepts involved, particularly of space and place. At their heart is the idea that space is not a neutral, objective container for social life, but that it is itself produced through relationships (Soja 1989). The **materialist** and power-infused elements of processes of producing space have been highlighted in particular by Lefebvre (1991) and Massey (1994), who suggest that spaces are produced in dynamic, shifting and temporal ways.

While most human geographers acknowledge that both space and place are relationally constructed, there is a tendency to view **space** as broader social and relational structures and **place** as produced by more specific social practices and relationships, and given meaning by the individuals involved (Bartos 2013). At the same time, space and place do not relate to a distinction of macro and micro levels. They can both be seen as abstract and concrete at the same time. For example, while a place can be linked to a specific location, it can gain particular meanings for children through their experiences of its environment (Bartos 2013). Places can have multiple meanings for different people, and these meanings can be changing over time (Massey 1994).

- How do space and place feature in the lives of children who you are living, working or researching with?
- What might a spatial lens add to your understanding of childhoods in particular contexts?

Children's geographies are a dynamic field with a history of engaging in debates about its disciplinary identity and purpose (see, for example, Holloway 2014; Horton and Kraftl 2006; Robson et al. 2013). Such debates focus on moving forward theoretical concepts (such as agency or 'voice') or discussions around representations of childhood. There are particular affinities between children's geographies and emotional geographies (e.g. Blaisdell et al. 2021; Blazek and Kraftl 2015; Blazek and Windram-Geddes 2013). There are also synergies between children's geographies and **post-humanist** or new materialist perspectives on childhoods (Taylor and Pacini-Ketchabaw 2018) which emphasize the entanglements of children's lives with nature, animals, and human and non-human entities. This in itself constitutes an interdisciplinary endeavour by seeking to expand beyond purely sociological or geographical understandings of childhood. Writers at the crossroads of childhood studies and children's geographies have also stressed the local and global dimensions of childhood, including aspects of power and colonialism in constructions and experiences of childhoods (Abebe 2007; Twum-Danso et al. 2019).

In terms of broader interdisciplinary considerations, the case of children's geographies illustrates the merits of scholars within a discipline (in this case, human geography) coming together with a particular focus (childhood). On the other hand, the creation of any sub-disciplinary field also carries the risk that the learning from within it – such as the critical focus on childhood – is not mainstreamed into wider disciplinary debates. Thus, there are balances to be struck between creating specialized and supportive communities of research and practice while at the same time proactively challenging the creation of academic silos.

Exploring concepts further: Identity and belonging

Children's **social identities** (in terms of **gender**, race, ethnicity, social class, disability and so on) have been the subject of much research. Research framed by positivist epistemologies views identity as something that is fixed, singular and 'acquired' by children (e.g. if viewing gender identities as the logical consequences of a child's biology). **Social constructionist** or **post-structuralist** research, on the other hand, tends to recognize identities as fluid, situated and **intersectional**. This also raises questions on how social identities come into being along debates of agency and structure, and to what extent children (and indeed all human beings) can 'choose' their identities.

The answers to these questions depend on how researchers position themselves in terms of their ontological and epistemological frameworks around childhood and social identities. Childhood studies scholars have usefully drawn on ideas from gender studies or race and ethnicity studies, bringing discussions around agency and other core childhood studies concepts into dialogue with frameworks such as **queer theory**, post-colonial theory, intersectionality or feminist post-structuralist theory (see, for example, Breslow 2021; George 2014; Renold 2005; see also Chapter 5).

The concept of **belonging** is useful for researchers to explore children's identities, experiences of space and place, homes, families, communities and migration. A sense of belonging can come into existence in relation to individuals or groups, to spaces and places, in concrete or abstract ways and through processes of self-identification or identification by others. As Yuval-Davis (2011) suggests, belonging tends to be naturalized and part of everyday practices. It is constituted by emotions and relationships, as well as by complex intersectional **positionalities** (Yuval-Davis 2011). Children's sense of belonging extends beyond their immediate environments and is shaped by their links to wider places and spaces (Kustatscher 2017).

Childhood studies and psychology

The discipline of psychology has for over a century held a central place in global North understandings of childhood (Rose 1989; Walkerdine 2015). The opposition to developmental (or age-based) ways of thinking about children, illustrated, for example, in the work of foundational child psychologist Piaget, was a core element of setting up alternative thinking in childhood studies. Piaget's work contained assumptions about age and stage and about contrasting children to adults in deficit ways, from which childhood studies differentiated itself by emphasizing children's competence and agency, and childhood as a social construction.

Many writers within childhood studies have called for a less simplistic, more nuanced understanding and collaboration with child psychologists. For example, Thorne (2007) writes:

> How can the approaches clustered within the 'new social studies of childhood' be brought into more fruitful dialogue with the well-established, better funded and much more **hegemonic** approaches of developmental psychology? [. . .] I regret the continuing wall of silence between the 'new social studies of childhood' and the field of child development because I believe that the complex articulation of different types of temporality – historical, generational, chronological, phenomenological, developmental, biological – should be central to the study of children and childhoods. (150)

Woodhead (2009) provides an overview of child development theories and how their critique has been linked to the emergence of childhood studies. He highlights the salience of developmental, or age-based, ways of thinking about childhood in most global North societies – for example, by celebrating birthdays as key markers in children's (and adults') lives or by giving priority to age in children's identities and institutional locations. This is not inevitable, he suggests, as historically birth dates were not always registered, and age did not play such an important part in children's lives. Thus, the assumed naturalness and inevitability of children's age-based development, including inherent assumptions which may **universalize** particular constructions of childhood, need to be challenged (see Chapter 5).

While developmental psychologists have often highlighted children's active role in their own development, psychological research designs tend to be less child-centred than is common in childhood studies (Woodhead 2009). However, Woodhead suggests that this should not be cause for disregarding such research, which can give insights into important issues such as children's **wellbeing**. In order to provide holistic pictures of children's lives, differing ontological and epistemological approaches may need to be employed.

Childhood studies as a field has paid much attention to power, for example, in terms of inter- and intra-generational power relations in children's lives. This attention extends to how disciplinary perspectives, such as those of early developmental psychologists, are always produced under specific conditions of power. Drawing on the work of Foucault, Walkerdine (2015) analyses how early developmental psychology work was informed by the socio-historical context of technologies of population control at a time of rapid industrial expansion (e.g. by producing the adult workforce needed to feed this economic development (see also Cunningham 2005; Hendrick 1997, for a historical perspective)). She highlights:

> The issue is [. . .] to understand that childhood is always produced as an object in relation to power. Thus, there can be no timeless truth, sociological or psychological, about childhood. There can rather be understandings of how childhood is produced at any one time and place and an imperative to understand what kinds of childhood we want to produce, if indeed we want childhood at all. (Walkerdine 2015: 117)

Thus, viewing psychology – and other disciplines – as technologies of **knowledge production** enables scholars to remain reflexive about the socio-historical power relations underpinning any type of research.

There has been a tendency in childhood studies to 'throw the baby out with the bathwater' (Lee 2001: 54) with regard to dismissals of developmental psychology. Such dismissals run the risk of reifying and stereotyping 'other' disciplines while failing to recognize the diversity of perspectives within them. Indeed, developmental psychology has evolved into a dynamic field with critical debates around its origins and directions. A key example is Burman's (2017) *Deconstructing Developmental Psychology* which utilizes **feminist post-structuralist theories** to critically analyse the development of the discipline itself. Rather than merely questioning 'facts' produced by the discipline of psychology, Burman invites scholars to engage critically with the methods and discourses under which they were produced, including questioning of certain gazes and foci (e.g. the focus on women as children's caregivers, concerns around attachment, the production of 'normal' childhoods and the exclusion of voices and perspectives from the global South). Similarly, Tatlow-Golden and Montgomery (2021a: 14) suggest that more should be made of the opportunities to collaborate between childhood studies and psychology, particularly with those strands of psychology which 'incorporate genuinely ecological, contextual and cultural approaches in their models of childhood' (see also Tatlow-Golden and Montgomery (2021b)).

Childhood and the body

Some of the debates between sociological and psychological perspectives tie into wider discussions on the entanglements of the social and biological elements which come to define childhood. Prout (2019) suggests that it is in the breaking down of dichotomies (such as body/mind, nature/**culture**) that the very opportunities for interdisciplinary childhood studies can thrive. Drawing on Pinker (2003), he suggests that acknowledging biological factors in children's lives does not need to imply a deterministic lens or one that accepts inequalities as given.

The dichotomy of the biological and the social has been reconciled, for example, in the concept of **embodiment**: it highlights that 'bodies are a dynamic and complex admixture of the social, the cultural and the biological, in which none of these elements can be effectively disentangled from the others' influences' (Lupton 2013: 38; see also Prout and Campling 2000).

Theoretical debates around childhood and the body, and their practical implications for children's lives, have been particularly illuminated by writers bringing together the fields of childhood studies and disability studies. For example, Tisdall (2012: 183) highlights that both children's and people with disabilities' contributions have been historically under-recognized due to an assumed lack of competences in comparison with a 'mythical gold standard' of 'normal' or 'adult'. Watson (2012) suggests that only an approach which captures the biological, physical, social, political, psychological and cultural aspects of the lives of children with disabilities can do justice to their lives. The experiences of children with disabilities cannot be reduced to either the biological aspects of their impairments or the social aspects which may hinder or enable their social **inclusion**. Thus, for writers in the field of disability studies, 'embodiment is discussed as a social practice', which neither ignores children's embodiment nor positions them as 'other' (Curran and Runswick-Cole 2014: 1622).

Activity: Social and biological aspects of childhood: Thinking about gender

An example that brings to life questions around social versus biological elements of childhood is gender. A wide range of theories and conceptualizations have taken different approaches by viewing gender as biological, developmental, social or performative. Many writers have challenged binary views of gender and highlighted heteronormative constructions (see Kustatscher (2020) for an overview). While children are often seen as too 'innocent' or 'ignorant' to be knowledgeable about gender, they are at the same time hyper-gendered ('boys and girls') with very real gendered implications for their lives (from limited access to education for girls, to restrictive emotional ideas around masculinity for boys, or by positioning trans-children as threats).

Individually or in groups, consider debates presented in the special issue by Xu, Warin and Robb (2020) on gender pedagogies and practices in **early childhood**:

- What role do social and biological aspects play in conceptualizations of gender in these articles? How do these ideas align with or contradict your own views on gender?
- How can dichotomies between social and biological aspects of gender be reconciled, and what are the implications of doing this?
- To what extent do childhood practices and policies recognize children's own assertions of gender?

Childhood studies and economics

There are many important crossovers between childhood studies and economics, and economists increasingly form part of debates in childhood studies (Alanen 2012). Children are – as other groups in society – exposed to the dynamics of socio-economic inequalities which shape their lives. In broader economic terms, children often tend to be viewed as 'futurity' (James 2010: 492) or as 'future human capital' (Morrow 2012: 5). This implies a view of childhood as a site of investment – of capital, education and **early intervention** – not only for the benefit of individual children but also to produce future economic citizens for the good of society as a whole. Capitalism and **neoliberalism** heavily shape children's lives globally but are rarely explicitly highlighted within childhood studies (with notable exceptions such as del Solar et al. 2021; Perez and Canella 2011).

One area in which debates from childhood studies and economics converge is the area of child labour, although within childhood studies this tends to be discussed through a children's rights or philosophy lens rather than economically (e.g. Cook 2018; Liebel et al. 2012; see also Chapter 4). An emerging field of research recognizes children's role within economics not only as consumers but also as economic actors, for example through youth-led social entrepreneurships (Calderón et al. 2021).

More practically, there has been much interest in children and consumption, in terms of accessing children themselves, as well as their parents, as consumers. As is often the case, views of children in this sphere tend to be polarized and range from seeing them as active and empowered consumers (of goods and media) to seeing children as passive victims of commercial exploitation and consumer culture (Buckingham 2007; Cook 2005). Considering children's agency as consumers becomes even more complex as media cultures and digital data-shaped advertising continue to evolve rapidly. Finally, Collins (2014) suggests businesses should have an obligation to respect children's **human rights**, as this could lead to better outcomes in terms of business sustainability and social responsibility.

Critical challenge: Childhood studies and children's rights

There are affinities and tensions between childhood studies and the children's rights field (see Mayall (2005) for a detailed discussion, for example, on children's agency and structure, intergenerational relationships, children's contributions to labour systems and debates about rights as individual or collective). After reading Chapters 2 and 4, return to the following questions:

- What do you consider to be the main synergies between childhood studies and children's rights?
- What does each of the fields contribute to the other?
- Can you identify any tensions and, if so, which?
- What other fields or disciplines are involved in the alignment of childhood studies and children's rights (e.g. social policy, social work) and how?

My research is underpinned by children's rights, and I use theory from childhood studies to help understand the topics that I research. For example, how does a concept like children's agency apply in social work practice? In what ways do children shape the encounters that they have with social workers and how does social work practice constrain or support children's agency in this context? Childhood studies provides me with a range of theoretical lenses that help me understand my research in the areas of social work and social policy.

Fiona Morrison, Senior Lecturer at the Centre for Child Wellbeing and Protection, University of Stirling, UK

Arts and Humanities: Methodologies, histories and philosophies

Childhood studies has collaborated with many disciplines in the arts and humanities field, such as architecture, arts, cultural studies, dance, design, drama, history, languages and literatures, music or philosophy. On the one hand, synergies are often methodological: childhood studies has drawn from arts disciplines with regard to developing arts-based methodologies which have become central to much research involving children. The benefits of utilizing arts in participatory methods with children have been well documented (and there are crossovers with areas such as play therapy): they range from enabling children to exercise their agency, to improving wellbeing, to building self-esteem and strong relationships (Lee et al. 2020). They also assist researchers in challenging traditional modes of knowledge production by enabling different forms of self-expression and can make research processes more inclusive (Blaisdell et al. 2019).

On the other hand, childhood studies principles of centring children's views through participatory approaches have influenced arts and humanities disciplines. For example, it is increasingly becoming good practice to consult children in urban planning or architectural developments. Hackett et al. (2015) highlight how architecture can improve children's access to spatial justice by including them in the design process and designing in ways that continuously enable children to exercise their agency in everyday life. Krishnamurthy (2019) highlights how elements of flexibility and playfulness can improve children and their families' experiences of public space and should be included in town planning.

Languages and linguistic scholars have provided important insights into children's communication and how it may demarcate boundaries of class, ethnicity or gender (e.g. through speech that involves particular phrases) (Stephens et al. 2018). Fruitful discussions have also taken place at the overlap of childhood studies and children's literatures, for example, with regard to children's representation in past and contemporary children's books and how it positions children (and adults) through text and illustrations (Christensen 2003).

History and philosophy are further disciplines which have been instrumental in shaping the contemporary sociology of childhood (see

Chapter 2). Engaging with the works of philosophers such as Hobbes, Rousseau or Locke has enabled historians such as Ariès (1962) and Cunningham (2005) to delineate evolving constructions of childhood and their co-existing manifestations today (e.g. children as tabula rasa, as 'savages' or 'innocents'). Childhood studies continue to engage with broader philosophical thought, such as post-human or new materialist perspectives (Malone et al. 2020; see Chapter 2).

While these examples are by no means exhaustive, they shine some light on the rich debates across childhood studies, arts and humanities and the potential for mutual interdisciplinary learning. The following section now turns to discussing children and childhoods within medical sciences.

Medical sciences: Research ethics, public health and early intervention

More recently, there have been increasing collaborations between childhood studies and the medical sciences. Defined very broadly, the medical sciences involve disciplines aimed at the science of dealing with the maintenance of health and with a focus on prevention and healing. This includes fields of inquiry related to biology, chemistry, clinical psychology, medicine, pharmacology or public health. This section covers examples of conceptual thinking at the intersections of medical sciences and childhood studies and encourages students to think of collaboration in new areas.

Medical sciences – The evolution of research ethics involving children

The history of research within the medical field provides some alarming and important lessons about the real-life consequences for children of ignoring the lessons from childhood studies and children's rights. Many earlier unethical studies have included children: from Nazi experiments on children and adults in concentration camps, to testing and knowingly infecting children with rabies and herpes (Murphey 2003), to active ridicule to trigger stuttering in children with additional support needs (Silverman 1988). Medical research history is full of examples of unethical and harmful research with children, and many of our current ethical guidelines are a result of these studies, including the concept of **informed consent**, balancing risks and benefits for participants, fair selection of participants and the need for an independent external review of ethics of studies.

In the late 1800s, with the growth of the medical research field, some of the first recorded unethical research trials involving children came to light, such as the case of the French-based scientist Pasteur who tested his new rabies vaccine by injecting a nine-year-old with live rabies and freely published the documentation of his results including the names, addresses, personal circumstances and outcomes of his subjects (Murphey 2003). Historical documents highlight how his methods drew scientific criticism even at that time but also how many parents pleaded with Pasteur to give injections to their children (Murphey 2003). However, these types of experiments were not unusual or isolated cases. The central ethical debate this brought to the fore was whether it is acceptable to perform a harmful experiment on a person who will themselves see no benefit from it.

Following unethical and often lethal experiments on children and adults being held and tortured in concentration camps, twenty Nazi doctors were sentenced in the 1945–6 Nuremberg Trials for unethical research. The process resulted in the first ethics document, called the Nuremberg Code, which serves as the basis for current thinking on research ethics (Grodin and Annas 1996). This ten-point code makes the voluntary consent of research participants, including having the legal capacity to consent, essential to ethical research (Nuremberg Code, cited in Shuster 1997: 1436).

The Nuremberg Code took a very protectionist stance towards children and argued that they do not have the capacity to consent. Many scientists at the time acknowledged that this did not move the medical field forward in terms of understanding diseases and medical conditions specifically as they impact on children. However, concerns for the involvement of children persisted, especially for institutionalized children (Lederer 2003). The World Medical Association (1964) took a different stance in the Declaration of Helsinki, allowing research on human beings without the capacity to consent, if consent can be obtained from a legally authorized representative.

Even after the Declaration of Helsinki, many within the medical scientific community as well as philosophers such as Ramsey (1976) argued that children should not be included as research participants when their own health is not at stake and when the research involves any physical aspect, due to their lack of ability to give consent. He and many others in the scientific community believed that children should be excluded from research unless the research carries some measure of benefit directly for them, in which case they believed parents should be entitled to consent on their behalf. While it was recognized that such an approach effectively stopped children's involvement in much medical research, it was believed to be better to avoid harm rather than expose children to risk (Murphey 2003).

These historical debates on the place of children in medical research have more recently led to debate on the tensions between the protection of children and children's rights for participation in research. Ennew and Pleateau (2005) suggest that the UNCRC, while not specifically focused on research, does articulate four articles that highlight children's 'right to be properly researched' (see Chapter 4). Over the last decades, ethical considerations have shifted from a predominant focus on protecting children and keeping them safe from research harms to an emphasis on recognizing children's agency and competency to fully participate in research of their own accord while highlighting **children's participation** rights (see, for example, the Ethical Research Involving Children compendium and case study: Graham et al. 2013).

Critical group challenge: COVID-19 vaccines for children

More recently, ethical debates have arisen around the administration of COVID-19 vaccines for younger children. In a group, take part in the following exercise:

Step 1: Divide into two groups: One group will advocate for COVID-19 vaccines for younger children and the other against them.

Step 2: Drawing on key ideas of this Chapter and the wider book, discuss and research the available evidence within your group to develop your position. This includes examining the following issues: children's consent versus parents' consent, promotion of children's rights, research involving children in the development of vaccines, children's views, children's agency, **decolonization**, conceptualizations of **vulnerability** but also the real-time protection of children and so on.

[Note for facilitator – you may want to provide short materials for each group if this is an in-class exercise or encourage them to research as homework and come back to the next class prepared to

debate. Potential readings: Goldman et al. 2022; Kamenetz 2021; Sidiq et al. 2020].

Step 3: Each group presents their case for five minutes and the other group can ask questions.

At the end, consider:

- Have your original views changed following this exercise? If so, how and why?
- How do your views link back to key concepts from this book?

The influence of the public health approach

While the medical sciences often focus directly on the maintenance of health and prevention of disease, a public health approach looks more broadly at health as physical, mental and social wellbeing and not merely the absence of disease (Telfair et al. 2020). The term 'public' also denotes the wider focus of the public health field, that is, looking at the health of entire populations (or specific sub-segments) rather than solely at the individual level. A large aspect of public health is focused on the concept of prevention. This may include prevention that seeks to stop a health problem before it even starts or preventative measures which lead to early diagnosis and prompt treatment (Baumann and Karel 2013).

Since the nineteenth century, child public health has increasingly become a major area of focus in public health. Today, significant resources and services are aimed at improving the health of children. Many public health approaches build on the theoretical efforts of life course theories and thinking around social determinants of health, often within systems frameworks. Key among these theorists is Bronfenbrenner (1979), whose concepts of social ecology and its effect on human development have been fundamental across a variety of disciplines working with children. Modern conceptualizations of this framework often describe how **risk and/or protective factors** for a particular issue happen at larger structural and societal levels and interact with those factors happening at community, interpersonal and individual levels (see Chapter 6 for an example from the field of childhood violence prevention).

Related to conceptualizations of public health are also notions of wellbeing – which is a field in and of itself with many theoretical constructs.

Chapter 4 provides a more detailed discussion on how wellbeing theories have been applied and adapted within the childhood studies and children's rights fields, such as the distinction between objective and subjective theories of wellbeing: objective wellbeing theories tend to define wellbeing in terms of external and universal notions of quality-of-life indicators such as social attributes or determinants (things like access to health, education, having strong social connections and networks, for example) and material resources (Watson et al. 2012). These so-called objective theories of wellbeing largely arise from Sen's work in welfare economics and tend to focus on agreed core human capabilities necessary for a quality life (Bourke and Geldens 2007). This school of thought is not without critics that argue that any notion of 'objective' wellbeing is of course political and influenced by larger structural factors (such as racism or conceptualizations of childhood and mental health) that are not at all objective but are historized experiences influenced by social, political and economic factors (Wright 2015). Research from longitudinal data suggests that **young people** may experience wellbeing as yet another dimension of life in which they must perform to **normative** standards and for which they are responsible (Wyn et al. 2015). Subjective wellbeing theories, on the other hand, focus on feelings and emotions as well as specific domains of wellbeing (such as school, work and family) (Deci and Ryan 2009). Public health has tended to utilize the former wellbeing more since the main objective is to look at the health of populations, while other more individually oriented disciplines utilize conceptualizations related to subjective wellbeing (see Chapter 4 for discussion on wellbeing versus rights). With childhood studies critics argue that whatever notion of wellbeing is used, it needs to be grounded in children's lived experiences and perspectives, recognize and address intersectionality, take account of larger economic, political and social constructs and avoid labelling (Wright 2015; Wyn et al. 2015).

My research explores children's wellbeing in sport. Coming from a child rights background, the protection and promotion of children's rights are never far from my attention. The interdisciplinary approach childhood studies offers allows me to retain this commitment while drawing on rich sociological debates around such key concepts as agency, consent and even childhood itself.

Ruth Barnes, PhD Student, University of Edinburgh, UK

These theories have led to the evolution of various health behaviour models and several decades of work to better understand the reasons for people's health behaviours and how to change behaviour on a societal scale (through seatbelt laws, smoking cessation campaigns, etc.) (see Weston and Amiot 2020 for a description of key behaviour change models in health). Some of these models have been criticized, in a similar vein to the concept of **socialization**, as neglecting children's agency. However, these models highlight that there are increasingly areas of convergence between childhood studies and public health approaches.

In my research, I draw on key concepts from medical sociology, childhood studies and disability studies to make sense of children's experiences of living with cleft lip and palate in Colombia. In examining the social costs of having a bodily difference, I could see how children enact subtle and ambiguous agentic practices to resist those who stigmatize them, showing how stigma and agency ('mantras' of medical sociology and childhood studies respectively) converge. Working with different theories and disciplines is an overwhelming process. You must go deeply in your data analysis and critically scrutinize the literature to construct or find those linkages. Merging concepts also offers you different analytic angles and the potential to generate more impactful research.

Dr Liliana Arias-Urueña, Researcher, Colombia

Childhood and early intervention

One aspect of public health with salience for childhood studies is the concept of early intervention. 'Early' may refer to intervening at an early stage of the emergence of a health problem or to intervening at an early stage of the life course. Thus, childhood – and specifically early childhood – enters the gaze of policymakers as a key site of intervention and investment.

Because of early intervention policies, many countries (particularly in the global North) have developed universal services aimed at children and their families, such as **child protection**, education and health screening services. These often include a focus on parenting support, healthy schools, nutritional programmes or communication and wellbeing programmes for children and families (Blair et al. 2010). In recent years, studies around adverse childhood experiences (ACEs) have received much attention for highlighting how negative experiences in childhood (such as domestic abuse or substance misuse) can lead to negative outcomes later in life. While ACEs studies have found widespread reception in areas such as early childhood, child protection or education, their application has also been critically evaluated (Davidson and Wright 2020).

Activity: Critically evaluating ACEs research

Read the original ACEs study (Felitti et al. 1998) and a critical analysis of it (Edwards et al. 2019). Individually or in groups, consider the following questions:

- What categories of ACEs are identified by Felitti et al. (1998)?
- What are your reflections on these categories in relation to your own childhood experiences (or the experiences of children in your life)?
- Considering different points of view and different contexts of application, can you think of potential uses or misuses of ACEs?

While early intervention policies have led to widespread public health improvements, they have not been without critique in childhood studies. Scholars have pointed out how processes of standardization and normalization of children's development run the risk of becoming accepted truths about children's growth while being based largely on white, global North and middle-class samples of children (Burman 2017). In early childhood education, 'developmentally appropriate practice' has been described as a scientifically informed technology of government which seeks to produce healthy and productive future citizens and workers in line with neoliberal requirements (Dahlberg and Moss 2005). Simplistic policy interpretations of emerging neuroscience findings may lead to deterministic assumptions, such as the idea that a person's potential is irrevocably determined during the first few years of their life (Castañeda 2002). Finally, an often individualized focus on early intervention (e.g. by targeting 'parenting programmes' at families living in poverty) neglects **structural inequalities** and absolves governments from addressing these (Edwards et al. 2014). Thus, a childhood studies lens can provide useful critical insights into harvesting the benefits of early intervention approaches while not succumbing to deterministic neoliberal narratives about childhood and children's development.

Conclusion

As this Chapter has illustrated, the benefits of interdisciplinary work for more complex understandings and improvements of children's lives are significant. Working *across* and *with* multiple disciplines can open new perspectives and insights and is much needed in times of complex global problems. Connecting childhood studies with disciplines across the social sciences can expand theoretical and methodological understandings in the field and widen its scope of inquiry – for example, by placing importance on spatial aspects of childhood or by benefiting from critical contributions in disability, gender or race studies. Where cross-disciplinary conversations highlight tensions, such as with work in developmental psychology, they can bring childhood studies ontological assumptions into sharper focus and at the same time challenge their universality – for example, by contributing different perspectives on children's wellbeing research. Childhood studies aligns well with perspectives from the arts and humanities, whether through benefiting from arts-based methodologies, by focusing on child-led design or by critically analysing childhood through historical and philosophical lenses. Children's lives are heavily shaped by medical progress, such as in the form of public health and early childhood interventions, and childhood studies can draw from important learning with regard to the ethics of children's involvement in research and procedures, and the social determinants that shape children's health and wellbeing globally.

Despite all these benefits, there can be challenges to interdisciplinary work, similar to research across different geographies and cultures. Researchers may speak different languages, use different jargon and build on different ontological and epistemological assumptions about childhood. Tensions can be related to competitive dynamics between disciplines (e.g. linked to research funding) or in relation to values and assumptions about what constitutes children and childhoods. While some tensions may appear unresolvable, others can be brought together through fruitful discussions.

In the first place, it is important that researchers are mindful of any underlying tensions to make them visible and address them. This includes a need for researchers to be deeply reflexive about their own values and assumptions, and open to learning and debate. To truly address global challenges of childhoods, it is important to integrate interdisciplinary reflexivity and competence into the training of researchers and the development of new approaches. Another key challenge of interdisciplinary work is for researchers to refrain from being drawn into simplistic binaries or polarized views about childhood debates – a theme that rings true with wider cultural debates.

A core question related to interdisciplinary working is this: Which disciplines should be involved in the study of children and childhoods? Of course, this question can only be answered within the context of the particular research focus. The phenomenon under study should direct the disciplines that are involved, rather than the disciplines defining the subject of study. In practice, it is most likely not just one or the other: while we may seek to bring together relevant disciplines for particular research questions, as researchers we do not approach our research from a 'neutral' perspective but are always located already within our disciplinary upbringing.

Childhood studies have much to add to wider research on childhood. One core contribution is the centring of children's views and the highlighting of children's agency and competence, as well as the recognition that childhood is not merely a biological category. In recent years, childhood studies writers have called for a deeper engagement of childhood studies with other disciplines, in order to 'mainstream' a concern for childhood in social practices, relationships, interventions and institutions (Burman 2020; Punch 2020).

This Chapter has by no means provided an exhaustive list of interdisciplinary opportunities for childhood studies. For example, further disciplines to include can be found in the natural sciences (such as physics, life and earth sciences), and there is still much potential in these relatively novel disciplinary couplings of medical, natural and other 'hard' sciences, which we hope the Chapter inspires our readers to explore further.

Discussions around interdisciplinary work in the study of childhood are already taking place and for childhood studies researchers, there is a need to reach out and engage productively with those in different disciplinary contexts while holding true to the principles of centring children's views and recognizing children's agency. Childhood studies is well placed to do this: it is an open and dynamic field, always changing and expanding and looking for collaborations to better place children in this complex world in which we live.

References

Abebe, T. (2007), 'Changing Livelihoods, Changing Childhoods: Patterns of Children's Work in Rural Southern Ethiopia', *Children's Geographies*, 5 (1–2): 77–93.

Aitken, S. C. (1994), *Putting Children in Their Place*, Washington, DC: Association of American Geographers.

Alanen, L. (2012), 'Disciplinarity, Interdisciplinarity and Childhood Studies', *Childhood*, 19 (4): 419–22.

Ariès, P. (1962), *Centuries of Childhood*, London: Cape.

Bartos, A. (2013), 'Children Sensing Place', *Emotion, Space and Society*, 9: 89–98.

Baumann, L. C. and Karel, A. (2013), 'Prevention: Primary, Secondary, Tertiary', in M. D. Gellman and J. R. Turner (eds), *Encyclopedia of Behavioral Medicine*, 1532–34, New York: Springer.

Blair, D., Stewart-Brown, P., Waterston, D., and Crowther, D. (2010), *Child Public Health*, Oxford: Oxford University Press.

Blaisdell, C., Kustatscher, M., Zhu, Y., and Tisdall, E. K. M. (2021), 'The Emotional Relations of Children's Participation Rights in Diverse Social and Spatial Contexts: Advancing the Field', *Emotion, Space and Society*, 40: 100816.

Blaisdell, C., Arnott, L., Wall, K., and Robinson, C. (2019), 'Look Who's Talking: Using Creative, Playful Arts-based Methods in Research with Young Children', *Journal of Early Childhood Research*, 17 (1): 14–31.

Blazek, M. and Windram-Geddes, M. (2013), 'Editorial: Thinking and Doing Children's Emotional Geographies', *Emotion, Space and Society*, 9 (1): 1–3.

Blazek, M. and Kraftl, P. (2015), *Children's Emotions in Policy and Practice*, London: Palgrave MacMillan.

Bourke, L. and Geldens, L. M. (2007), 'Subjective Wellbeing and Its Meaning for Young People in a Rural Australian Centre', *Social Indicators Research*, 82 (1): 165–87.

Breslow, J. (2021), *Ambivalent Childhoods: Speculative Futures and the Psychic Life of the Child*, Minnesota: University of Minnesota Press.

Bronfenbrenner, U. (1979), *The Ecology of Human Development: Experiments by Nature and Design*, Cambridge, MA: Harvard University Press.

Buckingham, D. (2007), 'Selling Childhood?', *Journal of Children and Media*, 1 (1): 15–24.

Burman, E. (2020), 'Decolonising Childhood, Reconceptualising Distress: A Critical Psychological Approach to (Deconstructing) Child Well-Being', in M. Fleer, F. González Rey, and P. Jones (eds), *Cultural-Historical and Critical*

Psychology. Perspectives in Cultural-Historical Research, Vol 8, 99–111, Singapore: Springer.

Burman, E. (2017), *Deconstructing Developmental Psychology*, 3rd edn, London: Routledge.

Calderón, E., Kustatscher, M., Tisdall, E. K. M., Evanko, T., and Gomez Serna, J. M. (2021), 'Promoting Social Entrepreneurship Through Participatory Arts and Music with Young People: Creating Opportunities with Afrocolombian and Indigenous Youth During the COVID-19 Pandemic in Colombia. Changing the Story'. Available online: https://changingthestory .leeds.ac.uk/wp-content/uploads/sites/110/2021/08/Briefing-2_Social -Entrepreneuship.pdf.

Camponovo, S., Monnet, N., Moody, Z., and Darbellay, F. (2021), 'Research with Children from a Transdisciplinary Perspective: Coproduction of Knowledge by Walking', *Children's Geographies*, 1–14. Available online: https://www.tandfonline.com/doi/abs/10.1080/14733285.2021.2017405.

Cannella, G. S. (2002), 'Global Perspectives, Cultural Studies, and the Construction of a Postmodern Childhood Studies', in G. S. Cannella, J. L. Kincheloe, and K. Anijar (eds), *Kidworld: Childhood Studies, Global Perspectives, and Education*, 3–18, New York: Peter Lang Pub Incorporated.

Castañeda, C. (2002), *Figurations: Child, Bodies, Worlds*, London: Duke University Press.

Choi, B. and Pak, A. (2006), 'Multidisciplinarity, Interdisciplinarity, and Transdisciplinarity, Education and Policy: Definitions, Objectives, and Evidence of Effectiveness', *Clinical and Investigative Medicine*, 29 (6): 351–64.

Christensen, N. (2003), 'Childhood Revisited: On the Relationship Between Childhood Studies and Children's Literature', *Children's Literature Association Quarterly*, 28 (4): 230–9.

Christie, M. (2006), 'Transdisciplinary Research and Aboriginal Knowledge', *The Australian Journal of Indigenous Education*, 35: 78–89.

Collins, T. M. (2014), 'The Relationship Between Children's Rights and Business', *The International Journal of Human Rights*, 18 (6): 582–633.

Cook, D. T. (2005), 'The Dichotomous Child in and of Commercial Culture', *Childhood*, 12 (2): 155–9.

Cook, P. (2018), 'What's Wrong with Child Labor?', in Anca Gheaus, Gideon Calder, Jurgen De Wispelaere (eds), *The Routledge Handbook of the Philosophy of Childhood and Children*, 294–303, London: Routledge.

Cunningham, H. (2005), *Children and Childhood in Western Society Since 1500*, Harlow: Pearson Longman.

Curran, T. and Runswick-Cole, K. (2014), 'Disabled Children's Childhood Studies: A Distinct Approach?', *Disability & Society*, 29 (10): 1617–30.

Dahlberg, G. and Moss, P. (2005), *Ethics and Politics in Early Childhood Education*, London: Routledge.

Davidson, E. and Wright, L. H. V. (2020), 'Realising Children's Rights in an ACE-aware Nation', *Scottish Affairs*, 29 (4): 538–55.

del Solar, A. V., Llobet, V., and Nascimento, M. L. (eds) (2021), *South American Childhoods: Neoliberalisation and Children's Rights Since the 1990s*, Cham: Palgrave Macmillan.

Deci, E. L. and Ryan, R. M. (2000), 'The "What" and "Why" of Goal Pursuits: Human Needs and the Self-determination of Behaviour', *Psychological Inquiry*, 11: 227–68.

Edwards, R., Gillies, V., and Horsley, N. (2014), 'Policy Briefing: The Biologisation of Poverty. Policy and Practice in Early Years Intervention', *Discover Society*, 4. Available online: http://www.discoversociety.org/policy-briefing-the-biologisation-of-poverty-policy-and-practice-in-early-years-intervention/

Edwards, R., Gillies, V., and White, S. (2019), 'Introduction: Adverse Childhood Experiences (ACES) – Implications and Challenges', *Social Policy and Society*, 18 (3): 411–14.

Ennew, J. and Plateau, D. (2005), 'I Cry When I am Hit': Children Have the Right to be Properly Researched', *Paper Contributed to UNESCO, 2005, Eliminating Corporal Punishment – The Way Forward to Constructive Child Discipline*, Paris, France: UNESCO.

ERIC (Ethical Research Involving Children) (n.d.), 'ERIC'. Available online: https://childethics.com (accessed 1 March 2022).

Felitti, V. J., Anda, R. F., Nordenberg, D., Williamson, D. F., Sapitz, A. M., Edwards, V., Koss, M. P., and Marks, J. S. (1998), 'Relationship of Childhood Abuse and Household Dysfunction to Many of the Leading Causes of Death in Adults: The Adverse Childhood Experiences (ACE) Study', *American Journal of Preventive Medicine*, 14 (4): 245–58.

Gallagher, M. (2011), 'Sound, Space and Power in a Primary School', *Social & Cultural Geography*, 12 (1): 47–61.

George, A. A. (2014), *Making Modern Girls: A History of Girlhood, Labor, and Social Development in Colonial Lagos*, Athens: Ohio University Press.

Goldman, R. D. and Ceballo, R., International COVID-19 Parental Attitude Study (COVIPAS) Group (2022), 'Parental Gender Differences in Attitudes and Willingness to Vaccinate Against COVID-19', *Journal of Paediatrics and Child Health*, 58 (6): 1016–21.

Graham, A., Powell, M., Taylor, N., Anderson, D., and Fitzgerald, R. (2013), *Ethical Research Involving Children*, Florence: UNICEF Office of Research – Innocenti.

Grodin, M. A. and Annas, G. J. (1996), 'Legacies of Nuremberg: Medical Ethics and Human Rights', *JAMA*, 276: 1682–3.

Hackett, A., Procter, L., and Seymour, J. (2015), 'Introduction: Spatial Perspectives and Childhood Studies', in Abigail Hackett, Lisa Procter, Julie Seymour (eds), *Children's Spatialities*, 1–17, London: Palgrave Macmillan.

Hendrick, H. (1997), 'Constructions and Re-constructions of British Childhood: An Interpretive Survey, 1800 to the Present', in A. James and A. Prout (eds), *Constructing and Reconstructing Childhood*, 33–60, London: Falmer.

Holloway, S. L. and Valentine, G. (2000), *Children's Geographies: Playing, Living, Learning*, London and New York: Routledge.

Holloway, S. L. (2014), 'Changing Children's Geographies', *Children's Geographies*, 12 (4): 377–92.

Holt, L. (2003), '(Dis)abling Children in Primary School Micro-spaces: Geographies of Inclusion and Exclusion', *Health & Place*, 9 (2): 119–28.

Horton, J. and Kraftl, P. (2006), 'What Else? Some More Ways of Thinking and Doing Children's Geographies', *Children's Geographies*, 4 (1): 69–95.

James, A. (2003), 'Understanding Childhood from an Interdisciplinary Perspective', in P. Pufall and R. Unsworth (eds), *Rethinking Childhood*, 25–37, Ithaca, NY: Rutgers University Press.

James, A. L. (2010), 'Competition or Integration? The Next Step in Childhood Studies?', *Childhood*, 17 (4): 485–99.

James, A., Jenks, C., and Prout, A. (1998), *Theorizing Childhood*, Cambridge: Polity Press.

James, A. L. (2010), 'Competition or Integration? The Next Step in Childhood Studies?', *Childhood*, 17 (4): 485–99.

Kamenetz, A. (2021), 'Should Schools Require the COVID Vaccine? Many Experts Say It's Too Soon', *National Public Radio (NPR)*, 19 November. Available online: https://www.npr.org/2021/11/19/1056568867/should-schools-mandate-covid-vaccine-for-children.

Kehily, M. J. (ed.) (2013), *Understanding Childhood: A Cross Disciplinary Approach*, Bristol: Policy Press.

Krishnamurthy, S. (2019), 'Reclaiming Spaces: Child Inclusive Urban Design', *Cities & Health*, 3 (1–2): 86–98.

Kuhn, T. S. (1962 [2012]), *The Structure of Scientific Revolutions*, London: University of Chicago Press.

Kustatscher, M. (2017), 'The Emotional Geographies of Belonging: Children's Intersectional Identities in Primary School', *Children's Geographies*, 15 (1): 65–79.

Kustatscher, M. (2020), 'Gender', in D. T. Cook (ed.), *The SAGE Encyclopaedia of Children and Childhood Studies*, Vol. 2, 1–11, SAGE Publications. Available online: https://sk.sagepub.com/reference/the-sage-encyclopedia-of-children-and-childhood-studies.

Lee, N. (2001), *Childhood and Society: Growing Up in an Age of Uncertainty*, Milton Keynes: Open University Press.

Lee, L., Currie, V., Saied, N., and Wright, L. (2020), 'Journey to Hope, Self-expression and Community Engagement: Youth-led Arts-based Participatory Action Research', *Children and Youth Services Review*, 109: 104581.

Lederer, S. E. (2003), 'Children as Guinea Pigs: Historical Perspectives', *Accountability in Research*, 10 (1): 1–16.

Lefebvre, H. (1991), *The Production of Space*, Oxford and Cambridge: Blackwell.

Liebel, M., Hanson, K., and Nieuwenhuys, O. (2012), 'Do Children Have a Right to Work? Working Children's Movements in the Struggle', in Karl Hanson and Olga Nieuwnhuys (eds), *Reconceptualizing Children's Rights in International Development: Living Rights, Social Justice, Translations*, 225–49, Cambridge University Press, https://doi.org/10.1017/CBO9781139381796.

Lupton, D. (2013), 'Infant Embodiment and Interembodiment: A Review of Sociocultural Perspectives', *Childhood*, 20 (1): 37–50.

Malone, K., Tesar, M., and Arndt, S. (2020), *Theorising Posthuman Childhood Studies*, Singapore: Springer.

Matthews, H. and Limb, M. (1999), 'Defining an Agenda for the Geography of Children: Review and Prospect', *Progress in Human Geography*, 23 (1): 61–90.

Massey, D. (1994), *Space, Place and Gender*, Minneapolis: Polity/University of Minnesota Press.

Mayall, B. (2015), 'The Sociology of Childhood and Children's Rights', in W. Vandenhole, E. Desmet, D. Reynaert, and S. Lembrechts (eds), *The Routledge International Handbook of Children's Rights Studies*, 93–109, London: Routledge.

Mitchell, R. and Moore, S. A. (2018), 'Transdisciplinary Child and Youth Studies: Critical Praxis, Global Perspectives', *World Futures*, 74 (7–8): 450–70.

Morrow, V. (2012), 'Politics and Economics in Global Questions about Childhood and Youth, The Trouble with Numbers', *Childhood*, 19 (1): 3–7.

Murphey, T. (2003), 'The Ethics of Research with Children', *AMA Journal of Ethics Policy Forum*. Available online: https://journalofethics.ama-assn.org/article/ethics-research-children/2003-08.

Perez, M. S. and Cannella, G. S. (2011), 'Disaster Capitalism as Neoliberal Instrument for the Construction of Early Childhood Education/Care Policy: Charter Schools in Post-Katrina New Orleans', *International Critical Childhood Policy Studies Journal*, 4 (1): 47–68.

Philo, C. (1992), 'Neglected Rural Geographies: A Review', *Journal of Rural Studies*, 8 (2): 193–207.

Pinker, S. (2003), *The Blank Slate: The Modern Denial of Human Nature*, London: Penguin.

Prout, A. (2019), 'In Defence of Interdisciplinary Childhood Studies', *Children and Society*, 33 (4): 309–15.

Prout, A. and Campling, J. (eds) (2000), *The Body, Childhood and Society*, London: Palgrave Macmillan.

Prout, A. and James, A. (1990), 'A New Paradigm for the Sociology of Childhood? Provenance, Promise and Problems', in A. James and A. Prout (eds), *Constructing and Reconstructing Childhood: Contemporary Issues in the Sociological Study of Childhood*, 7–33, London: The Falmer Press.

Punch, S. (2020), 'Why Have Generational Orderings Been Marginalised in the Social Sciences Including Childhood Studies?', *Children's Geographies*, 18 (2): 128–40.

Oxford English Dictionary (n.d.), 'Discipline, n'. Available online: https://www.oed.com/view/Entry/53744?rskey=digVjB&result=1#eid (accessed 20 October, 2021).

Qvortrup, J. (1994), 'Childhood Matters: An Introduction', in J. Qvortrup, M. Bardy, G. Sgritta, and H. Wintersberger (eds), *Childhood Matters. Social Theory, Practice And Politics*, 1–23, Aldershot: Avebury.

Robson, E., Horton, J. and Kraftl, P. (2013), 'Children's Geographies: Reflecting on Our First Ten Years', *Children's Geographies*, 11 (1): 1–6.

Rose, N. (1989), *Governing the Soul: The Shaping of the Private Self*, London: Routledge.

Ramsey, P. (1976), 'The Enforcement of Morals: Non-therapeutic Research on Children', *Hastings Center Report*, 6: 21–30.

Renold, E. (2005), *Girls, Boys and Junior Sexualities: Exploring Children's Gender and Sexual Relations in the Primary School*, London: Routledgefalmer.

Shuster, E. (1997), 'Fifty Years Later: The Significance of the Nuremberg Code', *New England Journal of Medicine*; 337: 1436–40.

Sidiq, K. R., Sabir, D. K., Ali, S. M., and Kodzius, R. (2020), 'Does Early Childhood Vaccination Protect Against COVID-19?', *Frontiers in Molecular Biosciences*, 7: 120.

Silverman, F. (1988), 'The "Monster" Study', *Journal of Fluency Disorders*, 13: 225–31.

Skelton, T. (ed.) (2017), *Geographies of Children and Young People*, Singapore: Springer.

Stephens, N., Hall-Lew, L., and Ellis, V. S. (2018), 'I'm Like, "Really? You Were Homeschooled?" Quotative Variation by High School Type and Linguistic Style', *American Speech: A Quarterly of Linguistic Usage*, 93 (1): 108–38.

Soja, E. (1989), *Postmodern Geographies. The Reassertion of Space in Critical Social Theory*, London and New York: Verso.

Spyrou, S. (2018), *Disclosing Childhoods. Research and Knowledge Production for a Critical Childhood Studies*, London: Palgrave Macmillan.

Szostak, R. (2012), 'The Interdisciplinary Research Process', in Allen F. Repko, William H. Newell, and Rick Szostak (eds), *Case Studies in Interdisciplinary Research*, 3–20, United States of America: SAGE Publications, Inc. Available online: https://www.google.co.uk/books/edition/Case_Studies _in_Interdisciplinary_Resear/Lj97JT3bt1MC?hl=en&gbpv=1&printsec =frontcover.

Tatlow-Golden, M. and Montgomery, H. (2021a), 'Childhood Studies and Child Psychology: Disciplines in Dialogue?', *Children & Society*, 35 (1): 3–17.

Tatlow-Golden, M. and Montgomery, H. (eds) (2021b), 'Themed Section: Childhood Studies and Child Psychology: Disciplines in Dialogue?', *Children & Society*, 35 (1): 3–61.

Taylor, A. and Pacini-Ketchabaw, V. (2018), *The Common Worlds of Children and Animals: Relational Ethics for Entangled Lives*, London: Routledge.

Telfair, J., Trivedi, R., Bland, H., Reagon, V., and Williams, J. (2020), *Child Public Health*, American Psychological Association. Available online: https://www.oxfordbibliographies.com/display/document/obo -9780199791231/obo-9780199791231-0193.xml.

Thorne, B. (2007), 'Editorial: Crafting the Interdisciplinary Field of Childhood Studies', *Childhood*, 14 (2): 147–52.

Tisdall, E. K. M. (2012), 'The Challenge and Challenging of Childhood Studies? Learning from Disability Studies and Research with Disabled Children', *Children & Society*, 26 (3): 181–91.

Thrift, N. (2006), 'Space', *Theory, Culture and Society*, 23 (2–3): 139–55.

Twum-Danso Imoh, A., Bourdillon, M., and Meichsner, S. (2019), 'Introduction: Exploring Children's Lives Beyond the Binary of the Global North and Global South', in Afua Twum-Danso Imoh, Michael Bourdillon, and Sylvia Meichsner (eds), *Global Childhoods Beyond the North-South Divide*, 1–10, Cham: Palgrave Macmillan.

Walkerdine, V. (2015), 'Developmental Psychology and the Study of Childhood', in Kehily, M. J. (ed.), *An Introduction to Childhood Studies*, 112–23, London: McGraw-Hill Education (UK).

Watson, N. (2012), 'Theorising the Lives of Disabled Children: How can Disability Theory Help?', *Children & Society*, 26 (3): 192–202.

Weston, D., Ip, A., and Amlôt, R. (2020), 'Examining the Application of Behaviour Change Theories in the Context of Infectious Disease Outbreaks and Emergency Response: A Review of Reviews', *BMC Public Health*, 20: 1483.

Woodhead, M. (2015), 'Childhood Studies: Past, Present and Future', in M. J. Kehily (ed.), *An Introduction to Childhood Studies*, 19–33, London: McGraw-Hill Education (UK).

Woodhead, M. (2009), 'Child Development and the Development of
   Childhood', in J. Qvortrup, W. Corsaro, and H. Michael-Sebastine (eds),
   The Palgrave Handbook of Childhood Studies, 46–61, London: Palgrave
   Macmillan.

Woodhead, M. and Montgomery, H. (2003), *Understanding Childhood: An
   Interdisciplinary Approach*, London: Wiley.

World Medical Association (1964), 'WMA Declaration of Helsinki – Ethical
   Principles for Medical Research Involving Human Subjects'. Available
   online: https://www.wma.net/policies-post/wma-declaration-of-helsinki
   -ethical-principles-for-medical-research-involving-human-subjects/.

Wright, K. (2015), 'From Targeted Interventions to Universal Approaches:
   Historicizing Wellbeing', in K. Wright and J. McLeod (eds), *Rethinking Youth
   Wellbeing*, 197–218, Singapore: Springer.

Wyn, J., Cuervo, H., and Landstedt, E. (2015), 'The Limits of Wellbeing', in K.
   Wright and J. McLeod (eds), *Rethinking Youth Wellbeing*, 55–70. Singapore:
   Springer.

Xu, Y., Warin, J., and Robb, M. (2020), 'Beyond Gender Binaries: Pedagogies
   and Practices in Early Childhood Education and Care (ECEC)', *Special Issue
   of Early Years*, 40: 1.

Yuval-Davis, N. (2011), *The Politics of Belonging: Intersectional Contestations*,
   London: Sage.

Commentary on Childhood Studies Meets Other Disciplines

Tendai Charity Nhenga

Chapter Outline

The Chapter appropriately begins by pointing out what seems to be settled among scholars: that **childhood studies** is an **inter-**, **multi-** and **transdisciplinary** field of study. Indeed, advances in childhood studies debates have used knowledge and methodologies in research and teaching from an inexhaustive list of **disciplines**, in various ways, necessitated by the fact that children's issues often call for extensive dialogue among and inquiry by experts of different disciplines (in academia, public and private sectors, and civil society) such as medical scholars and practitioners, anthropologists, sociologists, political scientists, economists, practitioners and scholars in law and in international development studies, and policymakers and NGO workers from varied disciplinary backgrounds (Thorne 2007). Refreshingly, the Chapter goes on to demonstrate, with the use of examples, the inter-, multi- and transdisciplinary nature of questions that **childhood** scholars grapple with.

The challenge of defining inter-, multi- and transdisciplinarity

Most importantly, in putting the discussion into perspective, the Chapter makes evident the continuing challenges in defining what constitutes interdisciplinary, multidisciplinary or transdisciplinary inquiry. While the Chapter attempts to draw a distinction between the terms, which are often used interchangeably, there are clearly difficulties in providing concrete examples of research which is interdisciplinary, multidisciplinary or transdisciplinary. This points towards the challenges of defining and differentiating these terms.

Over the last fifty years, shifts have happened in the interpretation of inter-, multi- or transdisciplinary studies, which have a bearing on our understanding of the field of childhood studies today. Moreover, additional terminologies have been used in the field. For example, Stember offers a clear understanding of the different levels of disciplinarity simplified as follows:

- *Intradisciplinary*: working within a single discipline.
- *Crossdisciplinary*: viewing one discipline from the perspective of another.
- *Multidisciplinary*: people from different disciplines working together, each drawing on their disciplinary knowledge.
- *Interdisciplinary*: integrating knowledge and methods from different disciplines, using a real synthesis of approaches.
- *Transdisciplinary*: creating a unity of intellectual frameworks beyond the disciplinary perspectives. (Stember 1991)

This Chapter provides an entry point into some of these discussions, and readers are stimulated to consider further the opportunities and challenges presented by these different levels of disciplinarity where childhood studies meets with the other disciplines.

Interdisciplinary childhood studies: The example of children's rights

Kustatscher and Fry usefully delve into how different disciplines (such as social sciences, arts and humanities or medical sciences) are coming together with childhood studies, and what some of the opportunities and challenges of these encounters are. While the Chapter does not discuss in detail how childhood studies meets with the legal discipline (this is the focus of Chapter 4), this convergence provides an example of such encounters. Some scholars argue that there are certain aspects of childhood studies that have not been reconciled with legal scholarship. Huntington (2017: 755) avers that '[most] legal scholars do not engage with the wealth of interdisciplinary research on **early childhood**, nor are they part of the interdisciplinary dialogue and policy debates. As a result, that conversation does not include the voices of lawyers and legal scholars, who are uniquely positioned to add critical insights'. Huntington (2017: 759) even goes on to suggest the need for 'a subdiscipline of early childhood development and the law'.

However, since the coming into force of the **United Nations Convention on the Rights of the Child**, there has increasingly been scholarship where childhood studies meets with the legal discipline on issues around children's rights. Archard (2004) provides a key academic text for understanding the philosophical and moral basis of children's rights. The text relates children's rights to ideas about childhood, examining why children need particular rights and relationships among children, adults and the state. Freeman (2012), along with a number of other authors, has in recent years explored the interactions between legal thought and childhood studies. Freeman himself raises notable arguments that law has always been concerned with children, even before the emergence of childhood studies. He posits that law and childhood studies have much in common, most notably the emphasis on the child as a subject. However, on the flip side, he seems to agree with Huntington, when he argues that legal scholars, whose primary goal is to disseminate and propagate children's rights, are not so interested in understanding the construct we call 'childhood'. He concludes that there is room for more dialogue or collaboration between childhood studies and legal studies (Freeman 2012) (for further discussion on childhood studies and children's rights, see Chapter 4).

Applying interdisciplinarity: Examples from Zimbabwe

While the compartmentalized knowledge that emerges from childhood studies has provided many breakthroughs in understanding children's lives, it does not seem to be a match for the many complex problems facing children in the twenty-first century. Kustatscher and Fry rightly point out the increasing recognition that **child development** issues are interdependent with issues that are social, economic, geographic, medical, and so on, which has led to increasing calls for and funding that brings together different disciplines in multi-, inter- and/or transdisciplinary research. An example of that is the study 'Exploring Determinants of Violence in Childhood: Methodology of Research on Social Norms and Violence Prevention in Zimbabwe. Understanding Violence Against Children in Zimbabwe', collaboratively carried out by the University of Edinburgh and Women's University in Africa, with funding from UNICEF, Zimbabwe. This study drew together researchers from law, social sciences and humanities. While this research was successfully carried out, each researcher brought their own concepts and methods to the team, which shaped how they thought about children and childhoods and how they conducted the research. This made the interdisciplinary venture challenging yet overwhelmingly stimulating.

When childhood studies meets other disciplines in research, there will always be disciplinary differences in determining the 'methodological approach to follow; questions to ask; appropriate methods for collecting data; what actually constitutes data; applicable analytic tools; what evidence looks like' (Lach 2014: 88). A case in point would be where qualitative childhood studies meets with medical sciences which are predominantly quantitative. Early 2022, the Child Rights Research Centre of Africa University, with support from UNICEF and the Ministry of Health and Child Care in Zimbabwe, carried out a series of health-related studies which includes the unpublished 'Motivators and barriers to access to essential health care services during the COVID-19 pandemic in Zimbabwe'. This study, which employed a mixed-methods design, had a quantitative component carried out by public health researchers and a qualitative component (carried out by researchers from legal, social sciences, education and humanities disciplines) which takes into account the voices of different groups of people (people above sixty years of age, people with disabilities, key populations, community leaders, people with communicable and non-communicable diseases, among others). The study intentionally included girls of childbearing age who were accessing maternal health care and children with disabilities, an approach that is rarely used in public health-related research. The team that conducted this research was interdisciplinary and the different methodological approaches of their disciplines came under scrutiny during the development of the research proposal and even during ethical considerations. Concessions were made to come up with an all-encompassing and agreed research design.

Friedman (2013) points out the institutional and individual challenges of engaging in interdisciplinary research, arguing that

> [d]isciplines generate communities of **discourse**. However, interdisciplinary research breaks the bonds of community and seems to reject the solidarity of discourse and language that enable members of the community to recognize one another and to speak together. The discourse community may treat this as a signal of disrespect or a sign of ignorance. (54)

He adds that different disciplines determine criteria and judgement that involve norms, nomothetic values and standards. The communities of interest and practice that merge within disciplines constitute an identifiable peer group. Hence, he rightly points out that it is almost impossible for members of a particular discipline to judge the worth of research that does not originate from within the framework of their own discipline. An example of this kind of attitude was seen when the Child Rights Research Centre of Africa University was securing clearances for research by the relevant medical departments of the local authorities of Zimbabwe for the 'Motivators and barriers to access to essential health care services during the COVID-19 pandemic in Zimbabwe'. In some cases, the unit heads (who were from the medical field) felt that this kind of research was the exclusive domain of researchers from the medical field only. Some outrightly objected to the inclusion of qualitative researchers from non-medical disciplines on the research team (a decision which was vetoed by their parent Ministry of Health and Child Care). This clearly provided an example of how different disciplines determine criteria, judgement and standards to research involving children.

However, there have been encouraging developments in recent years in university colleges, departments and research institutes, where academics of a multiplicity of disciplines are increasingly constituting these various university bodies which were previously discipline-specific. Academics within these departments and institutes often find themselves supervising or examining postgraduate theses of disciplines not of their own or being included in multidisciplinary research teams or research institutes/centres. This meshing together of disciplines within the various faculties, colleges, departments and research institutes has proved more beneficial than problematic, as academics of different disciplines begin to appreciate the different research methodologies and develop new methodologies which take on board the best of the different disciplinary research approaches, and establish multidisciplinary communities of interest and practice, such as those relating to child development, children's rights, **violence against children** and access to essential health care services. A case in point is the Children's Institute of the University of Cape Town, South Africa, and the Child Rights Research Centre of Africa University, Zimbabwe, both of which have established a community of researchers of different disciplines, who are all bound by common interests – children.

Moving forward: Towards an interdisciplinary childhood studies

Having attended to the issues raised by interdisciplinary research, it is important, therefore, to note how local communities of practice can meet the challenges. An example of where local communities have met challenges brought on by interdisciplinary research would be where research institutes are intentionally established with the aim of harnessing the collective academic capability of a multiplicity of disciplines to collectively promote inquiry, to build capacity through teaching and training, and present evidence to guide the development of policies, laws and interventions for children. In such academic bodies, the focus would shift from the different methodologies used by different disciplines to the bigger picture – the welfare and development of children. Academics would pay more attention to how their discipline-specific methodological approaches complement each other and how to merge the methodologies of different disciplines and come up with new innovative ones, which are not discipline-specific, for the common good.

An example of this is the study 'Exploring Determinants of Violence in Childhood: Methodology of Research on Social Norms and Violence Prevention in Zimbabwe. Understanding Violence Against Children in Zimbabwe' (Fry et al. 2016) and the 'Protection Plus Cash: The Harmonised Social Cash Transfer Mixed Methods Study' (Nhenga-Chakarisa 2019), both of which culminated in the development, fine-tuning and implementation of the Round Robin Methodology, which took special consideration of child development from a social, cultural, economic and development perspective. It was designed to include a number of participatory activities exploring 'conceptualisations of childhood, pathways to violence, social norms and recommendations for responses' (Fry et al. 2016: 2).

This Chapter has begun an important discourse which childhood studies will benefit from in many ways going forward. Further work across the field on how local communities of practice can meet the challenges of inter-, multi- and transdisciplinarity will bring these opportunities to fruition.

References

Archard, D. (2004), *Children: Rights and Childhood*, Vol. 2, London and New York: Routledge.

Freeman, M. (2012), *Current Legal Issues*, Vol. 14, Oxford: Oxford University Press. doi:10.1093/acprof:oso/9780199652501.001.0001.

Friedman, K. (2013), 'C&C' 13: Proceedings of the 9th ACM Conference on Creativity & Cognition', *9th ACM Conference on Creativity & Cognition*, 11, New York: Association for Computing Machinery, June. doi:10.1145/2466627.2485920.

Fry, D., Casey, T., Hodzi, C., and Nhenga, T. (2016), *Exploring Determinants of Violence in Childhood: Methodology of Research on Social Norms and Violence Prevention in Zimbabwe. Understanding Violence Against Children in Zimbabwe*, Harare: UNICEF. Available online: http://preventingviolence .education.ed.ac.uk/areas-of-study/drivers-of-violence/social-norms -violence-zimbabwe/.

Huntington, C. (2017), 'Early Childhood Development and the Law', *Southern California Law Review*, 90: 755.

Lach, D. (2014), 'Challenges of Interdisciplinary Research: Reconciling Qualitative and Quantitative Methods for Understanding Human– Landscape Systems', *Environmental Management*, 53: 88–93.

Nhenga-Chakarisa, T. F. D. (2019), *Protection Plus Cash: The Harmonised Social Cash Transfer Mixed Methods Study*, Harare: Ministry of Public Services, Labour and Social Welfare, UNICEF.

Stember, M. (1991), 'Advancing the Social Sciences Through the Interdisciplinary Enterprise', *The Social Science Journal*, 28 (1): 1–14. doi:10.1016/0362-3319(91)90040-B.

Thorne, B. (2007), 'Editorial: Crafting the Interdisciplinary Field of Childhood Studies', *Childhood*, 14 (2): 147–52.

4

Childhood Studies Meets Children's Rights Studies

E. Kay M. Tisdall and

Kristina Konstantoni

Introduction

Children's rights has gained increased international policy traction with the near-universal **ratification** of the **United Nations Convention on the Rights of the Child** (UNCRC). Adopted by the UN Assembly in 1989, at the time of writing the United States is the only Member State that has not ratified the UNCRC.[1] The UNCRC is described as bringing together economic, social, cultural, civil and political rights, specified for children, into one document (UNICEF UK, no date). Once a country has ratified the UNCRC, they are obligated to implement its provisions. Thus, the UNCRC is a cornerstone for much of children's advocacy, from international non-governmental organizations to local initiatives.

The UNCRC is a core international **human rights** treaty. Human rights are particular forms of rights, which gained a political impetus after World Wars I and II. Human rights are **moral rights** above all others, recognized in international law (Donnelly and Whelan 2017). They are articulated in the Universal Declaration of Human Rights, adopted by the UN General Assembly in 1948, as a matter of inherent human dignity. Their international basis means they can be claimed even if not guaranteed or protected nationally. Human rights then are particularly powerful claims for victims and the dispossessed (Grear 2020). However, human rights are not always easily claimed and children can find them particularly hard to claim due to systemic and practical barriers.

The UNCRC is the current internationally agreed expression of children's human rights – but not necessarily a permanent one. This Chapter goes beneath and beyond a description of the UNCRC to consider children's rights and human rights more generally and conceptually. This is a perspective from the 'inside' – all of us writing the book work every day with the UNCRC and are advocates of children's human rights – and we do not want to undermine the UNCRC and its implementation. But there are benefits of respectful and well-grounded critique, which will only make current arguments stronger and potentially offer ways for change in the future.

While **childhood studies** researchers are not necessarily children's rights advocates, there is an affinity between asserting that children are **social actors** (see Chapter 2) and recognizing children have the full range of human rights. Further, childhood studies provides a lens to consider children's rights critically, in children's rights claims and in their realization (or not) in children's lives. This Chapter begins these discussions by considering the basis for human rights theory and whether children can have human rights. It goes on to outline key components of the UNCRC and then to consider common criticisms. It discusses potential alternatives to children's human rights for framing policy – theorizations of **vulnerability** and **wellbeing** – and their respective merits and problems. The Chapter then concludes.

What are human rights?

The history of rights is long, complicated and disputed. Historical experts trace discussions on rights back to Aristotle and the Stoics, as well as other heritages from ancient Babylon, India and Persia (see Freeman 2011). The Greek origins in particular were picked up, substantially modified and developed in the European Enlightenment intellectual movement of the late seventeenth and eighteenth centuries (for overviews, see Archard 2014; Jones 1994; Wall 2017). Links were made between natural rights, individuals and liberty, which are exemplified in the United States' Declaration of Independence:

> We hold these truths to be self-evident, that all men were created equal, that they are endowed by their Creator with certain inalienable Rights, that among these are Life, Liberty and the pursuit of happiness. (1776)

This sentence holds many of the cornerstones of rights theory that continue to influence human rights theory and applications today. First, certain rights are so fundamental that they are 'inalienable'. This means that these rights cannot be given away nor taken away from the person who possesses them. This does not apply to all rights but it does relate to certain rights. Second, these rights are so fundamental that they are universal. At the time of the Declaration of Independence, this principle was only ascribed to 'men' and – despite the wording of equality – only to certain men and not others. Thus, a range of people were excluded, such as children, women, Indigenous people and enslaved people. Third, there is a deep and strong theoretical thread that associates rights with individuals. While all these elements can be and are disputed, they capture some of the enduring strengths of human rights claims and **discourse** – that they are inalienable, fundamental and universal, protecting individuals from injustices – and some of the challenges, such as who and what is included or excluded.

Human rights are described as political 'trump cards' (Dworkin 1978; O'Neill 1988): that is, they are so fundamental that they trump, or supersede, other requests or demands. Rights set up entitlements and claims, so that an individual possessing rights can claim their entitlements (see Donnelly and Whelan 2017 for an accessible and more extensive discussion of rights relationships with claims and entitlements). A right typically means there is a corresponding duty, which the **duty-bearer**[2] is obligated to meet. If that claim were not met or the entitlement not respected, this is a special kind of violation and there should be accountability and substantial justification (if a justification were even possible). Rights thus set up strong relationships between the rights-holder and the duty-bearer, composed of claims, entitlement and accountability.

Critical challenge: Exploring distinctions between types of rights

A number of distinctions are made between types of rights, which can be fruitful categories to consider in their application to **childhood** and to children's human rights.

Legal rights: rights that are stated in law

Moral rights (also called **natural rights**): rights that are asserted but may or may not be in law

An example: A child's human right to be protected from physical punishment is a long-standing children's rights issue, but it is not recognized as a legal right in all countries.[3]

Can you think of another example of a moral right that is not a legal right?

Negative rights (also called **libertarian rights**): rights not to be interfered with by the state or others, unless for exceptional and justifiable reasons

An example: freedom of expression

Positive rights (also called **protection rights**): rights that require the state or others to act or provide

An example: right to education

Some would argue that positive rights cannot exist, as they place indefensible constraints on negative rights unless people agree by contract (e.g. Nozick 1974). Do you agree?

Some would argue that the distinction between negative and positive rights quickly falls down. For example, the right to a fair trial (typically considered a negative right) can require the right to legal aid (typically

considered a positive right) (e.g. Breakley 2015; Shue 1980). Can you think of other examples where a negative right is dependent on a positive right?

Will theories of rights: protect individual will (i.e. individual freedoms, liberties and **autonomy**) as long as such rights do not violate others' rights (e.g. Hart 1955)

Interest theories of rights: seek to advance human flourishing and all people deserve to be provided with basic human goods (e.g. MacCormick 1982; Nussbaum 1997)

Have a look at MacCormick's famous article in 1982. Do you agree or disagree with his arguments for children's rights based on interest theory?

While these elements help make human rights the political 'trump cards' described by Dworkin, they also lead to certain difficulties conceptually and practically: such as how to deal with seemingly irreconcilable conflicts between human rights (e.g. Kamm 2007), what matters are excluded from rights talk (can one have the right to love?) (e.g. Cowden 2016) and who (or what) is excluded from rights theory (e.g. Grear 2018). There have been questions, for example, of the privileging of humanity within rights theories and arguments to extend rights to animals, the environment and the world (e.g. Grear 2018; Stone 2010). Efforts have been made to go beyond the individualization of rights, to consider collective and group rights, drawing on feminist and Indigenous theorizing (e.g. Kymlicka 1989; Razack 1992; Wiessner 2011). Here, the assumptions of the rational, independent and autonomous individual are much critiqued. There are counter views that people are essentially social and therefore rights theory needs to recognize mutual dependence and relationality (e.g. Mackenzie and Stoljar 2000; Sandel 1988). But, arguably, the heritage of rights theory from the European Enlightenment continues into human rights discourse today: that such rights are inalienable, fundamental and universal, that rights are very particular types of claims and entitlements, which set up certain relationships between rights-holders and duty-bearers.

Can children have human rights?

Arguments for children having human rights are seeking to include children and childhood within a powerful moral and legal discourse. They are asserting that children, too, should be recognized as having inherent human dignity and children too should have claims and entitlements that duty-bearers are obliged to meet. Such arguments, though, need to counter the general absence of children and childhood from rights theorizations. If children and childhood are mentioned at all, they are 'largely a tool to illuminate the nature of the autonomous adult citizen by providing the perfect mirror within which to reflect the negative image of the positive adult form' (Arneil 2002: 74). In other words, children and childhood are only discussed in much of rights theory to exemplify how adults do have rights – but children and childhood do not (see Freeman 2020; Wall 2017).

The exclusion of children from rights, and particularly from human rights, has been challenged. Leading proponents in the past century or more include Eglantyne Jebb, who established an emergency relief organization, Save the Children Fund, to assist children in Europe affected by the World War I (Becker 2020). She drafted the five-point 'Charter for Children' in 1922; in due course this became the first Declaration on the Rights of the Child (see later). Janusz Korczak (the pen name for the Polish Jewish physician, writer and educator Henryk Goldszmit (d. 1942)) is noted for his ideas on children's rights, including children's right to respect and the right to be loved. These ideas were radical in their time and influenced the international children's rights movement of the twentieth century (see Council of Europe 2009). More recent agitators are the 'kiddy libbers' of the 1970s, who provocatively promoted equal rights for children. Children should have precisely the same rights as adults, such as the rights to work, to have lawful sexual relations and to vote (e.g. see Holt 1974). While the children's liberation movement is not largely accepted in the children's rights field today (see Freeman 1983), their arguments were another impetus to go beyond children's rights to protection, to consider children's rights to civil and political rights and to recognize children as social actors.

Activity: Should children have the same rights as adults?

You can test out your views by considering some issues that are debated currently:

- Should the voting age be lowered? If so, how low? Should babies have the right to vote?[4]
- Should children have the right to refuse life-saving medical treatment?[5]
- Should children have the right to work?[6]
- Should children have to go to school?[7]
- Should children be able to have lawful, consensual sexual relations?[8]
- Should children be held criminally responsible for their offences, as would adults?[9]

Consider the evidence and argument that you are using in answering the questions. What are your underlying constructions of childhood? How are you understanding rights?

If this were being undertaken in a group, you can organize a 'disagree/agree' activity. You can label, say, one end of a room 'disagree' and the opposite end of the room 'agree'. The space needs to be clear enough for people to be able to move around easily. You could similarly do this online with a visual online tool.

You can ask one of the questions (e.g. 'Should children have the right to work?') and invite group members to place themselves on an imaginary line between disagree and agree. For example, a group member who strongly thinks children should not have the right to work would stand close to the label 'disagree'. A group member who strongly thinks children should have the right to work would stand close to the label 'agree'. Other group members can distribute themselves between, depending on their own views for and against.

You can then encourage various group members to explain why they have placed themselves in a particular spot, asking them to expand on the underlying constructions of childhood and rights.

Table 4.1 Arguments against Children Having Rights and Responses

Children's rights pit children against parents, and children and society require parents to have rights and to have authority in order to protect and bring up their children (e.g. Guggenheim 2005).	Freeman is highly dismissive, judging this as only one step different from seeing children as their parents' property. However, according to Freeman, children do not have exactly the same rights as adults, children should have their best interests protected, and children's rights should not be set against parents' rights.
Obligations protect children better than children's rights and apply in a wider range of circumstances (O'Neill 1988).	Freeman counters O'Neill by arguing that she underestimates children's capacities, maturity and responsibilities. Children need to grow up in a rights-respecting context.
Rights do not encompass all that is important for children and childhood, such as relationships, love and friendship.	Freeman acknowledges this but states that, in the non-ideal world, rights establish important thresholds and parents (and other adults) do not always act in children's best interests nor ensure love, care and altruism. Rights can set up a framework in which such emotions can flourish, even if they cannot establish the right itself (Cowden 2016).
Children do not have rights because they lack the capacity to exercise them. Children are insufficiently competent, in terms of having neither the experience nor rationality to make decisions about their rights.	Some counter-arguments are evidential: children can be as rational or as competent as adults (Repucci and Crosby 1993); competency is context-specific, so children have been assessed as more competent when in familiar surroundings undertaking familiar tasks than unfamiliar ones (Donaldson 1978) and have shown considerable competency depending on their experience (Alderson 1993). Other counter-arguments are conceptual: that competency and its associated concepts of rationality and capacity are not the requirements to be a rights-holder or at least to hold certain rights. *An interest theory of rights*, for example, creates a basis for children to have human rights that is irrespective of such expectations (e.g. see Cowden 2016; Federle 2017).

Drawn from Freeman 2007 and 2020

The children's rights proponent Freeman (2007, with some arguments updated in 2020) neatly summarizes arguments against children having rights. A host of them are reviewed in Table 4.1.

These arguments and their rejoinders demonstrate how constructions of children and childhood (as well as parents and parenthood, and adults and adulthood) are entwined with debates about children having rights (see constructions of childhood, Chapter 2). Those who argue against children's rights tend to perceive children as lesser adults or as '**human becomings**', as insufficiently rational and competent, as dependents whose best interests need to be protected and who need to be educated into competency, citizenship and adulthood. For those who argue for children's rights, there are those – such as the children's liberation movement – who would refute these constructions of children and childhood entirely. More moderately, the predominant view of current children's rights advocates and studies recognizes children as both **human beings** and human becomings. Children need special assistance and protections, alongside respect and support for children as social actors.

Critical challenge: Arguments for and against children having rights

- What are the strongest arguments *against* children having rights? What are the strongest arguments *for* children having rights?
- How does your own experiences of childhood impact on your views of children's rights?
- If you consider the diversity of children – such as by age, **gender**, sexuality, **race**, **ethnicity**, disability, geographical location, socio-economic or religious background – does it make sense to group children together to discuss rights? Why or why not?

Working with young children and infants, I'm always struck by how children's rights really make me think about my practice. Take the example of a child needing a nappy change. Do I ask the child what they want? If I do, do I ensure I go down to their eye level and really ask, listening to what they actually say? If they do not want to, do I pause and think if indeed the nappy change can wait? And if the child says yes, do I ensure that the nappy change is fun, soothing and private? Just something as 'small' as a nappy change shows just how important children's rights are in some of the simplest and most basic routines in a child's day.

Laura Hill, Student on the MSc Early Childhood Practice and Froebel Pathway, University of Edinburgh Scotland

The international framework for children's human rights

Internationally, it has been accepted that children have human rights. The UNCRC entered into force on 2 September 1990 and has since become the most ratified of international human rights treaties ever. As a United Nations Convention, the UNCRC is international law and follows the rules, guidelines and procedures of the Vienna Convention on the Law of Treaties (1969).

The UNCRC builds on earlier international agreements on children's human rights.[10] For example, the predecessor to the United Nations – the League of Nations – adopted the Geneva Declaration of the Rights of the Child in 1924. Its text was brief, with five principles. A revised Declaration on the Rights of the Child was agreed by the United Nations Assembly in 1959, which was extended to ten principles (see the following suggested activity for comparing the two Declarations). While important steps in terms of articulating children's rights, UN Declarations are statements of intent rather than binding international law. In 1979, the International Year of the Child provided an impetus for Poland to recommend turning the 1959 Declaration into a convention. This proved a more extensive task than anticipated, growing to a much larger document, with the UNCRC finally emerging in 1989.

Activity: Comparing historical texts on children's rights

What are the similarities and differences between the texts of the Geneva Declaration on the Rights of the Child 1924 and the Declaration of the Rights of the Child adopted by the UN in 1959? (You can find the Declaration online in many places, through search engines.)

You may want to ask:

- What rights are included? (Consider the distinctions between negative and positive rights and/or economic, social, cultural, civil and political rights.)
- In what ways is childhood constructed by the wording?
- Who is responsible for ensuring children's rights are met?

The UNCRC consists of fifty-four Articles, with forty-two Articles outlining substantive rights for children and the other twelve procedural aspects around ratification, amendments and monitoring. For training and explaining, the substantive Articles are frequently grouped into the three Ps (provision, protection and participation) or the four Ps:

- Participation by children in decisions affecting them
- Protection of children against discrimination and all forms of neglect and exploitation
- Prevention of harm to children
- Provision of assistance to children for their basic needs (attributed to van Bueren 1995).

Article 1 defines a child, for the UNCRC, as 'every human being below the age of eighteen years unless under the law applicable to the child, majority is attained earlier'. At the time of writing, the UNCRC has three **Optional Protocols**, which are ways to expand upon or add to a Convention without reopening the negotiations on the full Convention. Optional Protocols are separately ratified by Member States, so it is possible that a country has ratified the UNCRC but not some or all of the Optional Protocols. The UNCRC's Optional Protocols are:

1. Optional Protocol to the CRC on the Sale of Children, Child Prostitution and Child Pornography
2. Optional Protocol to the CRC on the Involvement of Children in Armed Conflict
3. Optional Protocol to the CRC on a Communications Procedure

The third Optional Protocol allows for individual and interstate complaints against a State Party violating children's rights, as well as an inquiry procedure following 'reliable' information about serious or widespread violations of children's rights by a State Party (for discussion, see Child Rights Connect 2019). However, enforcement of children's rights remains largely at national or sometimes regional levels and can vary by the jurisdiction (see Lundy et al. 2013).

The UN Committee on the Rights of the Child has a key role in monitoring the UNCRC. It consists of eighteen experts that are first recommended by individual States Parties and then voted upon to serve a fixed term. Expected thereafter to act in a personal capacity, the UN Committee receives reports from States Parties in a reporting cycle (see Bergman, Fegan and Myers n.d.). After reports from a State Party and other organizations, requests for further information and plenary sessions, the Committee issues Concluding Observations to the State Party. States Parties are under an obligation, under Article 44(6) of the UNCRC, to publicize its reports. When ratifying the UNCRC or Optional Protocols, States Parties can make reservations, disapplying certain aspects of the UNCRC or declarations on how they will interpret certain rights.

Activity: How well are particular countries doing on children's human rights?

You can see the latest State Report and Concluding Observations for the State Party of your choice. These can be found on the official site for the UN Committee on the Rights of the Child.

Pick a UNCRC right that particularly interests you (e.g. children's right to an adequate standard of living (Article 27) or children's right to play, rest and leisure (Article 31)). Choose two or more countries to consider whether or how this has been addressed in the official reporting system. You can look at the States Parties' Reports, other submissions into the Committee and the Committee's Concluding Observations.

The Committee issues **General Comments**, which are authoritative interpretation, addressing key issues or particular UNCRC Articles. At the time of writing, there are twenty-six General Comments. One of the early General Comments from the UN Committee on the Rights of the Child (2003) outlined the General Principles of the UNCRC:

> Article 2: the obligation of States to respect and ensure the rights set forth in the Convention to each child within their jurisdiction without discrimination of any kind.

> Article 3(1): the best interests of the child as a primary consideration in all actions concerning children.

> Article 6: the child's inherent right to life and States parties' obligation to ensure to the maximum extent possible the survival and development of the child.

> Article 12: the child's right to express his or her views freely in all matters affecting the child, those views being given due weight. (para 12)

All the UNCRC Articles are to be considered holistically, as all are inalienable and indivisible. But the UN Committee on the Rights of the Child asserted that these Articles have an overarching role in reviewing and improving domestic legislation and practice.

The UNCRC is one of the nine core international human rights treaties.[11] The children's human rights field has gradually been integrating its advocacy and debates with broader human rights discussions, recognizing that these human rights equally apply to children and **young people**. This is encouraged by the introduction of the 'Universal Periodic Review',[12] under the auspices of the UN Human Rights Council. States Parties declare what actions they have taken to improve human rights and to fulfil their human rights obligations through a process of reports and review. Further, the United Nations and international development are currently framed by the seventeen **Sustainable Development Goals** (SDGs), which form the core of the 2030 Agenda for Sustainable Development. Many SDGs are directly applicable to children (e.g. SDG 4 on **inclusive** and equitable quality education), as well as pertinent to their circumstances (e.g. SDG 1 on ending poverty in all its forms everywhere). The SDGs are not part of international law and human rights, but a matrix has been produced by UNICEF to show the articulations between the SDGs and the UNCRC.[13]

For children's human rights, therefore, the UNCRC is currently the key reference point, intersecting with other international and regional human rights treaties as well as global initiatives like the SDGs (for a timeline of events, see Table 4.2).

Table 4.2: A List of Key Events for Children's Human Rights at the United Nations Level

1924	Geneva Declaration of the Rights of the Child adopted by the League of Nations
1948	Universal Declaration of Human Rights adopted by the UN
1959	Declaration of the Rights of the Child adopted by the UN
1979	International Year of the Child
1989	Convention on the Rights of the Child adopted by the UN
1990	World Summit for Children held at the UN
2000	Optional Protocols to the CRC are adopted by the UN, specifically On the Sale of Children, Child Prostitution and Child Pornography and On the Involvement of Children in Armed Conflicts
2014	A third Optional Protocol to the UNCRC is adopted by the UN, enabling children to make communications to the UN regarding violations of their rights
2015	The seventeen Sustainable Development Goals were adopted at an UN Summit, as part of the 2030 Agenda for Sustainable Development

While all human rights apply to children, the UNCRC was argued for because of the need to specify how universal principles and norms applied to children (for discussion, see Quennerstedt et al. 2018). The Preamble of the UNCRC itself repeats the words from the Declaration of the Rights of the Child, 'the child, by reason of his physical and mental immaturity, needs special **safeguards** and care, including appropriate legal protection, before as well as after birth'. Thus, debates about human rights – such as contentions about their **universality**, their enforceability and their alternatives – illuminate childhood studies just as childhood studies illuminates often unquestioned assumptions and constructions of childhood and children through the human rights framework.

Critiques of the UNCRC and the human rights framework

The UNCRC has played a significant role in shifting perceptions of children, from being innocent dependents to rights-holders, and has driven action on implementing children's rights globally (Todres and King 2020; Twum-Danso Imoh 2014). However, the UNCRC and the human rights framework more generally have been criticized. In the following, critiques from 'within' are first discussed: that is, the enforceability (or not) of the UNCRC; who and what is included (or not) within the UNCRC; and potential tensions within the UNCRC. Then critiques from 'without' are considered, such as whether the UNCRC is applicable to children around the world and if it can address the range of issues important to and for children.

How enforceable is the UNCRC?

The UNCRC is part of the international human framework, with both its strengths and weaknesses. States Parties are the primary duty-bearers in the UNCRC, with the obligations to respect, support and fulfil children's human rights.[14] While this has clarity, it can function less well in a range of contexts: when a country does not have a functioning national government; in federal and devolved contexts, where subdivisions of the state have responsibilities for key policy and service areas; for contexts outwith the state, such as the private or voluntary sectors, who are not directly duty-bearers under the UNCRC. One response is to extend regulation and contractual arrangements from the state or other funders to the private or voluntary sectors, making them responsible for relevant children's human rights issues. Efforts have been made more generally to include business within human rights[15] and specifically for children (UNICEF, Save the Children and the UN Global Compact 2012). The UNCRC thus does not guarantee that children's rights are covered in all contexts, but there are ongoing developments that are seeking to do so.

Even if children's human rights were legally covered, these rights are not always enforceable. Enforceability at the international level is relatively weak. The reporting cycle can encourage government and public analysis, scrutiny and critique, but ultimately it is up to the State Party to respond to any gaps found by the UN Committee in its Concluding Observations. The third Optional Protocol seeks to improve international enforceability of the UNCRC, and a growing number of cases are being considered.[16] However, the protocol has its own weaknesses, such as requiring domestic remedies to be exhausted first, creating barriers for a potential case to reach the UN Committee (see Vandenhole et al. 2019). National enforceability depends on the legal system within each country: Lundy and colleagues (2013; see also Kilkelly 2021) provide an accessible and legally accurate explanation of this. They explain how some countries have legal systems where international ratification automatically brings the UNCRC into domestic law, binding state authorities and may allow for rights violations to be adjudicated by domestic courts. In other countries, legal steps must be taken to incorporate the UNCRC expressly into domestic law, to create enforceable rights and duties. National enforceability thus can be easier or harder, depending on the particularities of each jurisdictions' legal context.

Like all UN human rights conventions, the CRC is not legally enforceable at the international level. Its force lies in almost all states in the world having agreed to follow these norms regarding children and in a continuous focus on making states comply – from the international community, national and international organizations, children's ombudspersons, the media and children themselves.
Kirsten Sandberg, former member of the UN Committee on the Rights of the Child, Professor at the Department of Public and International Law, University of Oslo, Norway

Even if children do have rights incorporated into national law, there are well-rehearsed barriers to children being able to enforce them, such as children's knowledge about their rights, access to legal advice and representation, the length of time of court procedures and the lack of a sufficient remedy (Liefaard 2019). As Lundy and colleagues (2013) rehearse, the children's rights community recommends a range of measures that can assist with incorporating rights, from national children's rights strategies, to information campaigns, to independent **children's rights commissioners**, to ensure the UNCRC is realized in children's daily lives (see UN Committee on the Rights of the Child 2003).

What are the criticisms of the UNCRC's contents?

The UNCRC itself has been criticized for what and who it does not cover. For example, the UNCRC does not directly address a range of important children's rights issues, from child marriage (where children are married below the age of eighteen) to the physical punishment of children by their parents/ caregivers. International children's rights advocacy has since articulated that both are human rights violations, according to the UNCRC and other human rights treaties; the advocacy has been successful internationally and with increasing national traction.[17] The UNCRC is accused of not going far enough to protect children's rights, in such areas as children working, the age of criminal responsibility and children becoming soldiers (for overviews, see Hanson and Nieuwenhuys 2013; Wells 2021). These issues interface with constructions of childhood (e.g. should children be in paid work?) and related age and stage debates (e.g. when can someone decide to fight for their country?), which remain highly contentious. While the UNCRC is described as covering all categories of human rights (i.e. economic, social, cultural, civil and political rights), its political rights are limited participation rights and do not include rights to vote or to take part in governance (for further discussion of children's participation and activism, see Chapter 5). **Intersectional** analysis (see Chapter 5) raises further issues about whether dimensions of gender, race, class, sexual orientation and national origin (among others) are sufficiently considered. Because of the concentration on the nation state, children who are 'out of place' can be at particular risk of rights violations: for example, Gypsy, Traveller and other communities who are nomadic (Aspinwall and Clements 2013), children associated with the street (Butler and Rizzini 2003; Hunter et al. 2018) and children who cross-national boundaries as migrants (Brittle and Desmet 2020). The list can be extended further; the UNCRC does not cover all issues for all children.

The formation of particular Articles within the UNCRC can also be critiqued. Of much discussion are the provisions for prioritizing a child's best interests (Article 3, see previous discussion). In itself, Article 3's existence suggests particular constructions of childhood, as it is only for children that 'best interests' are protected within the nine core international human rights treaties.[18] While a principle familiar internationally and to many national jurisdictions, it directs adult attention to protecting children – but also gives considerable discretionary power to whomever decides what is in children's best interests. What constitutes best interests may gradually accumulate through legal and practice decisions, but this is not necessarily backed up by defensible evidence (Vandenhole and Türkelli 2020). Protecting children's best interests are often described as in tension with children's participation rights in Article 12. For example, in humanitarian crisis and other **child protection** contexts, adults' concerns about children's vulnerability and children's needs for protection and provision lead adults to ignore or limit children's rights to participate (Collins et al. 2021; see Chapter 6). Adults remain key decisions-makers, presumably in relation to determining best interests in Article 3, deciding on how to weigh a child's views under Article 12, and in judging a child's evolving capacities under Article 5. Thus adults' views on children's best interests can easily squeeze out children's participation rights.

Activity: Debating particular rights

While it is now international law, the process of the UNCRC's creation was political – and thus is it a product of cross-national compromise and consensus. Interesting insights into these can be found in the working papers (called 'travaux préparatoires') for what became the UNCRC.

You can find collections of these working papers online (e.g. https://legal.un.org/avl/ha/crc/crc.html) or in edited versions by Detrick (1992) *The United Nations Convention on the Rights of the Child: A Guide to the 'Travaux préparatoires'*, The Netherlands: Martinus Nijhoff Publishers.

- The definition of a child (Article 1)
- The relationship between children's best interests (Article 3) and children's participation (Article 12)
- Parental guidance and children's evolving capacities (Article 5)
- Children in armed conflicts (Article 38).

The UNCRC can be accused of not addressing all issues important for children. King (1997) makes a stinging critique of the UNCRC, in how it narrows the focus on children's issues to ones that can be addressed by human rights. It thus turns international attention away from fundamental issues – such as natural disasters and armed conflicts – that children are particularly and disproportionately harmed by. In responding to the COVID-19 pandemic, policy responses prioritized people's right to survival and health but children's rights were often marginalized, with limited or no access to education during 'lockdowns' and restrictions on outdoor exercise and play (Adami and Dineen 2021; Tisdall and Morrison 2022). Human rights, then, may be pushed aside too quickly or are not sufficient to deal with these major events and situations that can be very detrimental to children.

There are potential responses to such critiques of the UNCRC. One response is that the UN Committee issues General Comments. For example, the General Comments have extensively considered how to interpret Article 3 and Article 12, and how they should work together (e.g. see numbers 12 (2009) and 14 (2013)). The General Comments can 'fill in' some of the gaps such as young children's participation (see number 7, 2005) and the rights of migrant children (see Joint General Comments numbers 3 and 4 (2017)). General Comments also provide a vehicle to address 'new' issues, such as on the digital environment (number 25 (2021)) and climate change (number 27 (not finalised at time of writing)). Another response is that UNCRC does not stand alone, so intersections with other international instruments can assist: for example, to recognize disability, with the UN Convention on the Rights of Persons with Disabilities, or to address gender, through the Convention on the Elimination of All Forms of Discrimination against Women. However, the power of these critiques and the ongoing debates as a result stand.

Is the UNCRC universally applicable?

Human rights make a claim to universal applicability. But the UNCRC has been much criticized for being based on childhoods of the **global North** rather than those of the **global South** (see discussion in Twum-Danso Imoh 2014; Wells 2021). For example, a global North construction of childhood as a time of play is protected by Article 31, whereas a global South construction of childhood as a contributor to their household economy through paid work is not. The UNCRC has been accused of privileging individualization, more commonly valued in the global North, at the expense of more interdependent

cultures and collective cultures in the global South (e.g. de Castro 2020). In response, the regional African Charter on the Rights and Welfare of the Child (1999) articulates children's responsibilities towards their 'family and society, the State and other legally recognized communities and the international community' (Article 31). Children's participation rights have proven particularly contentious. For example, Valentin and Meinert (2009) suggest the global North's emphasis on children's participation contradicts children's positions in generational hierarchies and social structures in parts of the global South, which have been built to cope with particular environmental, socio-economic and regional pressures. Thus, imposing the UNCRC on the global South risks not only being inappropriate or dysfunctional but potentially harmful to children themselves as well as their communities.

> Where I came from [Palestine], the perception of childhood and the boundaries between children and adults is not that fixed. The many constructions of childhood across time and place mean that children's *rights* too are constructed and interpreted differently by different groups. There is a need to investigate how rights and children's rights are perceived and experienced before assuming universality of rights.
>   *Mohammed Alruzzi, Lecturer in Childhood Studies, University of Bristol*

Human rights generally, and children's human rights in particular, have been accused of being part of the neo-colonial project (Kapur 2006; Wells 2021; see **decolonization** discussion, Chapter 2). There are a number of potential responses. The UNCRC's Articles have considerable room for interpretation in their texts, which can be filled and used within local contexts (Twum-Danso Imoh et al. 2018). Liebel (2020) connects ideas of 'children's rights from below' (e.g. see Liebel 2012), **'living rights'** (e.g. Hanson and Nieuwenhuys 2013; van Daalen et al. 2016) and 'critical children's rights studies' (e.g. Vandenhole et al. 2015), which all explore how children's rights are understood, experienced, challenged and developed in their historically and socially situated contexts. For example, Rizzini (2011) writes powerfully of how Brazilian civil society used the international UNCRC framework to encourage fundamental changes in children's law (see Commentary Chapter 4). Legal expectations of implementation thus are joined by ideas familiar to childhood studies, of the need to also consider processes, contexts, relationships and structures. With such ideas of context, ongoing debate and change, understandings of human rights are possible from the perspectives of the global South as well as others (Hanson and Nieuwenhuys 2020; Liebel 2020).

The UNCRC's claim of universality is valid to the extent that it represents a starting point for the promotion of general norms and values applicable to all children, with due regard for the need to make sufficient allowance for contextual interpretations that take into account the practical realities at regional and domestic levels.

Usang Maria Assim, Associate Professor and Acting Coordinator, Children's Rights Project, Dullah Omar Institute for Constitutional Law, Governance and Human Rights, University of the Western Cape, South Africa

Whether these rejoinders are sufficient to meet the criticisms of human rights false universalism and neo-colonialism remains up for debate: such criticisms are difficult both conceptually and in practice.

Key concept: Living rights?

The concept of 'living rights' has inspired the children's rights field and subsequent research agendas. Living rights are defined by van Daalen and colleagues as follows:

> Living rights should be understood as, first, entitlements of agentic persons or collectives who can act upon the inevitable contradictions and tensions they often contain. This implies, second, that rights cannot be static and settled once and for all and that what were once only norms or even taboos may be transformed into legal rights and vice versa. Living rights are therefore continuously reinvented in the face of changed circumstances. Finally, even before they are codified and find their way into law, living rights are already there, in the daily lives and struggles of people confronting the challenges of everyday life and trying to make the most of their situation. (2016:18)

You may find it interesting to read how this and related concepts have been applied in their article, as well as by Hanson and Nieuwenhuys (2013, 2020) and Liebel (2012).

In summary, the UNCRC can be roundly criticized from several facets, from its lack of enforceability, to its tensions and gaps, to its false universality. These issues apply to international human rights more generally. Of particular interest here is how they interface with considerations for children and childhoods. The UNCRC is a product of particular constructions of childhood and perpetuates them, ranging from a limited extension of political (participation) rights to protecting children's right to play but not to work. The very advocacy for a separate convention on children's rights, even though children are covered by other international human rights treaties, reifies distinctions between childhood and adulthood (see King 1997). In light of these critiques, the next section will consider alternatives to children's human rights.

Activity: How childhood is constructed when promoting the UNCRC

In promoting the UNCRC over time, children and childhood have been presented differently. For example, have a look at these two videos and compare:

- A video from 1989, where a special event was held for children in the General Assembly Hall following the adoption of the UNCRC, https://media.un.org/en/asset/k1z/k1zhpqocgd.
- A video thirty years later that UNICEF produced for World Children's Day and the thirtieth anniversary of the UNCRC, https://www.youtube.com/watch?v=y4udqAY2Bqc.

Critical challenge: Delving into the details of the UNCRC

- What Articles in the UNCRC are most applicable to your area of work or of interest? How well are these rights met?
- If you had the power . . . how would you improve the UNCRC?
- Do you think that the UNCRC can be universally applied, given the diversity of children around the world?

Alternative frameworks to children's human rights?

Those who promote children's rights can be sharply protective of the human rights framework, as rights are entwined with (re)constructions of childhood and advocacy for children in policy and practice (see McMellon and Tisdall 2020; Thomas 2021). But there are alternatives, and their respective merits provide productive evidential and conceptual challenges. Two leading alternatives are explored here. The first framework – vulnerability – emerged from feminist and related critiques of liberal theories of rights. The second framework is wellbeing, a concept that has grown from public health and the social sciences and has become a popular policy focus for children as well as others. These frameworks pose worked-out and provocative alternatives to children's rights to organize policy and practice; their respective advantages and disadvantages are explored further.

The framework of vulnerability

Legal philosophy has developed 'vulnerability' as an alternative to **liberal theories of rights**. Liberal theory is criticized for incorrectly conceiving citizens as autonomous, self-sufficient and independent (Bedford 2020; Herring 2018). Instead, all people should be recognized as potentially vulnerable and dependent: vulnerability is a universal and inevitable condition of being human because people are **embodied** (Fineman 2008). Vulnerability is not solely negative but rather can open people to creativity, trust and relationships (Petherbridge 2016). The state has a more proactive role than in liberal theory, to ensure protection as needed, to value care and encourage social relations, and to provide resources to promote resilience (Bedford 2020; Fineman 2008).

Herring (2012) writes that, currently, law emphasizes adults protecting children from harm, children's lack of capacity and confines children to private or institutional spaces. Undue emphasis is placed on children being inherently vulnerable, rather than how relationally, situationally and structurally they are made particularly vulnerable.[19] Instead, if vulnerability were recognized as a universal state, commonalities between adults and children would be acknowledged, states Herring (2018), with the distinctions erased or largely blurred: people are all dependent on each other; people all have impaired capacity and lack rationality; and people's values are all influenced by others. With these distinctions between adults and children either erased or made irrelevant, Herring argues that children should be treated equally to adults but 'by treating adults more like children and not children more like adults' (2018: 2). There would be significant changes to law. For example, special concessions for disadvantaged groups, such as children, would become the norm rather than exceptions. Attention would focus on the (unwarranted) special privileges and accommodations given to able-bodied people or some adults. The emphasis would be on how social provision, from the state, can ameliorate people's vulnerability.

Reclaiming vulnerability as a universal condition is attractive. If most of liberal theory either ignores children or merely uses them to argue for adults' rights, children and childhood are central to vulnerability theories. Children and childhood are the quintessential examples of vulnerability, exemplifying the intergenerational and temporal claims for vulnerability and addressing dependency (e.g. Dodds 2013; Lotz et al. 2013). However, vulnerability has at least three problems for children and childhood, according to Tisdall (2017). First, key theoretical developments are situated within liberal democracies, with functioning and developed states. These and other concepts such as citizens and **agency** are not questioned for their **normative** values nor their applicability in contexts which are not democratic, where there are no functioning states and concepts of citizens and agency are not commonplace (see also Coyle 2013). Many children live in such contexts, so if vulnerability theorization were to be useful conceptually and practically, it needs to address such realities. Second, vulnerability can slide into ignoring control and power, despite what Herring argues – and especially when it is applied to groups who tend to be categorized as vulnerable. It can accept, for example, that children are inherently vulnerable rather than questioning and addressing the **structural inequalities** and other power hierarchies that make them so (Federle 2017; Sherwood-Johnson 2013). Third, vulnerability may garner considerable sympathy from the public and galvanize both charity giving and policy support, but it is not a position of strength for those categorized as vulnerable. Brown's research with young people (2011) found that few claimed the label of vulnerable voluntarily: vulnerability can be oppressive and paternalistic, it can be used to control people and it can stigmatize and exclude. For those already with less status in society, claiming the label of vulnerability does not challenge their low status nor power relations.

Thus, vulnerability theorizations are provocative in changing the frameworks for justice. Rather than the autonomous independent individual, they recognize all people as interdependent and potentially vulnerable. But when vulnerability is applied to children, and others on the 'margins' (Grear 2020), it leaves **adultism** and other power relations unchallenged. Vulnerability needs to be embraced first by the powerful before it is useful to support justice for children.

The framework of wellbeing

While the framework of vulnerability remains more theoretical than applied, children's wellbeing has grown from an area of academic interest to a driving concept for international and national policies. Its ascendancy can be attributed to at least two sources (Morrow and Mayall 2009). First, the World Health Organization asserted in 1946 that health was not solely the lack of disease or infirmity but also a 'state of complete physical, mental and social wellbeing'. This definition has had long-standing influence and brought wellbeing firmly into the lexicon. Second, children's wellbeing was argued as an alternative and improved concept over child poverty measures, to include a fuller range of domains and indicators (e.g. Bradshaw et al. 2006; OECD 2009). The ranking of countries by wellbeing indicators, in UNICEF report cards, firmly brought wellbeing to the children's field.[20] This combination of influential origins has resulted in children's wellbeing becoming a popular research concept and an increasingly dominant one in policy.

The definition of wellbeing is not settled across the literature (see Fattore et al. 2017). McAllister looked across the literature to identify certain commonalities and concludes:

> wellbeing is more than the absence of illness or pathology; it has subjective (self-assessed) and objective (ascribed) dimensions; it can be measured at the level of individuals or society; it accounts for elements of life satisfaction that cannot be defined, explained or primarily influenced by economic growth. (2005: 2)

This description recognizes the **dichotomy** between 'objective' and 'subjective' wellbeing (see Ben-Arieh et al. 2014; Hall 2013). Externally verifiable measures (e.g. material resources) constitute objective wellbeing, while subjective wellbeing recognizes that it may be significant to know people's own views on their wellbeing (e.g. perceived quality of life).[21]

Children's wellbeing has certain advantages over children's human rights. It has quickly gained a substantial depth of quantitative development, focused on indicators that appeal to outcome-focused policies. These can be easily turned to national or international objectives, such as monitoring the SDGs. Children's wellbeing can be flexible and adapted to the context (e.g. Ben-Arieh and Tarshish 2017; Camfield et al. 2009), in contrast to accusations that the UNCRC is part of the neo-colonial project and insensitive to specific contexts (see previous discussion). However, this flexibility can privilege certain expertise over others and can be swayed by those more powerful. It does not necessarily need to involve children and their families, finding their own and community solutions (Tisdall and Davis 2015), but can privilege experts' definitions of what counts, in indicators and outcomes, and professionals' solutions. Children's wellbeing thus has power politically in its quantification and sensitivity in its flexibility but risks masking power relationships.

Children's wellbeing can address some of the gaps in children's rights, discussed earlier. Wellbeing can include all issues important to children – from love to friendship to other relationships. Children's wellbeing conceptually and in practice has the potential to be maximizing, seeking to ever increase wellbeing. While some rights are expressed in maximizing ways (e.g. UNCRC Article 24, on a child's right 'to the enjoyment of the highest attainable standard of health'), a rights framework may not encourage duty-bearers consistently to maximize children's rights or exceed the UNCRC's requirements. Children's wellbeing thus provides a maximizing and encompassing alternative. But this can result in an utilitarian approach: as long as wellbeing is maximized in total, it does not matter if certain children have very poor outcomes. A rights perspective requires every children's rights to be met with strong claims on duty-bearers and requirements for accountability.

Are children's rights and children's wellbeing the same or different concepts? My experiences from undertaking a range of applied research projects, in Indonesia and in Scotland, suggest they are different but they can be complementary. Children's rights provide the pathways to ensure efforts to achieve children's wellbeing and respect all children as rights-holders.

Harla Octarra, Child Rights Expert, Associate Researcher at Atma Jaya Catholic University of Indonesia

Thus, children's wellbeing provides a provocative challenge to children's rights conceptually as well as practically. It has the benefits of statistical investment and expertise, a relationship with outcomes popular currently and has maximizing potential. But it lacks the elements of children's human rights that help change the status of children, such as rights as entitlements and claims, the accountability of duty-bearers, the requirements of non-discrimination. As these frameworks continue to evolve, their articulation becomes of increasing practical as well as theoretical importance.

Activity: Considering 'lockdown' during the COVID-19 pandemic

In 2020 and 2021, many countries responded to the COVID-19 pandemic by restricting people to their houses (called 'lockdown'). Schools were closed and, at best, children had schooling online.

- What were the main children's human rights issues of these policy responses?
- Would children's lives have been improved during 'lockdown' if policies had been framed by vulnerability or by wellbeing?

(If you would like resources to consider these questions, see Tisdall and Morrison (2022) and UN Committee on the Rights of the Child (2020), Special Issue vol 29 (issue 2), on COVID-19 in the *International Journal of Children's Rights* (2021)).

Conclusion

Children's rights has become an increasing intellectual, policy and research issue, leading to and encouraged by the UNCRC. For its proponents, the UNCRC provides a basis to recognize children as rights-holders themselves, to ensure their full range of economic, social, cultural, civil and political rights, as part of the international human rights framework.

Children's rights, and more specifically the UNCRC, can also be considered as particular constructions of childhood, historically and contextually specific and including some but not all issues that matter to children and childhood. The UNCRC can be critiqued for its unexamined focus on children as particularly vulnerable, its exclusion of certain rights for children that are recognized for adults and its presumed universalism. Rejoinders have been developed that acknowledge localized interpretations of the UNCRC or that further improvements can be made to the UNCRC. But these critiques have traction.

Alternative frameworks for policy and practice have been suggested in this Chapter: that is, vulnerability and wellbeing. Each addresses certain weaknesses for children's human rights but are problematic in all too easily positioning children as solely dependent on adults/parents and not recognizing nor supporting their roles as social actors. The latter is a key precept of the **paradigm** for childhood studies (see Chapter 2), so the affinity as well as debates between childhood studies and children's rights studies are likely to remain fruitful areas of stimuli and cross-fertilization.

Notes

1. The United States has signed the UNCRC but not ratified it. Signing indicates an intention to ratify. Meanwhile, signing creates an obligation to refrain from acts that would defeat the object and purpose of the Convention.
2. Duty-bearers refer to all those who must respect, promote and fulfil human rights and to abstain from human rights violations.
3. See https://endcorporalpunishment.org/ (accessed 11 March 2023).
4. See https://www.youthrights.org/issues/voting-age/top-ten-reasons-to-lower-the-voting-age/. (accessed 11 March 2023); Munn (2021).
5. See https://blogs.bmj.com/medical-ethics/2020/11/25/refusal-redux -revisiting-debate-about-adolescent-refusal-of-treatment/ (accessed 11 March 2023).
6. See Boudrillon and Carothers (2019) and https://www.tdh.ch/en/media -library/documents/time-talk-report-its-time-talk-childrens-views -childrens-work (accessed 11 March 2023).
7. See Wyness (2019), especially Chapter 7.
8. See https://www.unfpa.org/sites/default/files/pub-pdf/UNFPA_ ASRHtoolkit_english.pdf (accessed 11 March 2023).
9. See Lynch and Liefaard (2020).
10. The history of the UNCRC is fascinating in its interaction with other happenings – such as World Wars I and II – and its political tensions – such as overtones of the Cold War between USSR and the West, which

played out in the UNCRC's formation. For historical reviews, see, for example, Becker 2020, Van Bueren 1995 and Veerman 1992.

11. The nine core international human rights treaties are: International Covenant on Economic, Social and Cultural Rights; International Covenant on Civil and Political Rights; Convention Against Torture and Other Cruel, Inhuman or Degrading Treatment or Punishment; International Convention on the Elimination of All Forms of Racial Discrimination; International Convention on the Protection of the Rights of All Migrant Workers and Members of their Families; International Convention for the Protection of All Persons from Enforced Disappearance; Convention on the Elimination of All Forms of Discrimination Against Women; Convention on the Rights of the Child; and Convention on the Rights of Persons with Disabilities.

12. https://www.ohchr.org/EN/HRBodies/UPR/Pages/BasicFacts.aspx (accessed 11 March 2023).

13. See https://www.unicef.org/media/60231/file (accessed 11 March 2023).

14. Not all areas in the world are accepted as Member States of the UN, with contentions around places like Taiwan, Palestine and the Vatican (Holy City) at the time of writing.

15. UN Guiding Principles on Business and Human Rights, https://www. ohchr.org/Documents/Publications/GuidingPrinciplesBusinessHR_ EN.pdf (accessed 11 March 2023).

16. See information on the UN Committee on the Rights of the Child's website https://www.ohchr.org/EN/HRBodies/CRC/Pages/CRCIndex.aspx (accessed 11 March 2023)

17. For ending child marriage, see https://www.unicef.org/protection/child-marriage (accessed 11 March 2023); for banning physical punishment of children, see https://endcorporalpunishment.org/ (accessed 11 March 2023).

18. In addition to Article 3 of the UNCRC, 'best interests' is found in Principle 2 of the 1959 Declaration of the Rights of the Child, 'interest' in Article 5(b) and 'interests' in relation to children in Article 16(d), (f) of the Convention on the Elimination of All Forms of Discrimination against Women, Articles 7(2), 23(2) and (4) of the Convention on the Rights of Persons with Disabilities.

19. See similar arguments by Wyness (2012) from a childhood studies perspective, discussed in Chapter 2.

20. See https://www.unicef-irc.org/publications/226-a-league-table-of-child-poverty-in-rich-nations.html (accessed 11 March 2023).

21. See Camfield and colleagues (2009) for a critique of this dichotomy and White (2010) for an alternative distinction between material, subjective and relational dimensions of wellbeing.

References

Adami, R. and Dineen, K. (2021), 'Discourses of Childism', *The International Journal of Children's Rights*, 29 (2), 353–70.

Alderson, P. (1993), *Children's Consent to Surgery*, Buckingham: Open University Press.

Archard, D. (2014), *Children: Rights and Childhood*, 3rd edn, London: Taylor and Francis.

Arneil, B. (2002), 'Becoming versus Being: A Critical Analysis of the Child in Liberal Theory', in Archard, D. and Macleod, C. M. (eds), *The Moral and Political Status of Children*, 70–96, Oxford: Oxford University Press.

Aspinwall, T. and Clements, L. (2013), 'The Rights of Gypsy and Traveller Children and Young People in Wales', in J. Williams (ed.), *The United Nations Convention on the Rights of the Child in Wales*, 1st edn, 149–66, Cardiff: University of Wales Press.

Becker, J. (2020), 'The Evolution of the Children's Rights Movement', in J. Todres and S. M. King (eds), *The Oxford Handbook of Children's Rights Law*, 32–48, Oxford: Oxford University Press.

Bedford, D. (2020), 'Introduction: Vulnerability Reconfigured', in D. Bedford and J. Herring (eds), *Embracing Vulnerability*, 1–28, Abingdon: Routledge.

Ben-Arieh, A., Casas, F., Frønes, I., and Korbin, J. (2014), 'Multifaceted Concept of Child Well-Being', in A. Ben-Arieh, F. Casas, I. Frønes, and J. Korbin (eds), *Handbook of Child Well-Being*, 1–27, Dordrecht: Springer.

Ben-Arieh, A. and Tashish, N. (2017), 'Children's Rights and Well-Being', in M. D. Ruck , M. Peterson-Badali, and M. Freeman (eds), *Handbook of Children's Rights*, 68–79, Abingdon: Routledge.

Bergman, L. T., Fegan, R., and Myers, L. (n.d.), 'The Reporting Cycle of the Committee of the Rights of the Child'. Available online: https://www.ohchr.org/Documents/HRBodies/CRC/GuideNgoSubmission_en.pdf (accessed 11 March 2023).

Bourdillon, M. and Carothers, R. (2019), 'Policy on Children's Work and Labour', *Children & Society*, 33 (4): 387–95.

Bradshaw, J., Hoelscher, P., and Richardson, D. (2006), *Comparing Child Well-Being in OECD Countries*, UNICEF Innocenti Research Centre. Available online: http://www.unicef-irc.org/publications/pdf/iwp2006_03_eng.pdf (accessed 11 March 2023).

Breakey, H. (2015), 'Positive Duties and Human Rights: Challenges, Opportunities and Conceptual Necessities', *Political Studies*, 63 (5): 1198–215.

Brittle, R. and Desmet, E. (2020), 'Thirty Years of Research on Children's Rights in the Context of Migration?', *The International Journal of Children's Rights*, 28 (1): 36–65.

Brown, K. (2011), 'Vulnerability: Handle with Care', *Ethics and Social Welfare*, 5 (3): 313–21.

Butler, U. and Rizzini, I. (2003), 'Young People Living and Working on the Streets of Brazil', *Children, Youth and Environments*, 13 (1): 182–201.

Camfield, L., Streuli, N., and Woodhead, M. (2009), 'What Is the Use of "Well-Being" in Contexts of Child Poverty?', *International Journal of Children's Rights*, 17 (1): 65–109.

Child Rights Connect (2019), 'Towards Better Implementation of the UNCRC Through Its Third Optional Protocol on a Communications Procedure'. Available online: https://www.childrightsconnect.org/wp-content/uploads/2019/08/report_-opic_roundtable_discussion.pdf (accessed 11 March 2023).

Collins, T. M., Rizzini, I., and Mayhew, A. (2021), 'Fostering Global Dialogue: Conceptualisations of Children's Rights to Participation and Protection', *Children & Society*, 35: 295–310.

Council of Europe (2009), 'Janusz Korczak'. Available online: https://rm.coe.int/janusz-korczak-the-child-s-right-to-respect/16807ba985#:~:text=Children%20are%20not%20the%20people,treated%20with%20tenderness%20and%20respect.&text=For%20Korczak%20two%20rights%20were,and%20the%20right%20to%20respect (accessed 11 March 2023).

Cowden, M. (2016), 'A Right to be Loved', in *Children's Rights*, 133–52, New York: Palgrave Macmillan.

Coyle, S. (2013), 'Vulnerability and the Liberal Order', in M. A. Fineman and A. Grear (eds), *Vulnerability: Reflections on a new Ethical Foundation for law and Politics*, 61–75, Farnham: Ashgate.

de Castro, L. R. (2020), 'Why Global? Children and Childhood from a Decolonial Perspective', *Childhood*, 27 (1): 48–62.

Dodds, S. (2013), 'Dependence, Care and Vulnerability', in C. Mackenzie, W. Rogers, and S. Dodds (eds), *Vulnerability: New Essays in Ethics and Feminist Philosophy*, 181–203, Oxford: Oxford University Press.

Donaldson, M. (1978), *Children's Minds*, London: Fontana.

Donnelly, J. and Whelan, D. J. (2017), *International Human Rights*, 5th edn, New York: Routledge.

Dworkin, R. (1978), *Taking Rights Seriously*, London: Bloomsbury.

Fattore, T., Mason, J., and Watson, E. (2017), *Children's Understandings of Well-being Towards a Child Standpoint*, 1st edn, Netherlands: Springer.

Federle, K. H. (2017), 'Do Rights Still Flow Downhill', *International Journal of Children's Rights*, 25 (2): 273–84.

Fineman, M. A. (2008), 'The Vulnerable Subject: Anchoring Equality in the Human Condition', *Yale Journal of Law and Feminism*, 20 (1): 1–18.

Freeman, M. D. (1983), *The Rights and Wrongs of Children*, London: Francis Pinter.

Freeman, M. D. (2007), 'Why It Remains Important to Take Children's Rights Seriously', *The International Journal of Children's Rights*, 15 (1): 5–23.

Freeman, M. D. (2011), 'The Value and Values of Children's Rights', in A. Invernizzi and J. Williams (eds), *The Human Rights of Children from Visions to Implementation*, 21–34, Franham: Ashgate.

Freeman, M. D. (2020), 'Taking Children's Human Rights Serious', in J. Todres and S. M. King (eds), *The Oxford Handbook of Children's Rights Law*, 49–70, Oxford: Oxford University Press.

Grear, A. (2018), 'Human Rights and New Horizons? Thoughts Toward a New Juridical Ontology', *Science, Technology, & Human Values*, 43 (1): 129–45.

Grear, A. (2020), 'Embracing Vulnerability', in D. Bedford and J. Herring (eds), *Embracing Vulnerability: The Challenges and Applications for Law*, 153–74, Abingdon: Routledge.

Guggenheim, M. (2005), *What's Wrong with Children's Rights*, Boston: Harvard University Press.

Hall, J. (2013), 'From Capabilities to Contentment', in J. Helliwell, R. Layard, and J. D. Sachs (eds), *World Happiness Report 2013*. Available online: https://s3.amazonaws.com/happiness-report/2013/WorldHappinessReport2013_online.pdf (accessed 11 March 2023).

Hanson K. and Nieuwenhuys O. (2013), 'Living Rights, Social Justice, Translations', in K. Hanson, and O. Nieuwenhuys (eds), *Reconceptualizing Children's Rights in International Development*, 3–26, Cambridge: Cambridge University Press.

Hanson, K. and Nieuwenhuys, O. (2020), 'A Child-Centred Approach to Children's Rights Law', in J. Todres and S. M. King (eds), *The Oxford Handbook of Children's Rights Law*, 100–18, Oxford: Oxford University Press.

Hart, H. L. A., (1955), 'Are There Any Natural Rights?', *The Philosophical Review*, 64 (2): 175–91.

Herring, J. (2012), 'Vulnerability, Children and the Law', in M. Freeman (ed.), *Law and Childhood Studies*, 243–63, Oxford: Oxford University Press.

Herring, J. (2018), *Vulnerability, Childhood and the Law*, Cham: Springer.

Holt, J. (1974), *Escape from Childhood*, New York: E.P. Dutton & Co.

Hunter, J., van Blerk, L., and Shand, W. (2018), 'The Rights of Street Children and Youth'. Available online: https://discovery.dundee.ac.uk/ws/portalfiles/portal/29636331/Briefing_Paper_12_Rights_May_2018_nb.pdf (accessed 5 June 2022).

Jones, P. (1994), *Rights*, Basingstoke: Macmillan.

Kamm, F. (2007), *Intricate Ethics*, Oxford: Oxford University Press.

Kilkelly, U., Lundy, L., and Bryne, B. (eds) (2021), *Incorporating the UN Convention on the Rights of the Child into National Law*, Cambridge: Intersentia.

King, M. (1997), *A Better World for Children?*, Abingdon: Routledge.

Kapur, R. (2006), 'Human Rights in the Century: Take a Walk on the Dark Side', *Sydney Law Review*, 28 (4): 665–87.

Kymlicka, W. (1989), *Liberalism, Community, and Culture*, Oxford: Oxford University Press.

Liebel, M. (2012), *Children's Rights from Below*, Basingstoke: Palgrave.

Liebel, M. (2020), *Decolonizing Childhoods: From Exclusion to Dignity*, Bristol: Policy Press.

Liefaard, T. (2019), 'Access to Justice for Children', *The International Journal of Children's Rights*, 27 (2): 195–227.

Lotz, M. (2013), 'Parental Values and Children's Vulnerability', in C. Mackenzie, W. Rogers and S. Dodds (eds), *Vulnerability*, 242–65, Oxford: Oxford University Press.

Lundy, L., Kilkelly, U, Byrne, B., and Kang, J. (2013), 'The UN Convention on the Rights of the Child: A Study of Legal Implementation in 12 Countries'. Available online: https://www.unicef.org.uk/publications/child-rights -convention-2012-report/ (accessed 11 March 2023).

Lynch, N. and Liefaard, T. (2020), 'What is Left in the "Too Hard Basket"? Developments and Challenges for the Rights of Children in Conflict with the Law', *The International Journal of Children's Rights*, 28 (1): 89–110.

MacCormick, N. (1982), *Legal Right and Social Democracy*, Oxford: Clarendon Press.

Mackenzie, C. and Stoljar, N. (2000), *Relational Autonomy*, Oxford: Oxford University Press.

McAllister, F. (2005), *Wellbeing Concepts and Challenges*. Available online: http://www.sd-research.org.uk/sites/default/files/publications/Wellbeing %20Concepts%20and%20Challenges_0.pdf (accessed 28 November 2014).

McMellon, C. and Tisdall, E. K. M. (2020), 'Children and Young People's Participation Rights', *The International Journal of Children's Rights*, 28 (1): 157–82.

Morrow, V. and Mayall, B. (2009), 'What Is Wrong with Children's Well-being in the UK? Questions of Meaning and Measurement', *Journal of Social Welfare and Family Law*, 31 (3): 217–29.

Munn, N. (2021), 'The Trap of Incrementalism in Recognising Children's Right to Vote', *Nordic Journal of Human Rights*, 39 (2): 113–27.

Nussbaum, M. C. (1997), 'Capabilities and Human Rights', *Fordham law Review*, 66 (2): 273–300.

Nozick, R (1974), *Anarchy, State, and Utopia*, New York: Basic Books.

OECD (2009*), Doing Better for Children*, Paris: OECD.

O'Neill, O. (1988), 'Children's Rights and Children's Lives', *Ethics*, 98 (3): 445–63.

Petherbridge, D. (2016), 'What's Critical About Vulnerability? Rethinking Interdependence, Recognition, and Power', *Hypatia*, 31 (4): 589–604.

Quennerstedt, A. Robinson, C., and I'Anson, J. (2018), 'The UNCRC: The Voice of Global Consensus on Children's Rights?', *Nordic Journal of Human Rights*, 36 (1): 38–54.

Razack, S. (1992), 'Collective Rights and Women', *The Journal of Human Justice*, 4: 1–12.

Repucci, N. D. and Crosby, C. A. (1993), 'Law, Psychology and Children', *Law and Human Behaviour*, 17 (1): 1–10.

Rizzini, I. (2011), 'The Promise of Citizenship for Brazilian Children', *The ANNALS of the American Academy of Political and Social Science*, 633 (1): 66–79.

Sandel, M. (1998), *Liberalism and the Limits of Justice*, 2nd edn, Cambridge: Cambridge University Press.

Sherwood-Johnson, F. (2013), 'Constructions of "Vulnerability" in Comparative Perspective', *Disability & Society*, 28 (7): 908–21.

Shue, H. (1980), *Basic Rights*, Princeton, NJ: Princeton University Press.

Stone, C. D. (2010), *Should Trees Have Standing? Law, Morality and the Environment*, 3rd edn, Oxford: Oxford University Press.

Thomas, N. P. (2021), 'Child-led Research, Children's Rights and Childhood Studies: A Defence', *Childhood*, 28 (2): 186–99.

Tisdall, E. K. M. (2017), 'Conceptualising Children and Young People's Participation', *The International Journal of Human Rights*, 21 (1): 59–75.

Tisdall, E. K. M. and Davis, J. M. (2015), 'Children's Rights and Wellbeing', in A. Smith (ed.), *Enhancing the Rights and Wellbeing of Children*, 214–27 Basingstoke: Palgrave Macmillan.

Tisdall, E. K. M. and Morrison, F. (2022), 'Children's Human Rights Under COVID-19: Learning from Children's Rights Impact Assessments', *The International Journal of Human Rights*, doi:10.1080/13642987.2022.2036135.

Todres, J. and King, S. M. (2020), 'Children's Rights in the Twenty-First Century: Challenges and Opportunities', in J. Todres and S. M. King (eds), *The Oxford Handbook of Children's Rights Law*, 718–28, Oxford: Oxford University Press.

Twum-Danso Imoh, A. (2014), 'Realizing Children's Rights in Africa: An Introduction in Children's Lives in an Era of Children's Rights', in A. Twum-Danso Imoh and N. Ansell (eds), *The Progress of the Convention on the Rights of the Child in Africa*, 1–16, Abingdon: Routledge.

Twum-Danso Imoh, A., Bourdillon, M., and Meicsner, S. (eds) (2018), *Global Childhoods Beyond the North-South Divide*, Basingstoke: Palgrave Macmillan.

UN (1924), 'Geneva Declaration on the Rights of the Child'. Available online: http://www.un-documents.net/gdrc1924.htm (accessed 11 March 2023).

UN Committee on the Rights of the Child (2003), 'General Comment No. 5 General Measures of Implementation of the Convention on the Rights of the Child'. Available online: https://tbinternet.ohchr.org/_layouts/15/treatybodyexternal/Download.aspx?symbolno=CRC%2fGC%2f2003%2f5&Lang=en (accessed 11 March 2023).

UN Committee on the Rights of the Child (2005), *General Comment No. 7: Implementing Child Rights in Early Childhood*. Available online: https://www2.ohchr.org/english/bodies/crc/docs/AdvanceVersions/GeneralComment7Rev1.pdf (accessed 11 March 2023).

UN Committee on the Rights of the Child (2009), *General Comment No. 12 The Right of the Child to be Heard*. Available online: http://www.coe.int/t/dg3/children/participation/CRC-C-GC-12.pdf (accessed 11 March 2023).

UN Committee on the Rights of the Child (2013), *General Comment No. 14 on the Right of the Child to Have his or her Best Interests Taken as a Primary Consideration*. Available online: https://tbinternet.ohchr.org/_layouts/15/treatybodyexternal/Download.aspx?symbolno=CRC%2fC%2fGC%2f14&Lang=en (accessed 11 March 2023).

UN Committee on the Protection of the Rights of All Migrant Workers and Members of their Families and UN Committee on the Rights of the Child (2017), *Joint General Comment on the General Principles Regarding the Human Rights of Children in the Context of International Migration*. Available online: https://documents-dds-ny.un.org/doc/UNDOC/GEN/G17/343/59/PDF/G1734359.pdf?OpenElement (accessed 11 March 2023).

UN Committee on the Rights of the Child (2020), *CRC COVID-19 Statement*. Available online: https://tbinternet.ohchr.org/_layouts/15/treatybodyexternal/Download.aspx?symbolno=INT/CRC/STA/9095&Lang=en (accessed 11 March 2023).

UN Committee on the Rights of the Child (2021), *General Comment No. 25 on Children's Rights in Relation to the Digital Environment*. Available online: https://tbinternet.ohchr.org/_layouts/15/treatybodyexternal/Download.aspx?symbolno=CRC%2fC%2fGC%2f25&Lang=en (accessed 11 March 2023).

UN Committee on the Rights of the Child (2022), (Draft) *General Comment No. 26 on Children's Rights and the Environment with a Special Focus on Climate Change*. Available online: https://www.ohchr.org/en/documents/general-comments-and-recommendations/draft-general-comment-no-26-childrens-rights-and (accessed 11 March 2023).

UN Human Rights (1959), 'Declaration of the Rights of the Child'. Available online: https://www.ohchr.org/en/resources/educators/human-rights-education-training/1-declaration-rights-child-1959 (accessed 11 March 2023).

UNICEF, Save the Children, and the UN Global Compact (2012), *10 Children's Rights and Business Principles*. Available online: http://childrenandbusiness.org/the-principles/introduction/ (accessed 11 March 2023).

UNICEF UK (n.d.), 'How We Protect Children's Rights'. Available online:
https://www.unicef.org.uk/what-we-do/un-convention-child-rights/
(accessed 11 March 2023).

Valentin, K. and Meinert, L. (2009), 'The Adult North and the Young South',
Anthropology Today, 25 (3): 23–8.

Van Bueren, G. (1995), *The International Law on the Rights of the Child*,
Dordrecht: Nijhoff.

van Daalen, E., Hanson, K., and Nieuwenhuys, O. (2016), 'Children's Rights as
Living Rights: The Case of Street Children and a New Law in Yogyakarta,
Indonesia', *International Journal of Children's Rights*, 24 (4): 803–25.

Vandenhole, W., Desmet, E., Reynaert, D., and Lembrechts, S. (eds) (2015),
Routledge International Handbook of Children's Rights Studies, Abingdon:
Routledge.

Vandenhole, W. and Türkelli, G. E. (2020), 'The Best Interests of the Child', in J.
Todres and S. M. King (eds), *The Oxford Handbook of Children's Rights Law*,
204–21, Oxford: Oxford University Press.

Vandenhole, W., Türkelli, G. E., and Lembrechts, S. (2019), *Children's Rights: A
Commentary on the Convention on the Rights of the Child and Its Optional
Protocols*, Cheltenham: Edward Elgar.

Veerman, P. E. (1992), *The Rights of the Child and the Changing Image of
Childhood*, Dordrecht: Nijhoff.

Wall, J. (2017), *Children's Rights: Today's Global Challenge*, Lanham: Rowman &
Littlefield.

Wells, K. (2021), *Childhood in a Global Perspective*, 3rd edn, Cambridge: Polity
Press.

Wiessner, S. (2011), 'The Cultural Rights of Indigenous Peoples', *European
Journal of International Law*, 22 (1): 121–40.

Wyness, M. (2019), *Children and Society*, 3rd edn, London: Red Globe Press.

Commentary on Childhood Studies Meets Children's Rights Studies

Irene Rizzini

Can children have **human rights**? Chapter 4 starts with a provocative question. That question was the subject of the **paradigm** shift that finally recognized children as entitled to rights in the last decades of the twentieth century, legitimized by the **ratification** of the **United Nations Convention on the Rights of the Child (UNCRC)** in 1989. The debate remains relevant as much of the world's population, including children and **young people**, routinely experience denials and violations of rights while paradoxically the legal frameworks of human rights continue to expand globally (Assy 2018; Douzinas 2000; Pahuja 2011; Santos 2021).

The authors present a rich introduction to the debates between **childhood studies** and children's rights studies, taking into account international debates and **interdisciplinary** approaches. They explore proponents and critical arguments about children's rights in the academic literature. This by itself is a very useful exercise to inform academics but also a broader, non-academic audience.

Questioning the universality of children's rights

The authors revisit fundamental critiques of the UNCRC, despite its undoubted importance in the struggle for children's rights, particularly interrogating the idea that one version of children's rights can be applied to all children. One of the points made is that the Convention – and the human rights framework at large – is based on a Western- and northern-centric notion of **childhood** that should not, in fact, be considered universal. This argument seems to be broadly accepted internationally, although it tends to resonate more in voices of the so-called **global South** (Balagopalan 2019; Castro 2020; Imoh and Okyere 2020).

However, what still needs to be more strongly contested is the idea of a world divided into two, as if all the countries in the North and those in the South necessarily shared common features. The assumption that rights based on notions that largely come from northern frameworks can be considered applicable to the global South is clearly a problem but so is the assumption that the realities of childhood in either of those halves are uniform (Balagopalan 2019). In some **cultures**, even the notion of childhood as a transitional stage towards adulthood does not translate, calling for a more comprehensive approach to their statuses of subjects of rights and active **social actors** (Tabak 2020; Twum-Danso Imoh and Okyere 2020).

From a decolonial perspective, one could argue about the limitations of discussions based on sources published only in English. This issue has been recognized for years, with authors arguing for the **decolonization** of knowledge (Grosfoguel 2012; Connell 2013). Despite the growing literature on decoloniality, particularly by authors from countries that experienced brutal processes of colonial occupation in Latin America, Africa and Asia (Galeano 1997; Ndlovu-Gatsheni 2015; Quijano and Ennis 2000; Spivak 1994),[1] the mainstream **discourse** still tends to prioritize some local knowledge as global, based on contributions from largely English-language material.

Decolonization refers to contesting given assumptions about historical power imbalances that persisted over time (Ballestrin 2017; Castro-Gómez and Grosfoguel 2007; Mignolo 2012). The Peruvian sociologist Quijano (2000) developed the concept of decoloniality of power to discuss economic and political relationships of domination and structures of control and **hegemony** that continue to produce colonial forms of domination. Tensions that result from power imbalances also appear in **knowledge production** in the academic and research spheres focusing on children as discussed by Jamieson and colleagues (2022), reflecting on a study carried out in partnership with scholars from southern and northern countries.

Related to this homogenization and **universalization** of ideas of childhood across geographies is the problem that these notions overemphasize children's experiences as distinctive and separate from the world of adults, a notion that travelled from Western Europe to other parts of the world and was expanded in the twentieth century as highlighted by Twum-Danso Imoh and Ame (2012). Universal notions of what childhood should or does look like are embedded in the UNCRC, imposing those generalities on signatory countries where childhood may well differ from those universal notions.

Despite the assumption of universality of childhoods and the universal applicability of human rights implied in the Convention, that does not mean that some of the critical aspects of childhood are the same in every culture nor that the violation of rights in different cultures have been or can be treated in the same way. In most Latin American countries, for example, there was a particular development in the discourse of rights as the region started to emerge from dictatorships in the 1980s. A growing wave of resistance led by social movements fought against these authoritarian regimes; while they were doing so, they also fought against poverty and inequality and advocated for children´s rights and **wellbeing** (Pilotti 2001).

An example from Brazil

The important particularities of these experiences can be seen in Brazil. In that country, coinciding with the political moment of 're-democratizing' the country, a new constitution was drawn up with, for the first time ever, intense popular participation.[2] The promise of citizenship also included children and youth who were moved in law to being the 'subjects', that is, the holders of rights (Rizzini 2011).

A key feature of the movement towards democracy and of the constitution was the notion of citizen participation, which also connects to the idea of children and youth's social participation and engagement as citizens.[3] With the institutionalization of children-specific rights, the Statute on the Child and the Adolescent enacted in 1990 included a comprehensive set of provisions to promote and defend children´s rights. In line with the emphasis on participation the statute also included provisions for creating new democratic institutional structures such as the children's rights councils to promote more equal decision-making processes, balancing power forces between governmental and civil society representatives (Assis 2009). These councils, which exist at the federal, state and municipal levels, are made up of half government officials and half non-profits devoted to children's issues. Recently, the National Children's Rights Council has advanced the notion of **children's participation** one step further by requiring each council to reserve two seats for young people. These features of the Brazilian process towards defining and ensuring children's growing **protagonismo**, and examples from other countries at the margins of the dominant global circuits, should complement and inform any international enunciation of rights. Though these examples stem from a particular context, they tell us about relevant knowledge based on research and experiences in a large number of countries that to date have insufficiently contributed to the dialogue and would inspire others. This provides ways to decolonize children's rights and childhood studies more generally.

Key concept: Protagonismo

Protagonismo (protoganism in English) can be defined as a concept closely related to participation that emphasizes children and young people's place and roles in society as proactive actors having competence and a sense of **autonomy** (Cussianóvich 2013; Rizzini 2019).

Conclusion

There is much pathbreaking theory debated in this Chapter and those theories have shaped new ideas and standards for children's rights. Theorists from a variety of **disciplines** will continue relevant debates about the merits of those theories and, at the same time, those theories should be exposed to and challenged by the lived and concrete realities of the lives of children in different countries and cultures.

Notes

1. Galeano (1997) and Spivak (1994) being some of the precursors in this growing field.
2. A movement known as the 'Constituinte' and the constitution popularly called 'the citizen Constitution'. The constitution was adopted in 1988 and included provisions about children and young people's rights in its Article 227m, as follows: 'It is the duty of the family, the society and the Government to assure children, adolescents, and youths, with absolute priority, the rights to life, health, nourishment, education, leisure, professional training, culture, dignity, respect, liberty and family and community harmony, in addition to safeguarding them against all forms of negligence, discrimination, exploitation, violence, cruelty and oppression.'
3. In the Latin American literature on children and youth's participation, citizen participation emphasizes the link between participation as a right and children as subject of rights (Acosta and Pineda 2007; Corvera 2011; Lay-Lisboa 2018).

References

Acosta, A. and Pineda, N. (2007), 'Ciudad y Participación Infantil', in Y. C. Caraveo and M. E. L. Pontón(eds), *Participación Infantil y Juvenil en América Latina*, 147–77, Bogotá: Cinde.

Assis, S. G. (2009), *Teoria e Prática dos Conselhos Tutelares e Conselhos de Direitos da Criança e do Adolescente*, Rio de Janeiro: Ed. Fiocruz.

Assy, B. A. (2018), 'The Subject of Discrimination: Factual Life, Empowerment, and Being Political', *La Revue des Droits de L'Homme*, 13. Available online: https://journals.openedition.org/revdh/3625?lang=en (accessed 20 March 2021).

Balagopalan, S. (2019), 'Childhood, Culture, History: Redeploying "Multiple Childhoods"', in S. Spyrou, R. Rosen and D. Cook (eds), *Reimagining Childhood Studies*, 23–39, London: Bloomsbury.

Ballestrin, L. M. D. A. (2017), 'Can Modernity/Coloniality Exist Without "Imperiality"? The Missing Link in the Decolonial Shift', *DADOS: Revista de Ciencias Sociais*, 60 (2): 505–40. doi:10.1590/ 001152582017127.

Castro, L. R. (2020), 'Why Global? Children and Childhood from a Decolonial Perspective', *Childhood*, 27 (1): 48–62.

Castro-Gómez, S. and Grosfoguel, R. (eds) (2007), *El Giro Decolonial: Reflexiones Para una Diversidad Epistémica más Allá del Capitalismo*

Global, Bogotá: Siglo del Hombre Editores; Universidad Central, Instituto de Estudios Sociales Contemporáneos y Pontificia Universidad Javeriana, Instituto Pensar.

Connell, R. (2013), 'Using Southern Theory: Decolonizing Social Thought in Theory, Research and Application', *Planning Theory*, 13 (2): 210–23.

Corvera, N. (2018), 'Participación Ciudadana de los Niños Como Sujetos de Derechos', *Persona Y Sociedad*, 25 (2): 73–99.

Cussianóvich, A. (2013), 'Protagonismo, Participación y Ciudadanía Como Componente de la Educación y Ejercicio de los Derechos de la Infancia', in A. Cussianóvich (ed.), *Historia del Pensamiento Social Sobre la Infancia*, 1–53, Lima: Universidad Mayor de San Marcos.

Douzinas, C. (2000), *The End of Human Rights*, Oxford: Hart Publishing.

Galeano, E. (1971 [1997]), *Open Veins of Latin America: Five Centuries of the Pillage of a Continent*, New York: Monthly Review Press.

Grosfoguel, R. (2012), 'Decolonizing Western Uni-versalisms: Decolonial Pluri-versalism from Aimé Césaire to the Zapatistas', *Transmodernity*, 1 (3): 88–102.

Jamieson, L., Rizzini, I., Collins, T. M., and Wright, L. H. V. (2022), 'International Perspectives on the Participation of Children and Young People in the Global South'. *Third World Thematic*, doi:10.1080/23802014.2022.2050940.

Lay-Lisboa, S., Araya-Bolvarán, E., Marabolí-Garay, C., Olivero-Tapia, G., and Santander-Andrade, C. (2018), 'Protagonismo Infantil en la Escuela: Las Relaciones Pedagógicas en la Construcción de Ciudadanía', *Sociedad e Infancias*, 2: 147–70.

Mignolo, W. D. (2012), *Local Histories/Global Designs*, Princeton, NJ: Princeton University Press.

Ndlovu-Gatsheni, S. (2015), 'Decoloniality as the Future of Africa', *History Compass*, 13 (10): 485–96.

Pahuja, S. (2011), *Decolonising International Law: Development, Economic Growth and the Politics of Universality*, Cambridge: Cambridge University Press.

Pilotti, F. (2001), *Globalización y Convención Sobre los Derechos del Niño: El Contexto del Texto*, Santiago de Chile: CEPAL.

Quijano, A. and Ennis, M. (2000), 'Coloniality of Power, Eurocentrism and Latin America', *Nepantla: Views from South*, 1 (3): 533–80, Project MUSE muse.jhu.edu/article/23906..

Rizzini, I. (2011), 'The Promise of Citizenship for Brazilian Children', *Annals of the American Academy of Political and Social Science*, 633 (1): 66–79.

Rizzini, I. (2019), 'Young People's Participation in Public Spaces on Behalf of Their Rights', *6th International Conference on Geography of Children, Youth and Families*, UNICAMP, Brazil, 22–24 May.

Santos, B. S. (2021), 'Human Rights, Democracy and Development', in B. S. Santos and B. S. Martins (eds), *The Pluriverse of Human Rights: The Diversity of Struggles for Dignity*, 21–40, New York: Routledge.

Spivak, G. C. (2015), 'Can the Subaltern Speak?', in P. Williams and L. Christman (eds), *Colonial Discourse and Post-Colonial Theory*, 66–111, London: Routledge, https://doi.org/10.4324/9781315656496.

Tabak, J. (2020), *The Child and the World: Child-Soldiers and the Claim for Progress*, Athens: The University of Georgia Press.

Twum-Danso Imoh, A. and Ame, R. (eds) (2012), *Childhoods at the Intersection of the Local and Global*, Basingstoke: Palgrave.

Twum-Danso Imoh, A. and Okyere, S. (2020), 'Towards a More Holistic Understanding of Child Participation: Foregrounding the Experiences of Children in Ghana and Nigeria', *Children and Youth Services Review*, 112: 104927.

5

Intersectional Perspectives on Childhood

Marlies Kustatscher and

Kristina Konstantoni

Chapter Outline

Introduction

In recent years, **intersectionality** has emerged as a key concept of the social sciences and has started to feature also in scholarship and policy in the field of **childhood studies**. As previous Chapters have illustrated, there has been ample debate in the field of childhood studies on the diversity of children and the lives they lead. There has also been plenty of discussion on inter- and intra-generational power dynamics and their implications for children expressing **agency** and their experiences within families, institutions and society more broadly. This Chapter highlights how intersectionality, with its focus on power and complexity, provides a key framework for critically evaluating children's social positions and experiences. While there are many debates about how intersectionality should be defined and operationalized, this Chapter puts forward a view of intersectionality as both a critical theoretical framework (with implications for methodology and analysis) and a social-change-oriented **radical praxis**.

This Chapter begins by introducing the history and definitional debates around intersectionality, highlighting some of its critiques and challenges. It then delves into the links between childhood studies and intersectionality and discusses some of the synergies and tensions between both fields – what they can learn from each other, how they can be usefully brought together and what some of the challenges of this work might be. In the following section, the Chapter provides reflections on what intersectional approaches mean for conducting research and producing **knowledge(s)** with children and about childhoods. Finally, it considers the implications of applying an intersectional approach in **childhood** practice and policy.

Conceptualizing intersectionality: Histories, definitions and tensions

This section provides an overview of intersectionality's histories and origins as well as current debates, including the place of **race** (and whiteness), in discussions around its operationalization.

Intersectionality's origins

Hill Collins (2019) describes a familiar 'story of origin' that is often utilized in writings about intersectionality. In this story, Crenshaw, an **anti-racist** and legal scholar from the United States, is generally cited as the person who 'coined' the use of the term 'intersectionality' in her influential paper 'Demarginalizing the Intersection of Race and Sex':

> Because the intersectional experience is greater than the sum of racism and sexism, any analysis that does not take intersectionality into account cannot sufficiently address the particular manner in which Black women are subordinated. Thus, for feminist theory and antiracist policy **discourse** to embrace the experiences and concerns of Black women, the entire framework that has been used as a basis for translating 'women's experience' or 'the Black experience' into concrete policy demands must be rethought and recast. (Crenshaw 1989: 140)

Crenshaw's work was indeed significant for bringing ideas about intersectionality into wider academic circles and highlighted the need to centre the experiences of women of colour and the importance of aligning anti-racist and feminist projects. However, as Hill Collins and Bilge (2016) suggest, it built on decades of work undertaken by social activists. Some trace intersectionality's origins back to Sojourner Truth's *Ain't I a Woman?* speech in 1851, which questioned the essentialist notion of the 'white woman' and its social consequences (Brah and Phoenix 2004; Emejulu 2011). In the 1960s and 1970s, African-American women within the civil rights and Black Power movements, Mexican-American women in Chicana movements as well as Asian-American and Native women's groups expressed core ideas of intersectionality. Hill Collins and Bilge (2016) highlight important texts from this area, such as Cade Bambara's (1970) *The Black Woman* or Beal's (1969) *Double Jeopardy: To Be Black and Female*, which set out intersectional arguments. A little later in 1977, the Combahee River Collective – a Black feminist lesbian organization – published *A Black Feminist Statement* that focused on the interlocking systemic oppression of sexism, racism, capitalism and homophobia (Hill Collins and Bilge 2016).

These are just a few of the many examples of Black feminist activists and writers who were instrumental for shaping awareness and ideas around intersectionality. Thus, while it is oftentimes seen as an academic or theoretical framework, the origins of intersectionality are rooted in feminist and anti-racist activism of the past centuries. As can be seen from the above historical narrative, a key element of intersectionality is the centring of the experiences of women of colour and a challenge to interlocking systemic oppression based on **gender**, race, class and sexuality. These historical origins of intersectionality are crucial for making sense of ongoing debates over its definition and operationalization.

Critical challenge: The origins of intersectionality

- Have you heard the term 'intersectionality' before? Or have you perhaps seen or understood an event or movement from this perspective without using the term 'intersectionality'?
- When and where did you first hear about intersectionality?
- How, if at all, has the history of the concept been represented in your encounter(s) with it?
- Why does it matter to pay attention to how the histories of concepts are told? What is at stake?
- What is your own contribution – as a student, writer, researcher, practitioner – to the **genealogy** of intersectionality and how do you position yourself within this process?
- Thinking about key concepts that you are utilizing as a childhood studies scholar/practitioner, how aware are you of their critical histories – who coined and shaped their usage, and what debates accompany their current meanings?

A travelling concept: Theoretical framework, analytical tool or radical praxis?

Crenshaw's work served to propel intersectionality into wider debates within the social sciences, and it began to travel both geographical and disciplinary boundaries, generating a wealth of debate on its definition and operationalization. Some of these debates are explored in this section: whether intersectionality should be seen as a theoretical or analytical framework, or a call to social action; whether intersectionality is about identities or inequalities; and which intersections should be considered within intersectionality – particularly the place of race.

From the 2000s onwards, intersectionality has become a 'buzzword' (Davis 2008) in social research and arenas beyond academia. It has been described through a number of images and metaphors, for example, as a crossroad (Crenshaw 1989), as prisms (Cho et al. 2013) or as axes of difference (Yuval-Davis 2006).

Activity: Visualizing intersectionality

Individually or in groups, use pens and paper to create a visualization of intersectionality. This could be in terms of your own experiences and identities or thinking about a particular study or context with children.

- Which image or metaphor do you find best illustrates intersectionality?
- (How) does this change depending on the context in which intersectionality is applied?

Addressing one fundamental concern of feminist scholarship, namely 'the acknowledgement of differences among women' (Davis 2008: 70), intersectionality has even been acclaimed as 'the most important theoretical contribution [of] women's studies' (McCall 2005: 1771). In her popular definition, Davis describes intersectionality as

> the interaction between gender, race and other categories of difference in individual lives, social practices, institutional arrangements, and cultural ideologies and the outcomes of these interactions in terms of power. (2008: 68)

Activity: Your own positionality and intersectionality

Individually or in groups, take a moment to consider your own identities and **positionality** in terms of what you have just read.

- How can intersectionality help you to understand your own identities, experiences and actions?
- How might your intersectional positionings shape the way you view children and childhoods? What views do these open up, and what biases might they bring?
- How can intersectionality help you to critically reflect on your research and practice with children?

There has been much debate about which categories are the ones that should always be included in an intersectional analysis (such as race, gender, class, sexuality, disability) and whether these categories should be viewed as individual identities or **structural inequalities**. In addition, it has been highlighted that treating intersectionality merely as a synonym for complexity or diversity is problematic, and reducing it purely to the intersection of identities constitutes an overly simplistic approach. Cho et al. (2013) suggest that, while it is important to look at identities (such as race, gender, class):

> debates in intersectional studies will circulate less around categories and identities and more around how those categories and identities and their specific content are contingent on the particular dynamics under study or of political interest. (2013: 807)

Similarly, Tomlinson (2013) proposes:

> If critics think intersectionality is a matter of identity rather than power, they cannot see which differences make a difference. Yet it is exactly our analyses of power that reveal which differences carry significance. (1012)

These writers highlight the importance of looking at identities and structural categories always through a lens of power, which reveals complex dynamics of oppression and privilege, and that it is this analysis of power that should guide which categories should be prioritized. Anthias and Yuval-Davis (1983, 1992) suggest that intersectional analyses should focus on multiple levels: on individual experiences of advantage and disadvantage, on organizational and structural levels, and lastly on representational and discursive levels. As some authors have highlighted, the division of individual versus structural levels of inequalities can be seen as socially constructed anyway, since intersections of categories are 'simultaneously subjective, structural and about social positioning and everyday practices' (Brah and Phoenix 2004: 75).

Konstantoni and Emejulu (2017) further argue that operationalizing intersectionality needs to go beyond viewing it only as a framework for understanding complex interactions of categories of structural inequalities. They critique the application of intersectionality as merely an analytical tool to highlight the multidimensional nature of social identities while stripping intersectionality from the radical politics of its origins.

Numerous writers have pointed out the erasure of race, as intersectionality has travelled **disciplines** and continents, and became subsumed into different academic and political discourses (Bilge 2013; Lewis 2013; Tomlinson 2017). For example, Bilge (2013) analyses how intersectionality has been depoliticized and commodified, and how there has been a process of 'whitening' intersectionality. This process ignores the contributions of women of colour and prioritizes gender over race, thus often emphasizing a 'common' feminist project that is being 'diluted' by focusing on processes of **racialization** and racism within it. However, this line of argument ignores **hegemonic whiteness** (the idea that dominant (but often unnamed) social practices associated with 'being white' define our social world) and how it shapes both individual standpoints and wider power dynamics. Thus, a focus on race (including whiteness) needs to be central to any operationalization of intersectionality.

Recognizing that intersectionality is more than a tool to analyse intersecting categories also acknowledges that academic debates, and the ways in which theories and concepts are defined and operationalized, are equally implicated in power relations. Thus, intersectionality can be seen as 'a **counter-hegemonic praxis** that seeks to challenge and displace hegemonic whiteness in the naming and legitimating of particular kinds of politics, policymaking and **knowledge production**' (Konstantoni and Emejulu 2017: 8). Hill Collins (2019: 3) suggests that intersectionality as a 'critical social theory sits in a sweet spot between critical analysis and social action', and this way of conceptualizing intersectionality is drawn upon in this Chapter.

Exploring concepts further: Intersectionality, whiteness and anti-racism

It is important to acknowledge that this Chapter has not been written in a social vacuum or speaks about the topic of intersectionality from a 'neutral' place. Located within the **neoliberal** academic context of the UK, as authors we are working in particular conditions that favour certain types of knowledge production and application. This context tends to involve the **commodification of knowledges** and often utilizes extractive processes of knowledge generation. As white middle-class heterosexual cis-women authors of this section, we write about intersectionality from a particular positionality, and we need to reflect on how this impacts on our writing, the implications for the space we occupy and how this is being recognized. Viewing intersectionality as a radical praxis which challenges white hegemony and white supremacy (Konstantoni and Emejulu 2017) aligns with other areas of anti-racist work that require us to critically reflect on whiteness and its impact, including white privilege. Related but distinct concepts include:

Anti-racism is a stance that recognizes that racism is pervasive and systemic, and that aims to identify and actively oppose racism (for further readings, see, for example, Eddo-Lodge (2018) or Saad (2020), and follow the Movement for Black Lives).

Decolonization aims to challenge and undo historical and ongoing processes of colonialism, with a focus on the intellectual, emotional, economic and political reversal of colonial injustices (see definition and discussion in Chapter 2).

Epistemic justice (or sometimes **cognitive justice**) refers to justice in the ways in which knowledge is understood, produced and communicated. At the heart of this concept is the idea that what counts as knowledge is not neutral but infused with power dynamics and that different people have different experiences of having their views heard, recognized, respected and acted upon (Anderson 2017; Fricker 2007). The importance of epistemic justice goes beyond 'academic' environments. De Sousa Santos (2007) suggests that there can be no global **social justice** without global cognitive justice.

Operationalizing intersectionality: Contesting power

Different groups are racialized to different extents in society. Often, people who belong to a racial majority in a particular context – such as white people in many societies of the **global North** – tend to not be aware of their racial positioning because they do not experience racialization in their everyday lives. On the other hand, minority ethnic groups often experience racialization through racist stereotyping or discrimination.

If you identify as white or belonging to a non-racialized majority, consider how intersectionality might help you to critically reflect on and be proactive about complex injustices while being aware of and dismantling **hegemonic** viewpoints, including hegemonic whiteness (see also Mills' (2007) work on whiteness as ignorance):

- What aspects of your identity might privilege you, and how can you proactively use this privilege to challenge racial and other injustices?

- How reflective are you about your own whiteness (or other positions of relative privilege), and how does it shape your positionality and perspectives?
- What aspects of your identity might privilege or disadvantage you and shape your work and relationships?
- How can an intersectional framework help to draw attention to whiteness and white privilege while not **universalizing** or centring white experiences?

Intersectionality and childhood studies: Making the links

The Chapter now turns to discussing how childhood studies and intersectionality can come together, and what the synergies of this work can be and what the implications are.

Intersectional childhood studies

Recognizing differences within children's lives is certainly in line with one of the key tenets of childhood studies, namely the emphasis on the heterogeneity of children as a social group (James and Prout 1997). And, indeed, numerous studies have explored how different categories such as race, **ethnicity**, gender, social class, disability and age shape children's lives (e.g. Evans and Holt 2011; Morrow and Connolly 2006). However, fewer writers have explicitly used an intersectional framework (exceptions include von Benzon and Wilkinson 2019, special issue edited by Konstantoni et al. (2017); O'Neill Gutierrez and Hopkins 2015) and studies vary in how seriously they consider intersectionality's politics and practices.

To date, little theorization or analytical debate exists about the implications of bringing the fields of childhood studies and intersectionality together. As Chapter 2 has illustrated, childhood studies has traditionally foregrounded the category of age/generation over other aspects of difference. Numerous scholars have recognized children's specific social positions in terms of power due to the minority status of 'childhood' and stressed the importance of reframing **children's participation** in research and more widely through an intergenerational lens, considering the specific power relations produced in child–adult relationships (Blaisdell 2019; Mannion 2007; Mayall 2002). Indeed, drawing out the importance of the category of age/generation as a structural property, and the different ways in which it has been constructed (e.g. in relation to maturity, capability or development), is a central contribution of childhood studies. However, while differences within childhood have been the focus of the field for some time, more theorization is needed of how different categories are inflecting each other and how the category of 'the child' is both being abstracted and reified in this process (Burman 2013). Intersectionality can provide the tool to support critical attention to, yet also **deconstruction** of, the various categories that come to constitute children and childhoods.

> I appreciate intersectionality as a framework informed by **Black feminist thought**. I am interested in policy and practice in education and the way that this can sustain and recreate existing inequalities. My thesis explores the social determinants of adolescent boys' mental health and **wellbeing** in education. I am particularly interested in focusing on lived experience at the intersection of gender and age.
>
> *Parise Carmichael-Murphy, PhD Student, Manchester Institute of Education, the University of Manchester, UK*

Konstantoni and Emejulu (2017) have highlighted the risk of a depoliticization of intersectionality as it has become utilized more widely within childhood studies. They suggest that if the field of childhood studies is to take seriously the politics of intersectionality's origins, it needs to ensure that the anti-racist and feminist politics at its heart are maintained by continuing to insist on the importance of race, racialization and racism in children's lives. In addition, they suggest that childhood scholars who want to take intersectionality seriously need to go beyond using it as a theoretical or analytical framework and ensure that their work is aligned with emancipatory praxis and alliances which challenge intersectional inequalities in children's lives. This aligns well with the political agenda of the original childhood studies **paradigm** (see discussion in Chapter 2) and poises those in the childhood studies field to ensure they consider various social categories, including race, as well as to actively challenge inequalities experienced by children.

In summary, intersectionality and childhood studies share a commitment to deconstructing categories such as 'childhood'. Operationalizing intersectionality within childhood studies means to challenge assumptions and practices about *which* children are included and excluded (in research, theorizations, practices, representations), with a particular challenge to hegemonic whiteness and a clear agenda to contribute beyond academic circles to actual children's lives.

Knowing (with) children: Epistemological and representational issues

If intersectionality, as described earlier, is seen as not only a method but a call to radical praxis (Konstantoni and Emejulu 2017), what are the implications for how knowledge about childhoods is produced and how children are represented? It means that attention to intersectionality does not just begin when 'studying childhoods', but any field such as childhood studies is already situated within particular power relations (Tomlinson 2013) which shape the very conditions under which claims about children and childhoods are produced, including academic contexts, rhetoric and discourse. For example, Pérez (2017) highlights how the field of childhood studies, specifically **early childhood** studies, has historically been dominated by the views of white men from the global North, and while many **reconceptualist movements** have challenged taken-for-granted assumptions about childhoods, it is still rare that theoretical challenges in the field of childhood studies are informed by women of colour. In addition, current academic contexts (such as the Chapter authors' context of the UK) are characterized by a failure to challenge hegemonic whiteness, and Black and minority ethnic populations continue to be underrepresented (Rollock 2012).

Intersectionality is central in my work exploring racioling-uistic ideologies and anti-racist language education. Why are certain languages labelled 'modern', 'foreign' or 'community'? Are language, ethnic or national identities being conflated in the classroom? Which speakers of which languages are disadvantaged by the answers to these questions? Linguistic justice, cognitive justice and racial justice are not unrelated in language education.
Mariel Deluna, PhD Student and Researcher, Moray House School of Education and Sport, University of Edinburgh, Scotland

These conditions shape how knowledge about children and childhoods is produced and who the children are that this knowledge centres (or silences). **Epistemological** and representational questions about children and intersectionality revolve around who the children are that are included or excluded in research, who the people are that shape research agendas around childhood, how intersectional inequalities shape children's lives within different global contexts and institutions, and how children themselves make sense of their own and others' intersectional positions.

The childhood studies and children's rights fields in particular have been responsible for an increase in child-led research and knowledge production over the last twenty years (Cuevas-Parra and Tisdall 2019). Childhood studies shares with intersectionality a critical perspective on what constitutes knowledge and how knowledge agendas are shaped. For example, knowledge that is co-produced with children through participatory processes often constitutes a challenge to generally accepted research practices and criteria. And indeed, many forms of knowledge accepted in the dominant discourse around what constitutes knowledge exclude children through the very nature of their production processes (e.g. children may prefer oral over written knowledges or arts-based/relational/emotional over verbal or rationalized expressions).

The boundaries between research and activism tend to easily blur in participatory research with children, and there is a real opportunity for challenging generally accepted purposes of social research. Cuevas-Parra and Tisdall (2019: 13) suggest that child-led research tends to assume a more collective and distributed nature, as opposed to the image of the 'lone academic' researcher. This means that paying attention to the intersectional power relations within research teams, both intergenerational and racialized, gendered, classed and more, is essential for ensuring that child-led research can live up to its potential of centring intersectional childhoods as well as contribute to challenging dominant knowledge politics.

Activity: Centring children's knowledges in research

Blaisdell et al. (2019) write about using creative, playful arts-based methods in research with young children. In this piece, they reflect on a case study that explored what voice and listening meant to young children themselves. To facilitate this exploration, they drew on a combination of arts-based methods such as fine arts, video, puppetry, informal conversations and a 'play basket'. The authors also reflect on ethical issues and a mutual understanding and agreement between the intergenerational actors involved in the research on its direction and knowledge framework.

Reflecting on Blaisdell et al.'s (2019) approach, we invite you to consider:

- How have different studies involving children ensured (or not) that children's ways of expressing and conceptualizing knowledges are centred and respected?
- What challenges have researchers encountered, and how have they addressed them?
- What are the broader implications for how knowledge about childhood and children's experiences is produced and operationalized, for example, in practice and policy?

Applying intersectionality to key childhood studies concepts: Rebuilding foundations

It could be argued that the **interdisciplinary** field of childhood studies is defined by a shared scholarly interest in key concepts around childhood: generation/age, agency, participation and a rejection (or at least very critical evaluation) of deterministic and deficit notions of **child development** and children's competences (see Chapter 2). This section poses the question: What would it mean to re-imagine some of these core concepts of childhood studies through an intersectional lens?

A useful example is the critique of developmental notions of childhood, which is arguably a defining feature of childhood studies. This critique involves rejecting assumptions about 'age and stage' and links between children's age and assumed lack of competences. Foundational childhood studies texts in the 1990s (such as James and Prout 1997) highlighted the need to view childhood as worthy of study in its own right (rather than just as a preparation stage for adulthood) and to deconstruct **ontological** (what is a child?) and epistemological (how can we know about children and childhoods?) assumptions about childhood (Gallagher 2009).

In this process, some writers have highlighted how childhood has become 'colonized' by developmental psychology in a drive to inscribe **normative** ideas onto all children and pathologizing those that do not fit these norms. Rooted in positivist assumptions, child development discourses tend to ignore that 'child study experts are positioned socially and culturally to subjugate the child to their gaze, and hold the power to interpret the meaning of children's behaviours' (Varga 2011: 138). Indeed, foundational child development theories such as the work of Gesell are based on very limited white middle-class samples of children who he deemed superior to others in terms of providing evidence for developmental normality (Varga 2011). Yet, they continue to be applied to wide groups of children in universalizing ways. There are countless other examples of how developmental discourses are based on **whitewashed**, Euro-centric and colonial attitudes (e.g. see Burman 2008, 2012; Cannella 2004; Varga 2011; see Chapter 2 on decolonizing childhood and childhood studies).

Thus, a critique of child development foundations needs to be based not only on the normalizing and deterministic assumptions made about children's competences, agency and capabilities in relation to their age but also on the regulatory discourses around race and the tendency to whitewash childhoods and pathologize children of colour and children living in the global South. However, childhood studies as a broader field has focused mainly on the former, age-related critique. Childhood studies discourses have missed the opportunity to reject also the whitening and colonization of child development as part of this critique and to build this into foundational ideas of childhood studies (with notable exceptions, of course, such as Burman 2008, 2012; Pérez 2017; Varga 2011).

An intersectional perspective suggests that this is no accidental oversight but that in fact the relative absence of an awareness around race and hegemonic whiteness is constitutive of the discipline (see also Tomlinson 2013). As mentioned earlier, childhood studies (as many other disciplinary fields) has traditionally been dominated by the perspectives of white men from the global North (Pérez 2017), and academic discourses continue to be dominated by scholars in the global North. It is important to challenge the racialized, gendered/patriarchal and classed assumptions not only with regard to the critique of developmental psychology but also in terms of how they have shaped dominant understandings of agency, intergenerational relationships and children's participation – and other core concepts of childhood studies (Kustatscher et al. 2022). For example, in the field of participation, writers have described a tendency to include certain types of participation (such as participation within institutions which are ascribed status and value) into typologies, but less so participation in informal and non-institutionalized settings, particularly in the **global South** (such as participation of street children) (Savyasaachi and Butler 2014).

This requires, as Pérez et al. (2017) note, an onto-epistemological shift in childhood studies which challenges white hegemony and centres voices from the global South and those who occupy subaltern positions. Important work has already begun in the field (e.g. Pacini-Ketchabaw and Taylor 2015; Pérez and Saavedra 2017; Twum-Danso Imoh et al. 2019) and what it will require is no less than a shake-up not only of established understandings of core childhood studies concepts but also of the academic relationships that produce them.

Intersectional childhood research: Considering methodologies

As the previous debates illustrate, intersectionality has recently received more attention in the childhood studies field, and scholars have begun to critically discuss its application, particularly in relation to the politics and practices of importing and operationalizing intersectionality into childhood studies. What, then, does it mean to generate knowledge with, about and for children from an intersectional perspective? What are the implications for methodologies with children?

To date, the critical analysis of intersectionality within childhood studies has not been significantly extended to methodological approaches to researching childhoods (exceptions include Kustatscher 2016; O'Neill Gutierrez and Hopkins 2015; Rodó-de-Zárate 2017; Thorne 2004; von Benzon and Wilkinson 2019). This section, therefore, focuses on intersectionality as a methodological approach for conducting childhood research.

Researching power and complexity through intersectional approaches

Given that there is no one agreement on intersectionality's definition and operationalization, it is not surprising that there is also not one way of implementing intersectionality through research methodologies. In fact, Cho and colleagues (2013) propose that one of the ways in which intersectionality has been used across various disciplines is by drawing attention to complex methodological questions. Intersectionality is not considered a method or linked to a specific methodology. However, within the many debates in intersectionality studies, there have been some devoted to the question of methodology. These are informed by some of the key points of discussion within the field, particularly with regard to the conceptualization of 'intersectional categories', as summarized by Cho and colleagues (2013).

First, debates centre on whether intersectional approaches should view categories (such as age, race, ethnicity, gender, class, sexuality, dis/ability) as additive and **autonomous** or as interactive and mutually constitutive. Viewing categories as additive means seeing them as interacting but separable and fixed. Viewing categories as constitutive, on the other hand, means considering them to be dynamic, situated and contextual (Cho et al. 2013; Knudsen 2006; Yuval-Davis 2006). Constitutive, or sometimes called transversal, intersectionality approaches view categories as pervading and transforming each other (Knudsen 2006) and imply a critique of identity approaches for essentializing and prioritizing certain categories (Wright 2010).

Debates on additive versus constitutive views of categories are aligned to whether researchers utilize quantitative or qualitative methods. A constitutive view of intersectionality lends itself well to qualitative approaches, which endorse an open-ended investigation of the interacting and conflicting dynamics of age, race, gender, class, disability, sexuality, nation and others. Quantitative approaches, on the other hand, tend to be more often associated with additive intersectional categories. They need to embed intersectional representation into their design from the outset (e.g. consider age, race and gender in their sampling) and ensure that attention is paid to the analysis of how these intersect. For example, studies such as Young Lives (no date), a longitudinal mixed-methods research study with children in Ethiopia, India, Peru and Vietnam, generate data to understand how children's experiences are shaped by their gender, ethnicity and experiences of poverty.

Second, and related, researchers face the question of *which* categories should be included in an intersectional analysis. Lists of categories – such as age, race, gender, disability – inevitably fail to capture all the aspects of a child's life, and this is often addressed through an 'et cetera' at the end. As highlighted earlier in this Chapter, researchers need to examine carefully what are the relevant categories within the context of a study. Questions emerge with regard to 'who is intersectional' and whether intersectional analyses should focus on systems of oppression *and* privilege. In research with children, it is important to strike a balance: while it is crucial to highlight how structural oppression shapes children's lives, researchers need to avoid deficit approaches.

Third, as discussed in earlier sections, there is an ongoing debate over the place of race in applications of intersectional analyses and whether race needs to feature as part of any intersectional analysis or not. Some scholars argue that intersectionality has a wide application and does not necessarily have to include a focus on race. As intersectionality is rooted in the intellectual history and traditions of Black feminism, other scholars disagree and highlight that a focus on race is a defining feature of any intersectional research. If intersectionality as an analytical framework is operationalized in a way that is separated from the Black feminist tradition from which it emerged, then this act is considered as 'employing symbolic violence on Black women through the erasure of their history as knowing agents' (Konstantoni 2020: 1000). Additionally, when race is not explicitly foregrounded in intersectional research (say, for example, in a study on the intersections of gender and disability in young girls' lives), there is a risk that such research makes implicit assumptions, for example, about taken-for-granted whiteness. It is thus important that researchers make explicit the choices of their theoretical and methodological frameworks, and their own social positioning within them (Kustatscher et al. 2015).

Critical challenge: Positioning yourself in research

How scholars position themselves along the above lines of debate will shape their research design, including their choices of methods and the people who are invited into research as participants. Epistemological and methodological frameworks are not neutral, and it is widely accepted – especially within qualitative research – that attention to power dynamics is an integral part of the research process.

- How do you position yourself along these lines of debate?
- What implications might this positioning have for your research design, including research focus, choice of methods and invitation of research participants?

What unites intersectional research approaches, regardless of whether they seek to deconstruct categories, take them as given or interrogate their boundaries, is their ability to capture the complexity of social life (McCall 2005). In doing so, intersectional studies have employed a multitude of research methods, both quantitative and qualitative. O'Neil Gutierrez and Hopkins' (2015: 385) suggest that childhood studies which applies intersectional lenses of analysis are able to 'offer theoretical insights into the ways in which an intersectional framework allows researchers to better understand and re/present the everyday experiences and circumstances of their research participants'. Bringing together intersectional debates with the rich literature on childhood methodologies opens up critical opportunities for considering the complexity of research agendas, knowledge production and representation.

Activity: Methodological example by Rodó-de-Zárate (2017)

Rodó-de-Zárate (2017) has utilized 'Relief Maps' to explore **young people**'s experiences of their different identities and experiences of inequalities. The maps asked young people to draw how comfortable (or not) they felt in public spaces, based on their gender, sexuality, ethnicity, class and age. The maps provided a tool for the young people to discuss different aspects of their identities and how they shaped, and were shaped by, the various spatial contexts that they frequented. They also prompted discussion about political consciousness and political ideologies.

- Considering your field of interest, would such a mapping activity be appropriate? Why?
- Please identify a piece of childhood research that has been particularly influential for you. To what extent, and if so, how, has it considered children's and researchers' intersectional positions in the process of knowledge production?
- How do intersectional approaches align (or not) with the rich methodological repertoire employed in childhood studies (participatory methods, arts-based methods, ethnographic methods, etc.)?
- Which of these do lend themselves well, or not so well, to exploring intersectional complexity in children's lives – and why?

Child as method

As outlined earlier, intersectionality does not come with a prescribed set of methods. Rather, it is up to researchers to ensure that they pay attention to intersectional power dynamics through their research design. Burman suggests an approach called '**child as method**'. 'Child as method' does not actually imply specific methods but is a particular lens that enables researchers to centre, and critically evaluate, children and childhoods in any aspects of social relations or knowledge production. Drawing on Chen's (2010) influential text 'Asia as Method', and on **post-structuralist**, intersectional and **psychoanalytical** perspectives, Burman defines 'child as method' as:

> an analytical approach that addresses socio-political practices focusing on the positioning accorded the child/children. [. . .] It counters the abstraction of concern about (and for) children from other cultural-political contexts and dynamics, to attend to the ways these contexts and dynamics produce and interact with meanings and practices of childhood. (2020: 205)

Thus, 'child as method' is not actually a set of technical procedures or methods, but rather an 'epistemic angle' or 'narrative imaginary' that shapes research agendas and explores children and childhoods as a central element within social practices, relationships and institutions (Burman 2020). This implies a critical exploration of taken-for-granted cultural and political practices, including academic practices (Burman 2018).

A 'child as method' stance has two implications: on the one hand, it compels childhood researchers to bring an intersectional perspective into their research by critically analysing how children and childhoods are located in wider sociopolitical relations and how power operates in the constructing and shaping of childhoods in different situated contexts across time and space, in both local and global relations. On the other hand, 'child as method' is a call for *all* researchers to consider children and childhoods in their research. For example, researchers who are interested in issues such as the labour market, family life, social policy, health and wellbeing or social movements (to name a few examples) are reminded to consider how children are located within, impacted by and contributing to the issues at hand. This aligns with calls by Punch (2020) to include a focus on age and generation in 'mainstream' research, policy and practice (see Chapter 2 on considering **generational order**), in order to ensure that children and childhoods become a central concern beyond the field of childhood studies.

My work is informed by intersectional feminist decolonial commitments informing an approach I have called Child as method to attend to the complex geopolitical dynamics and agendas enacted by and in relation to children and childhoods, specifically drawing on the work of Frantz Fanon.
Erica Burman, Professor of Education, University of Manchester, UK

Intersectionality and ethical knowledge(s)

Researchers in childhood studies have devoted extensive attention to ethical issues (e.g. Christensen and James 2008; Gallacher and Gallagher 2008; Tisdall et al. 2008). These range from ensuring that children are respected in, and benefit from research, questions around **informed consent and assent**, **safeguarding** issues, to feedback and change resulting from research. Questions of ethics do not only apply to procedural aspects of research but are also important to consider for underlying research agendas, relationships with participants as well as broader dynamics of knowledge production and use.

Black feminist thought and intersectional perspectives are important resources for considering the ethics engrained in these epistemological questions. Hill Collins (2009) has developed a four-tenet analysis of Black feminist epistemology and ways of knowing which can be implemented while 'doing' childhood research. Hill Collins' (2009) Black feminist epistemology is based on: (1) knowledge that is built on lived experiences which come to be understood through a process of dialogue (which includes the researcher's presence in the research process, as no research can be value-free), where (2) knowledge is based on an ethics of caring, (3) evaluated with empathy and compassion and (4) requiring personal accountability. Hill Collins' approach suggests that knowing and knowledge cannot be separated from political values and individual beliefs, which is why **reflexive processes** are important to examine assumptions, values and systems of truth.

These ideas can be applied directly to intersectional childhood research. Similar to Black feminist epistemology, knowledge about children and childhoods is often based on understandings of lived and **embodied** experiences. Within Black feminist epistemology, the dialogical approach can implicitly centre 'voice' as part of a dialogue between the researcher and participant. For childhood researchers who apply intersectionality, all forms of communication need to be considered, including non-verbal communication (e.g. with babies and younger children). Researchers in childhood studies have been very sensitive to such nuanced aspects of the dialogical research process, for example, by highlighting problems with reliance on 'voice' or including a focus on silences and body language (e.g. Spyrou 2016; Tisdall 2018). Within childhood research, considering the role of the adult researcher and their intersectional positionings, including an analysis of whiteness, is an important element of applying intersectionality as part of research. Considering the 'intersectional dimensions of processes of knowledge production' can become part of ensuring academic rigour and integrity (Konstantoni 2020: 1000).

Exploring concepts further: Ethics and positionality in intersectional research

Childhood researchers have been sensitive to the ways in which research agendas and methodologies are generally set by adults. Different approaches have been proposed to make visible or de-centre adult power in research processes, with varying success. For example, Mandell (1988) suggested that researchers should adopt a 'least adult role', in which they reject ways of behaving that would usually be associated with being an adult and join into children's activities. Others have critiqued this as an illusionary attempt to shed one's adult power.

Christofferson (2018) suggests that taking an intersectional approach raises further ethical questions to be asked about our positionality as researchers, for example:

> Why am I researching this (Doucet 2008)? What is my relationship to the research topic? What are the politics around this topic? Do I have the right to research this? What gives me the right? Am I doing justice to the theorists whose work I am using? How will my positionality influence my relationships with research participants? With my epistemic communities? Will participants be made aware of my social position and relationship to the topic when they consent to participate? If not, is this 'informed consent'? Does my positionality present a barrier to attempts to equalize power and involve research participants? Is it realistic to aim for more equalized power? Is this the optimal social position from which to conduct this research? (Christofferson 2018: 419)

These questions are pertinent to consider in any research endeavour and resonate particularly with the sensitivity to both inter- and intra-generational relationships required in the field of childhood studies.

How would you answer them in relation to your research area?

The application of intersectionality in childhood policy and practice: The example of children's participation

A key feature of intersectionality is that it addresses power imbalances through collective action. Because intersectionality was born from Black women's social movements, there is an emphasis on thoughtful and committed action. Thus, a key challenge for childhood studies that adopts an intersectional approach is to use intersectionality in a way that recognizes and takes seriously the intellectual labour of Black women and preserves its original focus on action and change.

Critical challenge: Applying intersectionality in your own context

Consider the following questions by Emejulu (2013):

- Which 'children' count in the mainstream practices and campaigns in childhood studies, children's rights and **children's geographies**? Which children are silenced and why?
- How do the dynamics of race/class/gender/sexuality/disability shape children's lives?
- How do these dynamics serve as resources for children?
- What kinds of alliances need to be built across different groups to effectively address children's intersectional inequalities?

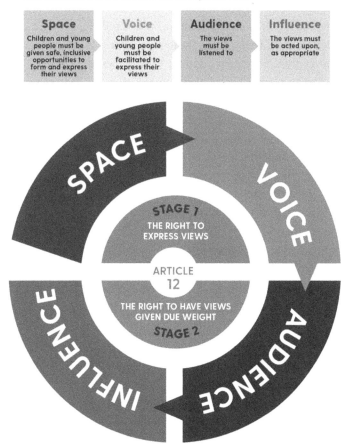

This model provides a pathway to help conceptualise Article 12 of the UNCRC. It focuses on four distinct, albeit interrelated, elements. The four elements have a rational chronological order.

Figure 5.1 The Lundy Model of participation. Reproduced from Government of Ireland, Department of Children, Equality, Disability, Integration and Youth 2021.

The focus on action aligns well with debates in childhood studies and in particular with the children's rights field, where change as a core element of participation has received much attention. A range of models have been developed to conceptualize what aiming for change or improved outcomes for children in the context of meaningful participation means (see Chapter 4). An example is the model developed by Lundy (2007).

The Lundy Model suggests that in order to conceptualize Article 12, four distinct and interrelated elements are required: Space, Voice, Audience and Influence. Followed in chronological order, these elements enable children to express their views and for their views to be given due weight. However, 'the implementation of processes of social change varies across childhood studies, as does recognition of the emancipatory and activist dimension of children's rights approaches' (Konstantoni and Emejulu 2017: 16). Models of participation can sometimes still be grounded in adult assumptions about children's 'voice' and 'agency', for example, by positioning them as rather passive (even if key) informants, who are not seen as capable of contributing to public debate or taking part in political decision-making structures (Houghton 2018). Houghton (2018) expands Lundy's participation model to include more active and **inclusive** roles for children. Furthermore, current models of participation would benefit from more nuanced analysis of how intersectional power relations between adults and children, and among children themselves, can affect participation processes.

Activity: Intersectionality and different participation models

Individually or in groups, compare the Lundy Model (Figure 5.1) to other children's participation models, for example Houghton (2018), Shier (2001) or others that you are regularly using.

- How (if at all) is intersectionality addressed in these models?
- Are there any gaps with regard to intersectionality?

More recently, there has been a move towards the recognition and re-conceptualization of children's participation to include concepts and practices linked to children's activism, moving beyond narrow understandings of political participation. For example, the work of Nolas (2015) expands notions of children's participation by linking it with social movements and social change through the idea of childhood publics. Tisdall and Cuevas-Parra (2020, 2021) show how child activism can provide a conceptual and practical challenge to the children's participation field by enabling a focus on children as political actors and highlighting the need for creating spaces and time that enable children's activism.

Activity: Children's climate justice activism

An increasing field of research explores children and young people's climate activism. Much of this activism is framed around climate justice (rather than climate change), recognizing that the burdens of and responsibility for the climate crisis are not shared equally among humankind. Applying social justice theories to debates on climate action means to centre the views of those most affected and to apply a **human rights** lens. As an example, you can listen to the views of young climate activists from different parts of the world here: https://linktr.ee/educationforclimatejustice (see also McGregor and Christie 2021).

Individually, or in groups, consider:

- What examples of children's climate activism have you come across, supported or been involved in?
- How are children positioned in these forms of activism, e.g. by the media or by key decision-makers?
- Whose children's views are most visible in climate activism and why? Whose children's views are not heard?
- How can theoretical models of activism and/or participation help us to understand and support children's climate activism?

Despite rising interest in children's activism, children's political participation (especially in the case of young children) is often ignored or considered as too 'soft' by adult activists (Bosco 2010; Taft 2019). Although there is a body of work that focuses on young children as active citizens involved in processes of change, more direct links to activism are rather limited as younger children are often viewed as 'innocent' and apolitical (exceptions include Konstantoni (2022), Rosen (2017) and Walker, Myers-Bowman and Myers-Walls (2008)).

> Because I work with young children, developing a social
> justice approach to my practice might be seen as too
> political, but children live in our world and have a complex
> and diverse range of experiences so I believe that a social
> justice perspective is invaluable to early years work.
>
> *Ruth Davidson, Early Years Officer, UK*

Children's activism does not take place in a social vacuum. As Tisdall and Cuevas-Parra (2020) highlight, it benefits from legal contexts as well as 'scaffolding' of wider stakeholders – such as NGOs, educators, parents or other significant adults. Considering intersectionality as praxis within childhood studies (Konstantoni and Emejulu 2017) commits various **social actors** to work together towards an emancipatory and activist agenda with the ultimate goal of challenging intersecting discrimination and multiple oppressions, including dismantling white privilege and promoting social justice. Intersectionality also serves as a key analytical tool for examining activist and participatory processes involving children through its focus on processes of inclusion and exclusion as well as power struggles (Konstantoni 2022).

There are numerous examples of how such alliances between children and civil society organizations can support children's activism, and they can follow different models of cooperation and leadership. In Scotland, for example, the organization Article 12 has developed practices for operationalizing intersectionality in their work with young Gypsy/Traveller women (Konstantoni and Emejulu 2017). More recently, a coalition of civil society organizations led by Terre des Hommes (including partners such as Save the Children, World Vision, Plan International, ChildFund Alliance, SOS Children's Villages and various academic partners) initiated the #CovidUnder19 campaign, which seeks to meaningfully involve children globally in responses to the COVID-19 pandemic (Terre des Hommes, no date).

The focus on collective action and activism raises questions about how childhood studies scholars should position themselves in these processes. Konstantoni and Emejulu (2017) state:

As scholars, we have an obligation to move from the academy to the streets. [. . .] The focus on practical work with groups both inside and outside academia is one of the most important aspects of the repoliticising of intersectionality for which Black feminists insist. The goal must be to produce knowledge with and for children and young people so that they can know, understand and take action in the world to address the multiple oppressions that impact on their everyday lives, on terms they define for themselves. (16)

As an academic field, childhood studies is well positioned to make such contributions on differing levels – to centre the views of children in knowledge production, to remind key stakeholders of the experiences of *all* children and to coalesce with children, communities and organizations beyond academia for enabling social change.

If a child is perceived based on a single label, often based on their gender, other categories that may be of strong significance may be overlooked. This impacts on the quality of provision received. References to intersectionality in the provision of services from the holistic perspective of children will have a positive impact on their overall development.

Chandrika Devarakonda, Associate Professor of Diversity and Inclusion, University of Chester, UK

Critical challenge: Intersectionality as praxis

Applying an intersectional approach in work with children implies that there is a commitment to processes of change.

- In your experience – whether as a child or young person, as a researcher, practitioner, educator or policymaker – how can intersectionality help you to analyse processes of children's participation or activism?
- Can you think of specific examples?
- Can you think of challenges that researchers might face in terms of contributing to policy and practice developments? What steps could they take to address these?

Finally, Konstantoni and Patsianta discuss the importance of adopting intersectionality as an approach not only in practice but also in policy. In particular, intersectionality can enable a questioning of 'who is benefiting and who is excluded from policy goals, agendas and priorities' (Konstantoni and Patsianta 2019: 153). Lombardo and Verloo (2009), drawing on Ferree (2009), warn of:

> policies that, by privileging the treatment of some inequities and ignoring the fact that inequalities are often mutually constitutive, end up marginalizing some people, reproducing power mechanisms among groups, and failing to address the creation of categories that are at the root of the constitution of inequities. (Lombardo and Verloo 2009: 479)

The application of intersectionality in itself becomes a political action, as it means to question taken-for-granted power relations in policy approaches and implies a commitment to improving inequitable conditions (Lombardo and Verloo 2009). Within childhood studies, practice and policy there is still a long way to go in order to meaningfully operationalize intersectionality across these different interlinked spheres.

Critical challenge: Operationalizing intersectionality in policy: Children's experiences in schools

A plethora of research has highlighted how children's experiences within schools in many countries are shaped by racialization, gender and social class, impacting on their educational attainment, relationships and emotional wellbeing (e.g. Crawford et al. 2017, Lareau 2011, Phoenix 2021). Educational policies – at institutional, local, national or international level – acknowledge this to different extents.

- In your own geographical context, can you identify educational policies that pay attention to and meaningfully address intersections of children's lives at school?
- How successful are these policies in doing so?
- What aspects of children's positionalities do they foreground or silence?

Children and pregnant people of colour are often excluded from spaces. Hence, I constantly ask early years practitioners and health professionals how they/we are seen. How is a Black autistic non-binary child treated in society? I also continue to ask why mostly white academics' work on 'race' is platformed in the early years across sectors.

Pavithra Sarma, Anti-racism consultant, Researcher and Co-founder of Scottish Anti-Racism Education, UK

Conclusion

This Chapter has brought together the fields of childhood studies and intersectionality, discussed the synergies and tensions between the two fields and what some of the opportunities and challenges are of combining them. The Chapter has introduced the history and definitional debates around intersectionality, alongside a discussion about some of its critiques and contestations. It has put forward a view of intersectionality as both a theoretical and analytical framework, as well as a radical praxis for childhood studies. An intersectional approach brings with it particular implications for epistemological, representational and methodological considerations in childhood studies, shaped by a focus on power, race and complex inequalities. Intersectional childhood studies are closely linked with the fields of children's rights, participation and activism, and are called to contribute to policy and practice. Doing intersectional work requires childhood scholars to carefully examine their own positionality, including their biases or privileges, and how this impacts on their constructions of childhood (and adulthood) and their normative connotations.

Important debates in childhood studies and the social sciences more widely have begun to grapple more seriously with questions of decolonization and epistemic justice, and what these mean for academic fields as well as for children's lives in diverse contexts. Taking an intersectional approach means to consider further how some groups of children are silenced, overlooked and marginalized. A key point of applying intersectionality is the attention to race and processes of racialization, alongside other categories of difference, while analysing children's lived and embodied experiences as situated within broader structural relations. It also means moving beyond a mere recognition of diversity and diverse childhoods (see Commentary Chapter 2) to seeking the transformation of institutions and processes that perpetuate discrimination and oppression (including academic and other sites of knowledge generation). Intersectional approaches focus on dismantling hegemonic whiteness and have at their heart a focus on change and activism.

Childhood studies in turn have much to offer to the wider debates about intersectionality. Ongoing debates about childhood activism, participation and children's agency can contribute to thinking about different ways of how individuals and collectives can effect change and what the barriers are. Childhood studies particular focus on age brings to intersectionality a focus on intergenerational relations and solidarity and allows the expansion of the application of intersectionality in different fields.

References

Anderson, L. (2017), 'Epistemic Injustice and the Philosophy of Race', in I. J. Kidd, J. Medina, and G. Pohlhaus Jr (eds), *The Routledge Handbook of Epistemic Injustice*, 139–48, London: Taylor & Francis.

Anthias, F. and Yuval-Davis, N. (1983), 'Contextualising Feminism – Gender, Ethnic and Class Divisions', *Feminist Review*, 15 (1): 62–75.

Anthias, F. and Yuval-Davis, N. (1992), *Racialised Boundaries – Race, Nation, Gender, Colour and Class and the Anti-Racist Struggle*, London: Routledge.

Beal, F. M. (1969), *Double Jeopardy: To Be Female and Black*, Manifesto. Available online: http://www.hartford-hwp.com/archives/45a/196.html (accessed 9 March 2020).

Bilge, S. (2013), 'Intersectionality Undone', *Du Bois Review*, 10 (2): 405.

Blaisdell, C. (2019), 'Participatory Work with Young Children: The Trouble and Transformation of Age-Based Hierarchies', *Children's Geographies*, 17 (3): 278–90.

Blaisdell, C., Arnott, L., Wall, K., and Robinson, C. (2019), 'Look Who's Talking: Using Creative, Playful Arts-based Methods in Research with Young Children', *Journal of Early Childhood Research*, 17 (1): 14–31.

Bosco, F. J. (2010), 'Play, Work or Activism? Broadening the Connections Between Political and Children's Geographies', *Children's Geographies*, 8 (4): 381–90.

Brah, A. and Phoenix, A. (2004), 'Ain't I a Woman? Revisiting Intersectionality', *Journal of International Women Studies*, 5: 75–86.

Burman, E. (2008), *Deconstructing Developmental Psychology*, New York: Routledge.

Burman, E. (2012), 'Deconstructing Neoliberal Childhood: Towards a Feminist Antipsychological Approach', *Childhood*, 19 (4): 423–38.

Burman, E. (2013), 'Conceptual Resources for Questioning 'Child as Educator', *Studies in Philosophy and Education*, 32 (3): 229–43.

Burman, E. (2018), 'Brexit, "Child as Method", and the Pedagogy of Failure: How Discourses of Childhood Structure the Resistance of Racist Discourse to Analysis', *Review of Education, Pedagogy, and Cultural Studies*, 40 (2): 119–43.

Burman, E. (2020), 'Child as Method', in D. Cook (ed.), *The Sage Encyclopedia of Children and Childhood Studies*, Vol. 1, 205–6, London: SAGE Publications, Inc.

Cade Bambara, T. (ed.) (1970), *The Black Woman: An Anthology*, New York: Washington Square Press.

Cannella, G. (2004), *Childhood and Postcolonization: Power, Education, and Contemporary Practice*, New York: Routledge.

Chen, K. H. (2010), *Asia as Method: Towards Deimperialization*, Durham, NC: Duke University Press.

Cho, S., Crenshaw, K. W., and McCall, L. (2013), 'Toward a Field of Intersectionality Studies: Theory, Applications, and Praxis', *Signs: Journal of Women in Culture and Society*, 38 (4): 785–810.

Christensen, P. and James A. ,(eds) (2008), *Research with Children: Perspectives and Practices*, London and New York: Routledge.

Christoffersen, A. (2018), 'Researching Intersectionality: Ethical Issues, Ethics and Social Welfare', *Ethics and Social Welfare*, 12 (4): 414–21.

Crawford, C., Macmillan, L., and Vignoles, A. (2017), 'When and Why Do Initially High-achieving Poor Children Fall Behind?', *Oxford Review of Education*, 43 (1): 88–108.

Crenshaw, K. (1989), 'Demarginalizing the Intersection of Race and Sex: A Black Feminist Critique of Antidiscrimination Doctrine, Feminist Theory and Antiracist Politics', *University of Chicago Legal Forum*, 1989 (1): Article 8.

Cuevas-Parra, P. and Tisdall, E. K. M. (2019), 'Child-Led Research: Questioning Knowledge', *Social Science*, 8 (2): 44.

Davis, K. (2008), 'Intersectionality as Buzzword: A Sociology of Science Perspective on What Makes a Feminist Theory Successful', *Feminist Theory*, 9 (1): 67–85.

De Sousa Santos, B. (2007), *Cognitive Justice in a Global World Prudent Knowledges for a Decent Life*, Plymouth: Lexington Books.

Doucet, A. (2008), '"From Her Side of the Gossamer Wall(s)": Reflexivity and Relational Knowing', *Qualitative Sociology*, 31 (1): 73–87. doi:10.1007/s11133-007-9090-9.

Eddo-Lodge, R. (2018), *Why I'm No Longer Talking to White People About Race*, London: Bloomsbury Publishing.

Emejulu, A. (2011), 'Re-Theorizing Feminist Community Development: Towards A Radical Democratic Citizenship', *Community Development Journal*, 46: 378–90.

Emejulu, A. (2013), 'Intersectionality: A Short Introduction', Paper presented at the Scottish universities insight institute seminar series 2013–2014, Children's Rights, Social Justice and Social Identities in Scotland: Intersections in Research, Policy and Practice, Seminar 1: Intersecting Childhood Identities, Inequalities and Rights: Unpacking concepts and exploring implications, Glasgow, 2 December.

Evans, R. and Holt, L. (2011), 'Diverse Spaces of Childhood and Youth: Gender and Other Socio-cultural Differences', *Children's Geographies*, 9 (3–4): 277–84.

Ferree, M. M. (2009), 'Inequality, Intersectionality and the Politics of Discourse: Framing Feminist Alliances', in E. Lombardo, P. Meier, and M. Verloo (eds), *The Discursive Politics of Gender Equality: Stretching, Bending and Policy-making*, 86–104, London: Routledge.

Fricker, M. (2007), *Epistemic Injustice: Power and the Ethics of Knowing*, Oxford: Oxford University Press.

Gallacher, L. A. and Gallagher, M. (2008), 'Methodological Immaturity in Childhood Research? Thinking Through Participatory Methods', *Childhood*, 15 (4): 499–516.

Gallagher, M. (2009), 'Data Collection And Analysis', in E. K. M.Tisdall , J. Davis , and M.Gallagher (eds), *Researching with Children & Young People. Research Design, Methods And Analysis*, 65–127, London: Sage.

Government of Ireland, Department of Children, Equality, Disability, Integration and Youth (2021), 'National Framework for Children and Young People's Participation in Decision-making'. Available online: https://hubnanog.ie/wp-content/uploads/2021/04/5587-Child-Participation-Framework_report_LR_FINAL_Rev.pdf (accessed 30 June 2021).

Hill Collins, P. (2009), *Black Feminist Thought: Knowledge, Consciousness and the Politics of Empowerment*, New York: Routledge.

Hill Collins, P. (2019), *Intersectionality as Critical Social Theory*, Durham, NC: Duke University Press.

Hill Collins, P. and Bilge, S. (2016), *Intersectionality*, Cambridge and Malden, MA: Polity Press.

Houghton, C. (2018), 'Voice, Agency, Power: A Framework for Young Survivors' Participation in National Domestic Abuse Policy-making', in S. Holt, C. Øverlien, and J. Devaney (eds), *Responding to Domestic Violence: Emerging Challenges for Policy, Practice and Research in Europe*, 1st edn, 77–96, London and Philadelphia: Jessica Kingsley Publishers.

James, A. and Prout, A. (eds) (1997), *Constructing And Reconstructing Childhood. Contemporary Issues in the Sociological Study of Childhood*, 2nd edn, London and Philadelphia: Routledge/Falmer.

Knudsen, S. (2006), 'Intersectionality – A Theoretical Inspiration in the Analysis of Minority Cultures and Identities in Textbooks', in E. Bruillard, B. Aamotsbakken, S. Knudsen, and M. Horsley (eds), *Caught in the Web or Lost in the Textbook?*, 61–76, Iartem: Int. Association for Research on Textbooks and Educational Media.

Konstantoni, K. (2020), 'Intersectionality', in D. Cook (ed.), *The Sage Encyclopedia of Children and Childhood Studies*, Vol. 1, 999–1001, Los Angeles, CA: SAGE Publications, Inc.

Konstantoni, K. (2022), 'Radical Democratic Citizenship at the Edge of Life: Young Children, Cafés and Intergenerational and Intersectional Activism', *Identities*, 29 (1): 80–7, doi:10.1080/1070289X.2021.2017591.

Konstantoni, K. and Emejulu, A. (2017), 'When Intersectionality Met Childhood Studies: The Dilemmas of a Travelling Concept', *Children's Geographies*, 15 (1): 6–22.

Konstantoni, K., Kustatscher, M., and Emejulu, A. (2017), 'Travelling with Intersectionality Across Time, Place and Space', *Children's Geographies*, 15 (1): 1–5.

Konstantoni, K. and Patsianta, K. (2019), 'Young Children's Rights in 'Tough' Times: Towards an Intersectional Children's Rights Policy Agenda in Greece and Scotland', in J. Murray, B. B. Swadener, and K. Smith (eds), *Routledge International Handbook of Young Children's Rights*, 145–57, London: Routledge.

Kustatscher, M. (2016), 'The Emotional Geographies of Belonging: Children's Intersectional Identities in Primary School', *Children's Geographies*, 15 (1): 1–15.

Kustatscher, M., Calderon, E., Tisdall, E. K. M., Evanko, T., and Gomez Serna, J. M. (forthcoming 2022), 'Decolonizing Participatory Methods with Children and Young People in International Research Collaborations: Reflections from a Participatory Arts-based Project with Afrocolombian and Indigenous Young People in Colombia', in M. Moncrieffe (ed.), *Decolonising Curriculum Knowledge: International Perspectives, Interdisciplinary Approaches*, 13–27, London: Palgrave MacMillan.

Kustatscher, M., Konstantoni, K., and Emejulu, A. (2015), 'Hybridity, Hyphens and Intersectionality-Relational Understandings of Children and Young People's Social Identities', in S. Punch and R. Vanderbeck (eds), *Families, Intergenerationality, and Peer Group Relations, Geographies of Children and Young People*, Vol. 5, 1–19, Singapore: Springer.

Lareau, A. (2011), *Unequal Childhoods*, Berkeley: University of California Press.

Lewis, G. (2013), 'Unsafe Travel: Experiencing Intersectionality and Feminist Displacements', *Signs: Journal of Women in Culture and Society*, 38 (4): 869–92.

Lombardo, E. and Verloo, M. (2009), 'Institutionalizing Intersectionality in the European Union?', *International Feminist Journal of Politics*, 11 (4): 478–95.

Lundy, L. (2007), 'Voice' Is Not Enough: Conceptualising Article 12 of the United Nations Convention on the Rights of the Child', *British Educational Research Journal*, 33 (6): 927–42.

Mandell, N. (1988), 'The Least-adult Role in Studying Children', *Journal of Contemporary Ethnography*, 16 (4): 433–67.

Mannion, G. (2007), 'Going Spatial, Going Relational: Why Listening to Children and Children's Participation Needs Reframing', *Discourse: Studies In The Cultural Politics Of Education*, 28: 405–20.

Mayall, B. (2002), *Towards a Sociology for Childhood: Thinking from Children's Lives*, London: Open University Press.

McCall, L. (2005), 'The Complexity of Intersectionality', *Signs: Journal of Women in Culture and Society*, 30 (3): 1771–800.

McGregor, C., and Christie, B. (2021), 'Towards Climate Justice Education: Views from Activists and Educators in Scotland', *Environmental Education Research*, 27 (5): 652–68.

Mills, C. (2007), 'White Ignorance', in S. Sullivan and N. Tuana (eds), *Race and Epistemologies of Ignorance*, 11–38, Albany, NY: State University of New York Press.

Morrow, V. and Connolly, P. (eds) (2006), 'Special Issue: Gender and Ethnicity in Children's Everyday Lives', *Children and Society*, 20 (2): 87–91.

Nolas, S.-M. (2015), 'Children's Participation, Childhood Publics and Social Change: A Review', *Children and Society*, 29 (2): 157–67.

O'Neill Gutierrez, C. and Hopkins, P. (2015), 'Introduction: Young People, Gender and Intersectionality', *Gender, Place and Culture*, 22 (3): 383–9.

Pacini-Ketchabaw, V. and TaylorA., (eds) (2015), *Unsettling the Colonial Places and Spaces of Early Childhood Education*, New York: Routledge.

Pérez, M. S. (2017), 'Black Feminist Thought in Early Childhood Studies: (Re) Centering Marginalized Feminist Perspectives', in K. Smith, K. Alexander, and S. Campbell (eds), *Feminism(s) in Early Childhood. Perspectives on Children and Young People*, Vol. 4, 49–62, Singapore: Springer.

Pérez, M. S. and Saavedra, C. M. (2017), 'A Call for Onto-Epistemological Diversity in Early Childhood Education and Care: Centering Global South Conceptualizations of Childhood/s', *Review of Research in Education*, 41 (1): 1–29.

Pérez, M. S., Saavedra, C. M., and Habashi, J. (2017), 'Rethinking Global North Onto-epistemologies in Childhood Studies', *Global Studies of Childhood*, 7 (2): 79–83.

Phoenix, A. (2021), 'What Did You Learn in School Today? Young People and Negotiations of Racialised Intersections', recorded webinar organized by RACE.ED, University of Edinburgh. Available online: https://www.race.ed.ac.uk/recorded-events/.

Punch, S. (2020), 'Why Have Generational Orderings Been Marginalised in the Social Sciences Including Childhood Studies?', *Children's Geographies*, 18 (2): 128–40.

Rodó-de-Zárate, M. (2017), '*Who Else* Are They? Conceptualizing Intersectionality for Childhood and Youth Research', *Children's Geographies*, 15 (1): 23–35.

Rollock, N. (2012), 'Unspoken Rules of Engagement: Navigating Racial Microaggressions in the Academic Terrain', *International Journal of Qualitative Studies in Education*, 25 (5): 517–32.

Rosen, R. (2017), 'Play as Activism? Early Childhood and (inter)generational Politics', *Contemporary Social Science*, 12 (1–2): 110–22.

Saad, L. (2020), *Me and White Supremacy: How to Recognise Your Privilege, Combat Racism and Change the World*, Naperville, IL: Sourcebooks.

Savyasaachi and Butler U. M. ,(2014), 'Decolonising the Notion of Participation of Children and Young People', in E. K. M. Tisdall A. M., Gadda, and U. M.Butler (eds), *Children and Young People's Participation and Its Transformative Potential: Learning from Across Countries*, 44–60, London: Springer.

Shier, H. (2001), 'Pathways to Participation: Openings, Opportunities and Obligations', *Children & Society*, 15 (2): 107–17.

Spyrou, S. (2016), 'Researching Children's Silences: Exploring the Fullness of Voice in Childhood Research', *Childhood*, 23 (1): 7–21.

Taft, J. K. (2019), 'Continually Redefining Protagonismo: The Peruvian Movement of Working Children and Political Change, 1976–2015', *Latin American Perspectives*, 46 (5): 90–110.

Terre des Hommes (n.d.), *#CovidUnder19 Campaign*. Available online: https://www.tdh.ch/en/projects/covidunder19 (accessed 15 October 2021).

Thorne, B. (2004), 'Theorising Age and Other Differences', *Childhood*, 11 (4): 403–8.

Tisdall, E. K. M. (2018), 'Applying Human Rights to Children's Participation in Research', in M. Twomey and C. Carroll (eds), *Seen and Heard: An Interdisciplinary Exploration of Researching Children's Participation, Engagement and Voice*, 17–38, Oxford: Peter Lang.

Tisdall, E. K. M. and Cuevas-Parra, P. (2020), 'Challenges for Children's Participation: Child Activism for Ending Child Marriage', *Children and Youth Services Review*, 108, 104568. Available online: https://www.sciencedirect.com/science/article/pii/S0190740919304712.

Tisdall, E. K. M. and Cuevas-Parra, P. (2021), 'Beyond the Familiar Challenges for Children and Young People's Participation Rights: The Potential of Activism', *The International Journal of Human Rights*, 26 (5): 792–810.

Tisdall, K., Davis, J. M., and Gallagher, M. (2008), *Researching with Children and Young People: Research Design, Methods and Analysis*, London: Sage.

Tomlinson, B. (2013), 'To Tell the Truth and Not Get Trapped: Desire, Distance, and Intersectionality at the Scene of Argument', *Signs: Journal of Women in Culture and Society*, 38 (4): 993–1017.

Tomlinson, B. (2017), 'Category Anxiety and the Invisible White Woman: Managing Intersectionality at the Scene of Argument', *Feminist Theory*, 19 (2): 145–64.

Twum-Danso Imoh, A., Bourdillon, M., and Meichsner, S. (2019), *Global Childhoods Beyond the North-South Divide*, 1st edn, Cham: Springer International Publishing; Imprint: Palgrave Macmillan.

Varga, D. (2011), 'LOOK - NORMAL: The Colonized Child of Developmental Science', *History of Psychology*, 14: 137–57.

von Benzon, N. and Wilkinson C., (eds) (2019), *Intersectionality and Difference in Childhood and Youth: Global Perspectives*, 1st edn, London: Routledge.

Walker, K., Myers-Bowman, K. S., and Myers-Walls, J. A. (2008), 'Supporting Young Children's Efforts Toward Peacemaking: Recommendations for Early Childhood Educators', *Early Childhood Education Journal*, 35 (4): 377–82.

Wright, C. (2010), 'Othering Difference: Framing Identities and Representation in Black Children's Schooling in the British Context', *Irish Educational Studies*, 29: 305–20.

Young Lives Research Study (n.d.), 'The Young Lives Study'. Available online: https://www.younglives.org.uk (accessed 15 October 2021).

Yuval-Davis, N. (2006), 'Intersectionality and Feminist Politics', *European Journal of Women's Studies*, 13: 193–209.

Commentary on Intersectional Perspectives on Childhood

Erica Burman

Intersectionality theories and practices both complement and contribute to **childhood studies** and practices of working with children, as Konstantoni and Kustatscher indicate. In this Commentary, I will elaborate on some key points raised in their accessible and wide-ranging account. In addition, I extend some of their analysis to suggest some mutual tensions and challenges ahead of us in childhood studies in putting intersectionality to work.

Positionality

A key point made by Konstantoni and Kustatscher throughout their Chapter is that **intersectional** approaches in general (notwithstanding their varieties) bring to the fore the importance of attending to one's own, and others', **positionality**. In a **childhood** research and practice context, this has, of course, typically been addressed in terms of trying to take account of how most of what we know about children and childhood – both in general and in relation to specific children – comes from adults with or even without consultation with children themselves. Clearly, **generational orders** have structured, and largely continue to structure, theories and understandings about children and childhood. Intersectional approaches complicate that adult–child binary in various ways. Alongside this adult–child, intergenerational power relation, in any specific context, many other axes of power and position come into play, including those structured around **gender**, racialized and classed positions, ablebodiedness and more. What marks intersectionality approaches as different from others that seek to attend to these diverse features is that they are not treated as additive but rather as situationally relevant and relational categories, whose relevance is organized and specified by particular, contingent situations.

This attention to specificity of context, as well as the co-constitution and interrelational status of the categories at play at any particular moment, disrupts the **hegemony** of any single axis of power in favour of showing how these cross-cut and inter-relate. In terms of childhood studies and practices, this enables more nuanced analysis of when and how questions of childhood status come into play and how and why they matter.

A telling example is the well-known scene in Fanon's (2008) book *Black Skin, White Masks* of the white boychild who hails Fanon with 'Look, a Negro!', that is, as a Black (man) who is also thereby rendered an object of fear. In his powerful account, this traumatically installs for Fanon, the now blackened subject, the panoply of meanings and subjective affects of **racialization**. These include activation of the memory of the history of slavery, of being rendered inferior, uncivilized, dangerous. Importantly, it also institutes an alienation, not only of the subject from the (dominant) social order but between the subject and their own body. Fanon offers a powerful, passionate evocation of the psychic, as well as social, impact of being dehumanized on the basis of his skin colour in 1950s France. What is interesting, for our purposes here, is that it is a child who is portrayed as exercising this impact. While Fanon's account maintains ambiguity about whether the child is a cypher for societal perceptions and practices in making his racist utterances (and he also includes an account of the ensuing conversation with the child's mother), he nevertheless accords the child agentic capacity to make such impact on him. In other words, child status, notwithstanding dominant societal motifs around childhood innocence or lack of responsibility (that doubtless Fanon was aware of and sometimes mobilized elsewhere, Burman 2017), was not sufficient to mitigate, or allow Fanon to dismiss, the insult and trauma of everyday interpersonal racism. The point here is not that racism 'trumps', or functions as a primary power relation over, others. Rather this example helps us see how the child's racialized privilege – and corresponding assumed and enacted sense of entitlement – at and for that moment, transcended other possible configurations of positions, including those structured around generational, gendered and classed positionings, although I have suggested that these do somewhat come into play in how Fanon subsequently navigates his way through this situation (Burman 2019).

As well as complicating understanding of children's and adults' positions and relationships, intersectional analyses therefore also offer practical analytical ways forward to consider when and how children may be enabled to be more agentic and with what effects. Equally, they prompt consideration of which children are able, and might be less able, to access those possibilities as also how desirable it is that they should. (This might also help us understand why and how children, like adults, may identify with oppressor positions and so have implications for **anti-racist** pedagogies.) At any rate, what intersectional debates bring to the fore is how we cannot presume *in advance of any particular enactment or relational context* which positions and axes of power relations will constellate or make salient.

Commonalities

As Konstantoni and Kustatscher clarify, there remain many unresolved discussions within intersectionality theory and practice. As they also highlight, intersectionality is best thought of as an approach, or way of thinking, that is put to work; that is, it only makes sense when applied to particular examples or contexts (as also indicated earlier). One particularly invidious debate within the intersectionality literature that connects with childhood studies is whether it concerns structure or experience. This is a particularly vexing or redundant binary since, in any materially sensitive constructionist model, experience is produced by, and moderated through, structures. Nevertheless, just as childhood studies aims to attend to and generate good accounts of children's experiences, so also we cannot access or interpret these outside of various structural relationships, including of course those that lie beyond, but intersect with, the adult–child axis. As usually a subordinate party in most institutional as well as interpersonal interactions, children are typically highly aware of, and skilled at, engaging with and navigating these. Hence, structure enters and informs experience, as well as constraining and producing the context for that experience.

Another commonality between childhood studies and intersectional approaches is the question of whether these are only analytical frameworks or carry further implications for practice. It has already been suggested that intersectionality only makes sense in the context of practice (as in the landmark successful legal case that prompted Crenshaw's, 1990, analysis demonstrating that Black women's positions as employees were distinct from – and structurally disadvantaged in relation to – both Black men's and white women's). Clearly, intersectionality's origins in Black feminist activism align with a politicized childhood studies that aims to go beyond analysing children's positions and generational orders, to doing something about challenging disadvantage, discrimination and marginalization. Quite what that politics is remains open. Nevertheless, there are clear parallels between debates in feminist research around attending to the gendered (and racialized, classed and heteronormative) structure of dominant forms and relations of **knowledge production**, and childhood studies critiques of adult-centric approaches and models. There is perhaps scope for further mutual learning between the two domains.

The role of race and gender

One key issue within intersectionality debates worthy of reflection upon here concerns the centrality (or otherwise) of **'race'**. In one sense, perhaps as a reflection of both the influence of and the 'mainstreaming' of intersectionality, it has become widely adopted as a tool for designing and analysing socially attuned research (Winker and Degele 2011). Since intersectional approaches apply everywhere and to everyone, there is a risk that its original focus on and from racially marginalized positionings could be displaced. This might appear to pose something of a double bind for white, privileged researchers whose anti-racist feminist commitments lead them to practice intersectional approaches. Yet what this invites us to recall is how its origins lie in Black feminist activist practices and that the approach must also in some sense remain shaped by that particular focus, even if it can be extended more generally. Without re-installing two-factor (race and gender) or three-factor (race, gender, class) sociological analyses, clearly any work that claims to be intersectional without attending to the role of gendered and racialized positions and relationships should be considered suspect. On the other hand, notwithstanding the ways capitalist imperialisms and colonialisms instituted racism as a global phenomenon, along with the hierarchy of 'development' that also aligned children with the colonized, what 'race' and racialization mean and their particular impacts and effects is also different in different places (Lutz 2014). It is important to attend to how topologies of racialization in Europe work differently from in the United States, as also very differently in the **global South** from the North.

There are some interesting parallels for childhood studies, whose knowledge base is formulated from the **global North** and by theorists and practitioners who have benefited from racialized (and often gendered) privilege. The activist Black feminist commitments of intersectionality theory and practice should invite childhood researchers and practitioners, including children's rights advocates, to reconsider the partialities not only of their own personal and institutional positioning but also of the **epistemological** basis, or knowledge base, on which they draw. Childhood studies, like other **disciplines**, is now very engaged with exploring and understanding children's lives outside the global hegemonic dominant childhood of the global North, documenting diversities and specificities of children's positions, lives and livelihoods. It is also involved with **decolonization** as a theory and practice that extends from our objects or topics of study to us as subjects. Alongside generating practices that position children as knowledge-producers and experts on the conditions of their lives, and attending to the different ways those child-related positions are moderated and mediated (or traversed) by other social significant axes and identities, we need also to practice intersectionality in our conduct and constitution of childhood studies, including the gendered, classed, racialized and regional positions of those considered its 'experts'.

This point also invites reflection on the tense relationship between feminist and childhood studies. This tension has, of course, a material historical basis in the ways in which women's oppression was (and often still is) linked to their childbearing and childcaring positions, such that women were aligned with and even treated as children legally and politically. If the 'woman and children' position led to an understandable need for some feminists to see as a key feature of feminist struggle the need to separate women's and children's interests (even as others asserted their inextricability), an attention to colonial **discourse** and practice shows how the oppressed, chattel status of both women and children within the emerging bourgeois nuclear family was both articulated alongside and worked explicitly to legitimize colonial domination. Heteropatriarchal paternalism of the 'benign' rule of the father over his wife and children was the template for colonial rule. In both cases, the natural basis of this rule was warranted by the mutual, that is, the presumed natural subordinate status of women, children and the colonized (McClintock 2013). Equally, Stoler's (2004, 2010) vivid analyses of the colonial archive of the Dutch East Indies highlight not only how colonial practices **deconstructed** as well as reconstructed the patriarchal bourgeois family but also how children – and in particular the mixed heritage status of many of those children – gave rise to anticolonial resistance even by the colonizers themselves. Such examples indicate how and why we need to think intersectionally in childhood studies, as elsewhere.

Particular challenges/asymmetries of/with childhood

While intersectional debates may usefully inform childhood studies theory and practices, childhood studies may also illuminate some wider presumptions and issues for intersectionality and other social research practices. One key feature is that childhood, unlike most other categorizations, is explicitly formulated as not only a relational but also a temporary category. Children by definition are constituted as not-yet-adult and as becoming-adult. This could be a challenge for more structural-oriented intersectional practice, but on the other hand it invites us, in all such analyses, to be more attentive to the ways categories and identities are shifting and fluid as well as situationally dependent. (Disability studies perhaps is a key aligned intellectual partner for childhood studies on this point.)

Konstantoni and Kustatscher generously, and in my view correctly, propose **child as method** as an intersectional frame that engages the mutual relationship and contributions of childhood studies to wider social and political theories and practices. We need to understand childhood intersectionally, and geopolitically, which means integrating childhood studies with – and insisting on its constitutive importance to – wider decolonial and transformative theory and practice.

References

Anthias, F. (2013), 'Intersectional What? Social Divisions, Intersectionality and Levels of ANALYSIS', *Ethnicities*, 13 (1): 3–19.

Burman, E. (2017), 'Fanon's Other Children: Psychopolitical and Pedagogical Implications', *Race Ethnicity and Education*, 20 (1): 42–56.

Burman, E. (2019), *Fanon, Education, Action: Child as Method*, London: Routledge.

Crenshaw, K. (1990), 'Mapping the Margins: Intersectionality, Identity Politics, and Violence Against Women of Color', *Stanford Law Review* 43: 1241.

Fanon, F. (2008), *Black Skin, White Masks*, Grove Press.

Lutz, H. (2014), 'Intersectionality: Assembling and Disassembling the Roads', in S. Vertovec (ed), *Routledge International Handbook of Diversity Studies*, 381–8, London: Routledge.

McClintock, A. (2013), *Imperial Leather: Race, Gender, and Sexuality in the Colonial Contest*, Routledge.

Stoler, A. L. (2004), 'Affective States', in D. Nugent and J. Vincent (eds), *A Companion to the Anthropology of Politics*, 4–20, Maldern, MA, Oxford, Carlton, VIC: Blackwell.

Stoler, A. L. (2010), *Carnal Knowledge and Imperial Power: Race and the Intimate in Colonial Rule*, University of California Press.

Winker, G. and Degele, N. (2011). 'Intersectionality as Multi-Level Analysis: Dealing with Social Inequality', *European Journal of Women's Studies*, 18 (1): 51–66.

6

Childhood Studies in Practice

M. Catherine Maternowska and

Deborah Fry

Introduction

This Chapter is meant to inspire students, demonstrating how the constructs of **childhood studies** can be applied in real-world settings to create positive change for children in both policy and practice and how practice can also challenge the field of childhood studies. An applied childhood studies approach can serve practitioners as well – in schools, in social welfare and in the allied health sciences – by offering space to reflect for professionals who work on the front line of child services.

Informed by theory largely from childhood studies, this Chapter takes a grounded approach to a technically complex and politically sensitive issue: ending **violence against children**. It recognizes childhood studies as an important source for learning and draws from other Chapters addressing the fundamentals of **childhood**, children's rights and **intersectionality**. It is also a functional example of 'where childhood studies meets other **disciplines'** given the **interdisciplinarity** required for a complex issue like violence prevention. Conducting academic research with **child protection** practitioners – placing practice-based knowledge alongside research-based knowledge – unveils the complexity of children's lives. When these findings are then translated into action designed to improve policy and practice, it becomes clear that, too often, prevention and response services, under the guise of a highly structured and professionalized child protection workforce, may not be delivering what children really need.

While there are some exceptions, child protection systems continue to face significant challenges around protecting children from violence, exploitation, abuse and neglect. Rates of physical, sexual and emotional violence remain stubbornly high and affect the lives of up to one billion children, with long-lasting and costly emotional, social and economic consequences (World Health Organization 2020). Drawing on examples from a multi-country study on the **drivers** of violence, this Chapter demonstrates how simplistic approaches to 'best practice' prevention and response services for children are questioned using public health data that is immersed in context. As a result, assumptions about the **universality** of childhood are interrogated and analysis becomes infused with meaning shaped by historical, political, economic and cultural contexts. Bringing concepts from childhood studies into the dialogue and debate with engaged policymakers helped national stakeholders navigate and interrogate assumptions made about what children experience. The study approach and its outcomes moved violence prevention practitioners away from simplistic, even dogmatic, models on how best to protect children to more nuanced, nationally driven interpretations of what drives violence and how to respond. The process introduced increasing complexity to the challenge of violence prevention, but at the same time offered more clarity around the potential for engaged multi-sectoral solutions. In the end, the research approach actively reversed the 'top-down' policies, strategies and programming into an agenda that prioritized national perspectives putting children's rights at the centre of the discussion.

The child and the child protection system

Across time and disciplines some of society's greatest thinkers have wrestled with the notion of childhood: what it is, when it starts, how it evolves and when it ends. In Chapter 2 of this book Tisdall asks the same: What is childhood? Her review of the foundations of childhood studies takes the reader through the rich history of how concepts of the child have evolved from 'demonic' to 'angelic' and from the child as a singular subject of psychological study to children as members of complex ecological systems where the environment, with all its relationships, affects how children grow and develop (Bronfenbrenner 1979).

'**Maltreatment**' – or violence against children including physical, sexual, emotional abuse and neglect – has occurred throughout history and across **cultures** (Mause 1994). The earliest legal forms of protecting children evolved in tandem with the Enlightenment's framing of the 'innocent child' (see Chapter 2; Jabeen 2013). Most of these efforts were situated in the **global North**. According to Finkelhor (1984), it was not until the twentieth century when two big social trends moved to create more formal protections. First, a large group of specialized professionals – nurses, social workers, schoolteachers and counsellors, legal advocates and family counsellors – took on the task of protecting children. Second, as women gained more freedom in their personal lives and more power in the workplace, they felt more empowered to advocate for children. Since then, the history of child abuse and child protection has been well documented in the global North. By the mid-twentieth century, distinct, professionally staffed child protection services with expertise in the assessment and treatment for cases of violence against children were well-established.

The evolution of the field of child protection has been influenced by scholars of childhood studies, most notably by defining childhood as a distinct social and developmental phase in the life course. In turn, this justified the development and introduction of policies aimed specifically at the particular and distinct needs of children as a social group (Elder 1998). Children were increasingly seen as not only needing but also deserving special measures to protect them from adversities (Metzler et al. 2017). Initially and largely in the global North, the focus was on physical abuse (often characterized as the 'battered baby syndrome') but over time, the focus of concern over the maltreatment of children has subsequently broadened to include emotional abuse, neglect and sexual abuse (Crane 2018).

The adoption of the **United Nations Convention on the Rights of the Child (UNCRC)** in 1989 acknowledged the more recent history of child abuse and protection, and notably in the **global South**. The UNCRC obligations coupled with the increase in data gave rise to an increased interest, in both practical interventions and research, in child protection. Accommodating these obligations, child protection systems are now considered essential and are typically designated as government-run services designed to protect children and **young people** while encouraging family stability. UNICEF, one of the key agencies behind the adoption and implementation of child protection as a field of practice, defines a 'child protection system' as:

> the set of laws, policies, regulations and services needed across all social sectors – especially social welfare, education, health, security and justice – to support prevention and response to protection-related risks. (United Nations Economic and Social Council 2008)

But child protection as a field of practice – and the systems that have been constructed to support children – is riddled with challenges. Critiques of childhood studies 'dominated by the perspectives of white men and scholars from the global North' hold similarly true for the field of child protection (also see Love 2002). One study examining the state of child protection systems in West Africa, for example, concluded that the systems reflect a 'preponderance of top-down policies, strategies and programmes into services that target specific groups of children, with an agenda and priorities largely influenced by the outside' (Child Frontiers 2011: IV).

The 'system' remains in question. At the Reconstructing Children's Rights Institute at Columbia University – an online institute about dismantling racism, neo-colonialism and patriarchy in humanitarian and development efforts to protect children and support families – a diverse group of practitioner-researchers are actively reviewing and unpacking the power imbalances inherent in the international development and humanitarian aid industries and, more specifically, the fields of children and youth rights and child protection. The institute engages a host of scholars who have studied – and challenged – ideas around what constitutes the child welfare system in Australia, New Zealand and Canada with Aboriginal, Māori and First Nations populations.

> Over the last few decades, as the international child protection field has developed, it has tended to transport, replicate, and export Anglo-Saxon models of child welfare and statutory services, rooted in structural racism and colonial ideologies, to areas all over the world. One could argue that the humanitarian aid industry has, in essence, exported and replicated models of child protection that are well documented to be racist in their treatment of Black and Brown children. These models are further layered on top of existing colonial structures of the international development and humanitarian aid industry – systems and structures imposed from the outside with an outsiders' lens. (Keshavarzian and Canavera 2021)

Naturally, systems can vary depending on geography, but many countries – particularly those in the global South – have inherited colonial models over the past several decades which have often displaced Indigenous systems of care and protection that are now being modified (Sampson and Daniel 2020). Not surprisingly, in countries around the world, there is a general lack of synergy and coordination between child protection actors, limited cross-sector collaboration with allied systems – notably, health, education, labour and poverty-reduction initiatives – and an absence of human and financial resources to support what the UNCRC demands. While there are exceptions, child protection systems overall face significant challenges protecting children from violence, exploitation, abuse and neglect.

Approaches to violence against children: Synergies with childhood studies

Globally, violence prevention research and implementation practice has grown substantially in the past two decades, fuelled largely by Article 19 of the UNCRC that provides an expanded definition for protection of children both in and out of the home and from all forms of violence, exploitation, abuse and neglect. The UNCRC situates child's rights, **wellbeing**, health and development as aspects of child protection (Bennet et al. 2009). The **Sustainable Development Goals** 2030 Agenda has upped the ante with a specific target to end all forms of violence against children (16.2). Abuse, neglect and exploitation of children are also mainstreamed across several other targets. The demand for data and evidence is huge: violence against children remains one of the world's most intractable challenges. Child protection workers, in the global North and South, are traditionally expected to correctly determine if a child is subject to maltreatment, to determine the severity of the abuse or neglect, the risk of future maltreatment and to develop effective means to ensure a child's safety. And yet, a major challenge is the availability of up-to-date, accurate and relevant information and data – all critical to coordinating, planning and strategic thinking for actors in the child protection sector.

In response to these challenges, governments have recognized that child protection response services in isolation (attempting to address violence after the fact) cannot provide adequate support to families (or communities) nor is it likely to reduce the risk of the occurrence or recurrence of child abuse and neglect. Over time, a public health approach to violence prevention (and reduction) has moved front and centre in the field of child protection. A growing body of statistical evidence documents children's widespread exposure to all forms of violence – in the home, school, and community and online (Cappa and Petrowski 2020). This shift, from monitoring single high-risk individuals to surveillance through a population-based approach, has significantly shifted the field of child protection. Previously siloed sectoral responses (e.g. through education, or health, or law enforcement) have increasingly moved towards a public health approach that monitors the scale, magnitude and trends against which coordinated, multi-sectoral programming can be measured. The Violence Against Children and Youth Surveys, initiated by the Centers for Disease Control, are government-led nationally representative surveys that measure the prevalence of sexual, physical and emotional violence in childhood, adolescence and young adulthood; these surveys have been at the forefront of this data-driven effort (Nace et al. 2021). Survey data measuring the magnitude, nature and consequences of violence has rapidly accelerated worldwide, thanks to committed coalitions of scientists, donors and policymakers. Alongside this is a growing body of evidence-based interventions that demonstrate that violence can be prevented. Global guidelines called INSPIRE, comprises seven evidence-supported strategies designed to help countries and communities to eliminate violence against children. Its implementation and an indicator handbook are recognized as the 'go to' resource for governments, bilateral aid agencies, other UN agencies and civil society organizations that are committed to ending violence against children (World Health Organization n.d.).

The challenge of translating global guidelines focused on implementing best practice violence prevention interventions is significant. Global inequalities between high-income countries and low- and middle-income countries exist in both **knowledge production** and exchange. Stakeholders in the global South face many pressing challenges given their lack of resources and voice. Technical and financial issues aside, values and practices shaped by the global North contribute to this imbalance.

Often policymakers charged with ensuring that child protection systems function work in under-resourced ministries or agencies. Without understanding why violence is happening and what can be done about it, policymakers feel disempowered to move prevention to the top of the national agenda for children (Hyman et al. 2016). At the level of the practitioners, typically, interventions will focus on one element of violence prevention or one type of intervention – such as a campaign to end corporal punishment or a parenting programme to reduce violence in the household, without fully understanding who the campaign or intervention is aimed at or how change is expected to take place. In many cases the theory of change or action underlying the intervention is underdeveloped – due to a lack of data and evidence. For effective prevention the whole of the system must be engaged: the upstream work to build political will for change as well as the downstream (frontline) work within different sectors – social work, education, health care and justice (World Health Organization 2016).

The evolution of child protection research: From simplicity to complexity

Central to the research questions on what causes violence against children is the work of ecological systems thinking. As Chapter 3 illustrates, **Bronfenbrenner's ecological systems theory** works across levels of the environment and originally focused on the microsystem, the meso system, the exosystem, the macrosystem and the chronosystem. The theory demonstrates how the interaction between the child, their immediate family/community environment and society impacts and steers the child's development. Changes in any one 'system' can affect the rest of the child's ecosystem.

Critical challenge: Thinking about the Brofenbrenner model and your research

In groups or individually, read Brofenbrenner's original work on the **socio-ecological system** model; (Brofenbrenner 1979) and some of the critiques (Elliot and Davis 2018 Houston 2017).

What factors or groups would you consider falling within each of Brofenbrenner's ecological systems (e.g. the microsystem, the meso system, the exosystem, the macrosystem and the chronosystem?)

Critics of Bronfenbrenner's theory cite a lack of fidelity in adaptations to the original theory as well as key elements being under-theorized such as connections with the natural world, power, **agency** and structure (Elliot and Davis 2018; Houston 2017). Adaptations to the framework in the field of violence prevention, however, have been impressive. It has been used by scholars and practitioners studying violence against women (Fulu and Miedema 2015; Heise 1998; Tekkas and Betrus 2020), by scholars studying violence against children (Khuzwayo and Taylor 2018; Pells et al. 2018) as well as by leading agencies such as the CDC to guide prevention efforts (Centers for Disease Control and Prevention n.d.). When applied in specific contexts, as will be demonstrated in the next section, the framework begins to account for how national and local politics influence the strength of violence prevention policy and practice. This **integrated approach** – one that considers the child's ecosystem more holistically – exposes the power of macro forces on the individual, demonstrating how **gender** and economic inequalities drive children's outcomes.

Tackling big concepts around **decolonization, structural inequities** and power – key themes in childhood studies – requires wrestling with who owns and who interprets data. The human-centred design and applied approach, described here, yielded national processes for data analysis and understandings of violence. Rather than (see Chapter 3) relying on an over emphasis on rigid socio-biological explanations of the child (e.g. deficit models of childhood including an over reliance on risk analysis) it places violence prevention and response within a more complex and dynamic construction of childhood. The process generated, in real time, a host of outcomes during the life of the study. As a result, national policymakers – the adults charged to protect children – were able to activate theory to improve policy and practice around violence prevention. Key to the success of this study approach – now reproduced in over twenty countries – has been it is working with, rather than trying to simplify or control, complexity.

Data that drives change: The multi-country study on the drivers of violence

Efforts to quantify and qualify violence through data and research have been powerful in the last twenty years. Increasingly, countries are developing baseline understandings of how much violence happens, where it occurs and its impacts on the health and well-being of children and youth in the field of violence prevention worldwide (Nace et al. 2021). In turn, the data has rallied significant political visibility to the problem, reflected in Sustainable Development Goal 16.2 to end abuse, exploitation, trafficking and all forms of violence and torture against children. And yet, uptake has been challenging. Bridging the gap between technical data teams and decision-makers, the *Multi- Country Study on the Drivers of Violence Affecting Children* – conducted in Italy, Vietnam, Peru and Zimbabwe – sought to disentangle the complex and often interrelated underlying causes of violence affecting children (VAC) in these four countries (Maternowska et al. 2018). A deliberate focus on the end-users for this study – national stakeholders – helped formulate context-appropriate understandings of the data leading, ownership of the challenges and engagement in the solutions.

Led by the Chapter authors with national study partners, the study was conducted by local research teams comprised of government, practitioners and academic researchers in each of the four countries. The study used an iterative approach which put national ownership and co-creation at its core. Reclaiming data sovereignty, secondary data analysis of existing surveys was conducted in-country by government statistics (Maternowska and Fry 2018).

Each national team used a common process involving three separate components, all of which build on existing data and research: a systematic literature review of academic and 'grey' literature (such as research reports), including both quality quantitative and qualitative research, secondary analyses of nationally representative data sets and an initial mapping of the interventions landscape. Analysed together, exploring the physical, emotional and sexual violence affecting children within each national context, these sources of information helped build initial hypotheses around what drives violence in each country. Facilitating and prioritizing national meaning-making through dialogue and joint data analysis and synthesis was key (Boyden et al. 2018). Working across and with multiple disciplines can open new perspectives and insights and is much needed in times of complex global problems.

Two key frameworks, both widely discussed in childhood studies, were applied to the analysis in this study: (1) a version of the socio-ecological model, which helps to understand the dynamic relationships between factors at the micro-, meso- and macro-levels, and (2) an age and gender framework, which recognizes that a child's **vulnerability** and ability to protect themselves from violence changes over time with their evolving capacities. Guided by findings from the four countries, the study importantly highlighted the dynamic and constantly changing and/or overlapping domains of what Bronfenbrenner called the 'chronosystem' that shapes violence in children's lives.

A child-centred socio-ecological model

The study approach was novel for the field; it built on the public health lens of understanding the **risk and protective factors** for violence affecting children – that is, the factors that reflect the likelihood of violence occurring due to characteristics most often measured at the individual, interpersonal and community levels (Maternowska and Potts 2017). Risk and protective factors alone, however, do not explain why violence is happening in any given society. Understanding the drivers of violence – those factors at the institutional and structural levels that create the conditions in which violence is more or less likely to occur – begins to explain the effects of broader structural forces or political factors that may fuel interpersonal violence (Maternowska et al. 2018). The approach brings a political economy lens to the field (see Hart and Boyden 2018).

Applying the socio-ecological framework paints the wider contextual picture of drivers and risk factors, how they intersect and interact. What I found particularly interesting was that presumed protective factors such as school can also be risk factors due to drivers such as national policies that encourage corporal punishment and lack of protection policies in institutions.

Charlotte Leonard-Wakefield, Student, 'Foundation of International Child Protection Course', University of Edinburgh

We analysed 'what' types of violence were occurring and where gaps in knowledge existed. We noted 'where' violence was happening and how violence in one setting might be reinforced in another. We also asked 'who' is involved in both perpetuating the problem and creating the solution. We used the socio-ecological framework as a critical tool to understand how factors that influence a child's likelihood of experiencing interpersonal violence interacts within and between several social and ecological levels (Vu 2016). The diagram here illustrates these various socio-ecological levels of influence adapted for use within the study (Brofenbrenner 1979; Heise 1998).

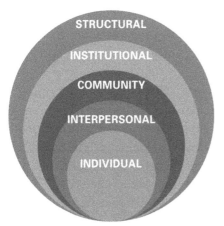

Structural: The macro-level political, economic and social policy environments.

Institutional: Formal organizations, institutions and services governed by a set of rules, policies or protocols expected to determine how things function.

Community: Social capital or networks influenced by particular opinions, beliefs and norms that may affect interpersonal relationships including in informal institutions and places of social gathering.

Interpersonal: The immediate context of violence and situational interactions between individuals, involving household, family or intimate or acquaintance relationships.

Individual: Personal history and individual developmental factors that shape response to interpersonal and community stressors.

Figure 6.1 The socio-ecological framework. *Source*: Maternowska and Potts 2017, copyright United Nations Children's Fund (UNICEF). This material (and all diagrams used in this Chapter) is available free of charge on the UNICEF Office of Research – Innocenti website: https://www.unicefirc.org/publications/991-drivers-of-violence-national-research.html.

National teams analysis and the study were practically focused on the pressing need to translate data into action. To address this, we proposed action-oriented ways to make violence visible by plotting examples from our secondary analysis of data sets, directly onto the socio-ecological framework (Pells et al. 2018). In each country we mapped our findings onto the framework to clarify what kinds of violence were happening and where potential points of intervention might be (LeHong et al. 2018). In the process, the dynamic relationships between factors at the micro-, meso- and macro-levels were made clear. Bringing the lens of childhood studies – a field of research that is generally small scale and qualitative – to large scale, population-based studies enhanced the interpretation of the data.

> As a student, the child-centred socio-ecological model empowered me to engage deeply and to look beyond drivers of violence at face value. Although the levels for examination are prescribed, this enhances your opportunity to flex criticality: preventing an obscuring of factors hitherto overlooked, recognizing a network of influences across interlocking levels and questioning which perpetrators have greater power at one level and not another, and *why*.
>   Morgan Tudor, Student, 'Foundation of International Child Protection Course', University of Edinburgh, UK

In the process of making meaning across the four countries, the socio-ecological framework shifted from a seemingly hierarchal representation of the levels (as it is traditionally presented) to one in which levels interact better representing the dynamic nature of children's lives (Maternowska et al. 2018). Our findings support the idea that no single level or domain within the socio-ecological model – and no single factors (drivers or risk factors) within or between those domains – determines or explains an act of interpersonal violence involving a child (Izumi and Baggo Rasmussen 2018). Instead, each factor, when combined with one or more other factors, may lead to a situation where a person perpetrates violence against a child. Further, when seeking to categorize various factors as 'risk' or 'protective' or institutional or structural they may be de-linked from the context in which they occur (either within the initial analysis or when results are synthesized at regional or global levels) (Boyden et al. 2018). The integrated framework helps connect these linkages.

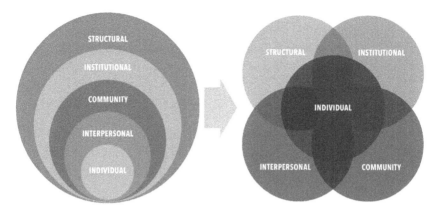

Figure 6.2 A child-centred and integrated framework for violence prevention. *Source*: Maternowska and Potts 2017, copyright United Nations Children's Fund (UNICEF).

This shift to a more integrated framework is an important contribution to childhood studies and practice. It squarely addresses what Tisdall notes in Chapter 2 (citing Wyness) that children are largely excluded from the economic realm and that their poverty is often hidden and unaddressed within households. The integrated framework makes clear that a driver of violence, such as poverty at the structural level, is not as distal as represented in the traditional socio-ecological model. Numerous other issues at the macro level, including, for example, economic and social policies that inadvertently increase poverty, inequality and migration, can have adverse effects on children – though children are rarely part of the calculus (Ames et al. 2018). Effectively applied, the framework can build inter-ministerial and cross-sectoral accountability, ensuring that legislature, policy and practice are child-centric.

When developing the integrated framework, we applied our backgrounds as researcher-practitioners who have seen first-hand the impact on children when actors from across these different levels fail to work together. In my work responding to violence against women and children in humanitarian settings, structural issues such as migration were often recognized yet disconnected from the everyday work of case workers and counsellors. The integrated framework makes visible how these larger forces impact children, their families and support systems. For

example, bringing practitioners, policymakers and researchers together to map risk and protective factors across these domains can bring
to light how the institutions tasked with support for refugees may be
failing to serve children of different ages and genders, and what
actions at the institutional as well as community level can support this
to change.

*Alina Potts, Research Scientist, The Global Women's Institute at the
George Washington University, United States*

Locating children at the centre of a myriad of levels or domains – both in terms of protective and risk factors as well as drivers – addresses the potential of their agency spatially, temporally and materially across a variety of settings (Oswell 2012). The relevance of children's position is more pronounced than ever with the added dimension of the online environment. Because most children today spend a great deal of time on social networking platforms or online games, perpetrators have new ways to contact children to groom or abuse them directly. In the advent of COVID-19, these risks have further increased (Lobe et al 2020). The framing of children's capacities to speak and act in different contexts, nearly two decades ago (see Landsdown 2005), is equally relevant for understanding the impact of the internet in childhood. Oswell foresaw children's capacities as 'networked, assembled or infrastructured with other persons and things in such ways as to endow them with powers, which they alone could neither hold nor use' (Oswell 2012: 3–8). Indeed, analysing children's social relations in terms of technologies and devices adds to debates in childhood studies around agency.

Commentators often focus on the associated risks of technology for children rather than focusing on how children can benefit from access to the internet as an opening into rich sources of knowledge and education. However, social media and computer games have the potential to enhance children's social spaces where they can fluidly form and sustain relationships, experiment with their social identities and engage in what Wilson (2016) calls an 'economy of dignity'. Recognizing that in children's worlds, technology and social problems interact, the field of global violence prevention is increasingly recognizing the connections between children's online and offline experiences of violence (Jones et al. 2013). The relevance of the integrated framework remains as it highlights the multiplicity and overlapping nature of issues requiring attention to make a child's world safe (Kardefelt-Winther and Maternowska 2020).

Critical challenge: Drivers versus risk and protective factors

In groups or individually, discuss the following:

- What are the main differences between risk and protective factors and drivers of violence?
- Why do you think this terminology makes a difference for policy and practice?

Applying the integrated framework: Vietnam

Drawing on a case study in Vietnam, the integrated framework highlights how children (rather than 'the individual' with a list of identified risk or protective factors) interact, interface and overlap with a variety of drivers and risk and protective factors – emphasizing the need for both protection and agency at once. In doing this, Vietnamese children move front and centre, so that they are represented more accurately as **social actors** poised to take part in the construction of childhood and how ultimately adults respond to these dynamic constructions (Konstantoni 2012; Prout and James 1997; Tisdall and Punch 2012).

Findings around physical violence in Vietnam indicate multiple reasons why corporal punishment is so widespread and illustrates the range of factors – macro to micro – that shape corporal punishment practice. Mapping data in this way shows the potential for more effective coordination and systems building, suggesting which stakeholders within or between domains need to be engaged. Too often social workers, for example, sit at the interface of the child, the interpersonal and the community and subsequently carry a heavy work burden across several domains. When plotted with data, the integrated framework makes clear where parents, as well as health, education, social welfare and law enforcement practitioners and their institutions, can and should play a part in children's wellbeing (Le Hong et al. 2018).

Finally, the framework is practice-friendly and can inform which prevention and response services can be most effective. It allows for national stakeholders to critically appraise potential interventions using global guidance while also

Child Centred and Integrated Framework for Violence Prevention:
Violent Discipline in the Home, Viet Nam

- Physical violence as a means of discipline is rooted in patriarchal values

- Parent's and teacher's own experiences of corporal punishment contributes to their view of its effectiveness as a form of discipline
- Boys are more likely than girls to experience violent discipline

- Children who are violent at school or more likely to be physically abused at home
- Alcohol is a risk factor for violence in the home

STRUCTURAL   INSTITUTIONAL

CHILD

INTERPERSONAL   COMMUNITY

- Confucianism and prescribed gender norms contributes to physical punishment in the home
- Weak legislation does not adequately prohibit corporal punishment
- Violence from teachers is one of the reasons students drop out of school

- Adults (teachers) remain silent about bullying to maintain authority
- Violence is viewed as a family matter
- Children from rural areas are more likely to be physically punished
- Beliefs about masculinity contribute to intergenerational violence

Figure 6.3 Applying the framework in Vietnam. *Source*: Maternowska and Potts 2017, copyright United Nations Children's Fund (UNICEF).

considering how to adapt interventions so that they are context-appropriate (Maternowska et al. 2018). When plotted against the child-centred and integrated framework for violence prevention, findings for Vietnam suggest that parenting programmes – a typical child protection response – is only one facet of a very entrenched issue. An intervention to reduce violent discipline in Vietnamese homes would require a series of simultaneous interventions at the level of the drivers and at the level of risk factors that engage stakeholders from multiple ministries in the government such as Education, Labour, Invalids and Social Affairs (official translation), including the Department of Gender Equality, the Children's Directorate and the Department of Social Evils Prevention (Le Hong et al. 2018). Each of these stakeholders plays a significant role in addressing the issue of violent discipline in the home. Good interventions are likely to require *both* an evidence base and cultural specificity.

We fully acknowledge that this framework is not new – it was used to explain human development by Bronfenbrenner (1979) and later was used to elucidate the complex issue of child abuse (Belsky 1980), sexual coercion (Heise et al. 1995) and domestic violence (Heise 1998). But describing an approach for systematically mapping existing qualitative and quantitative data is indeed innovative, especially when paired with discussions around structural and institutional violence, bringing the constructs of childhood studies into everyday practice.

Activity: The Integrated Child-Centred Framework

Applying the Integrated Child-Centred Framework helps build a holistic understanding of a particular child protection challenge.

Consider where you grew up – recall the town and community where you spent most of your childhood – and choose one type of violence (physical, emotional or sexual). While the framework relies on data, in this exercise, consider facts as you understood them and then plot them. At each level, draw on your experiences of childhood.

Facilitators note for group work: You may want to draw up the circles of the Integrated Child-Centred Framework (see Figure 6.2) on a large sheet of paper and have participants using sticky notes to write some answers to each level and place them on the diagram.

- Individual: What were the characteristics that typically defined more vulnerable children? What were the characteristics that defined more protected children?
- Interpersonal: In terms of a child's relationship to other adults (think: caretakers, parents, teachers, law enforcement, etc.) what were the relationships tended to be high risk for children in your community?
- Community: What were the community issues that shaped your childhood – that might have made you feel at risk for violence? What were the gender norms in your community?
- Institutional: Can you think of the institutions (and if possible the policies) that affected children in your community (think: education, health, police, justice)? Overall, did these institutions protect or put children at increased risk of violence? How?
- Structural: What were the big macro forces that were defining your childhood? For example: Was there an economic recession that created stress in your household? Were you required to migrate or move due to financial or other stressors? What were the defining gender norms of the day nationally that created inequalities?

Childhood as dynamic: Age, gender and power

The second critical childhood concept employed by the study addresses age and gender and how boys and girls grow and change as they move through childhood and into adolescence. Considering age and gender in childhood touches on several strands of childhood studies. Qvortrup and colleagues (1994) suggest that conceptually childhood can be considered a universal, structural phenomenon (see Chapter 2). In other words, all societies have a generational space marked out for children which is different from that of adults, albeit how that space is experienced by children themselves might differ markedly in different societies. Within this space, the principle of evolving capacities was first recognized in the UNCRC and then later championed by Lansdown (2005) with more specificity, recognizing that a child's vulnerability and ability to protect themselves change along with their evolving capacities over time (Lansdown 2005). This groundbreaking study, still relevant today, brings up critical questions about what levels of protection children are entitled to in recognition of their childhood. It also questions the impact of the cultural context, parental or community support and the role that children themselves play in their own protection. These are critical questions in childhood studies and proved important in our study of violence against children.

What is called 'generational space' or 'evolving capacities', in the field of public health, is more commonly referred to as the child's developmental life course. Working with practitioners we first established that while there is no global standard for categorizing children and young people's stages of life, and indeed that these can vary culturally, certain stages from pre-adolescence to young adulthood are predictable, based on biology and physiology alone. Too often, violence prevention theories and frameworks – and importantly practice – fail to consider the extraordinary implications of age and its nexus with socially ascribed gender roles based on biological sex. The disaggregation of data by both age and sex is critical for understanding the changing effects that violence can have on children in a variety of settings. As children grow, their capacities and vulnerabilities evolve and change – and these can vary widely across different cultural settings.

Learning more about the timing, nature and consequence of key transitions experienced by young adolescents and when these transitions

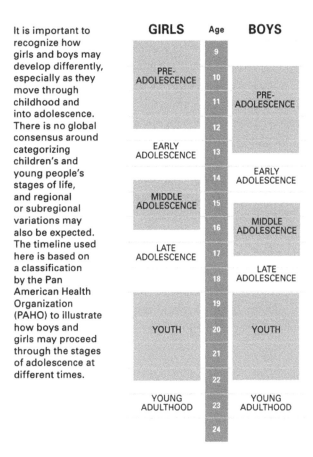

It is important to recognize how girls and boys may develop differently, especially as they move through childhood and into adolescence. There is no global consensus around categorizing children's and young people's stages of life, and regional or subregional variations may also be expected. The timeline used here is based on a classification by the Pan American Health Organization (PAHO) to illustrate how boys and girls may proceed through the stages of adolescence at different times.

Figure 6.4 Age and gender – Stages of adolescence (PAHO) classification. *Source*: Maternowska and Potts 2017, copyright United Nations Children's Fund (UNICEF).

typically occur in the life course is the grid upon which effective violence prevention should be built. It is important to acknowledge, however, that gender- and age-disaggregation of data is only the first step. Data and analysis of the power differentials or underlying causes for these differences are also needed. Using both a mix of quantitative and qualitative data and analysis provided insights into what the differences are and why those differences exist. To enhance the analysis, we drew on an intersectional approach to show how children, at the centre of this framework, are indeed multidimensional social beings – by their age and gender as well as other factors, including **race**, **ethnicity**, socio-economic class, family situation and other individual characteristics (see Chapter 5). Konstantoni et al. (2017) show how young children's social identities in relation to social class, gender and ethnicity can reveal ways that exclusion and inequality permeate childhood. Here again, childhood studies sheds light on what could be otherwise misinterpreted as simply a biological or physiological fact.

Gender roles are learned, changeable over time and, as previously noted, variable within and between cultures. Plotting data across the age and gendered lifecycle makes these changes visible over time, identifying who is most affected including the importance of same-sex groups, gender norms and inequalities, all issues that are well-documented in childhood studies (Blaise 2005). Intersectionality proposes that the basic aspects of one's identity – such as age and gender – need to be examined as simultaneously interacting with each other and affecting one's status or perception in society. Using a feminist lens enriches the analysis and places it within a broader understanding of power (UNICEF 2016). Understanding gender, gender relations and the power dynamics behind them is a prerequisite for understanding children's access to and distribution of resources, their ability to make decisions for themselves and importantly how boys and girls are affected by political processes and social development (MacNaughton 2000, 2006).

Critical challenge: Reflecting on age, gender and advocacy

Pick a specific advocacy issue (e.g. violence prevention, climate change, political activism) in a specific country/location and discuss the following questions:

- What are the age and gender implications for the advocacy issue including:
- How does the issue affect different ages or genders differently? How does the advocacy engage these groups in defining the problem and finding a solution?
- What can be changed to make solutions more **inclusive**?
- How do age and gender considerations impact on participation in political processes in your specific context? How do they impact on engagement in advocacy around this issue?

Our understanding of violence reinforces that individual and interpersonal risk and/or protective factors – for example, a child's ethnicity or disability or their relationship with the caretakers and other adults upon which they are dependent – need to be considered holistically with the lifespan in mind. In most public health analyses, factors that define a child are measured in relation to risk and largely from a biological perspective of age and gender (see Kustatscher 2015: 36). However, it is not always clear in what stage(s) in a boy's or girl's development this risk is most pronounced and when it may reduce – or what influences these changes. As children grow and change there are multilayered pressures in their lives that they must confront, particularly as expectations of who they are also change. As former Special Representative of the Secretary-General on Violence against Children (SRSG) Marta Santos Pais (in Lansdown 2005: vii) notes, 'childhood is not an undifferentiated period'. In the same vein, how violence affects the seventeen-year-old boy versus a six-month-old male infant will have very different individual and societal consequences. The role of power circumscribes this process and can shift in both positive and negative ways as a child gains capacity.

Activity: The Age, Gender, and Power Framework

Create a linear timeline of age from birth to the older adolescent.

Do some light research online to see if there are studies on violence against children in the country where you are currently residing.

Do a rapid assessment of these by reviewing each study you find and creating a document that lists that name of the study and (a) the age of the study population and (b) the type of violence the study was examining.

Plot these findings along your age and gender timeline and see if you can find patterns. Some of these patterns will be due to gaps in research: for example, you may find a cluster of studies focused on eleven- to fourteen-year-olds and not other ages, that's ok. Your goal here is to look for patterns.

- Did the studies pick up disaggregated gender differences?
- Compare results for boys and girls. Why do you think these differences exist?

By comparing boys' and girls' experiences of violence in four different countries, we know that gender inequality can be a marker of status which impacts on how children are treated (Maternowska et al. 2018). The predictive value of age and gender as risk and/or protective factors changes depending on a child's stage of development, social context and other circumstances. Some factors emerge during childhood or even earlier, whereas others do not appear until adolescence. Some become less important as a person matures, while others can persist throughout the lifespan. Some involve the family while others may involve members in the neighbourhood. The school and/or the peer group can also have considerable influence. One of the many important contributions made by childhood studies to understanding children and childhood comes from research into the social worlds that children construct with their peers (Rubin et al. 1998). Peer groups can be based on gender and around gender role expectations: in the global South this often reflects the different forms of economic activity that children are expected to engage in by the time they reach adolescence.

In our analysis gender was analysed as binary. In retrospect, we fully recognize that gender binarism can reinforce institutionalized structures of power and that children who may identify outside of traditional gender binaries often experience discrimination and harassment. Increasingly, evidence in the United States (Brown and Herman 2015) and in low- and middle-income countries (Kiss et al. 2020) demonstrates that LGBTQ+ youth and adults are much more likely to be victims of violence, and this violence can be repetitive, leading to re-victimization. This kind of evidence is a strong call for improved and inclusive analysis across the gender spectrum to ensure the design and delivery of gender-sensitive and, when needed, gender-specific approaches for interventions of all survivors of violence.

Key concept: What is the difference between sex and gender?

Review the Tolland and Evans (2019) article, which explores definitions related to sex and gender as they are explored for the UK national census which are aligned with World Health Organization definitions.

'Sex' and 'gender' are terms that are often used interchangeably, but they are two different concepts.

Sex can be defined as

- referring to the biological aspects of an individual as determined by their anatomy, which is produced by their chromosomes, hormones and their interactions

- generally male or female

- something that is assigned at birth. (Tolland and Evans 2019: 1)

Gender can be defined as

- a social construction relating to behaviours and attributes based on labels of masculinity and femininity; gender identity is a personal, internal perception of oneself and so the gender category someone identifies with may not match the sex they were assigned at birth

- where an individual may see themselves as a man, a woman, as having no gender, or as having a non-binary gender – where people identify as somewhere on a spectrum between man and woman. (Tolland and Evans 2019: 1)

Gender identity: A personal feeling of one's maleness, femaleness or being somewhere in between is known as gender identity (Young Scot n.d.).

Binary gender: When we talk about binary gender in this Chapter, we are referring to those categories that only include male and female.

Gender spectrum: Gender is increasingly understood as not binary but on a spectrum. Growing numbers of people are identifying as somewhere along a continuum between man and woman, or as non-gendered (neither man nor woman) (Young Scot n.d.). For example, it is anticipated that at least eighty different self-descriptions will be submitted in answer to the question about gender identity in the 2021 UK census (Gender Identity and Research Society 2022).

One criticism of traditional socio-ecological approaches from childhood studies is that, too often, the analysis is adult-driven causing significant power differentials (Taft 2015; Tesar 2016). Because this study was designed largely for policymakers and practitioners, the analysis was indeed adult-driven. However, in two of the four countries children and young people were directly involved. In Zimbabwe, a panel of youth advisors challenged the findings face-to-face with policymakers and programme managers in a lively forum around social norm change. In Vietnam, a children's organization created a study output – a youth-directed video – to promote the study's findings, bringing children's voices directly into the analysis. Moving children to the centre – not just of debate but within the research process itself – is gaining traction in the field (Boyden et al. 2018). In a recently produced resource pack for involving children in research, the authors review three approaches to **children's participation** in research: child-led research, collaborative research and consultative research (Jamieson et al. 2021). They are based on the 'continuum of participation' used by Landsdown and O'Kane (2014) to describe the type of engagement and balance of responsibilities between adult researchers and children and young people. Promoting this work is essential if children are to be more central in both practice and theory that defines their lives; likewise, bringing practice-based knowledge to inform theory is important.

Effective violence prevention hinges on identifying both risk and protective factors and determining when during a child's development they emerge, then recognizing and addressing the contextual issues that may exacerbate (or minimize) linked vulnerabilities, including power. Data disaggregated by age and gender can help visualize these changes while ensuring that the intersectionality of children's experiences is made more humane to reflect their development and their capacities. In the process, childhood in all its diversity becomes a living variable of social analysis. Even more importantly programming needs to be based on children's needs and ultimately their rights. Overlooking the dynamics of age, gender and power keeps interventions apolitical and technocratic, begging for a more intersectional approach across communities and across differences (Hart 2015).

The integrated framework was also informed by Young Lives longitudinal qualitative data and better reflects how children describe their experiences of, and responses to, violence in their everyday lives. In particular, the framework highlights how economic and social inequities related to gender, other forms of discrimination and poverty are embedded in institutional and community contexts giving rise to manifestations of violence. For example, poor children explained how a lack of clothes and school materials resulted in peer bullying as well as physical and emotional violence from teachers. Preventing violence against children, therefore, requires addressing the interconnections between multiple forms of violence as highlighted in this framework, rather than on a single layer (e.g. the interpersonal), as is often the case with such interventions.

Kirrily Pells, Associate Professor of Childhood, Social Research Institute, UCL, UK

Applying the age, gender and power framework: Peru

Drawing on a case study from Peru, data plotted against the age and gender timeline makes visible when (and where) violence affects children. Coupled with an analysis of where drivers and risk and/or protective factors fall against the integrated framework, this timeline helps practitioners identify both data gaps and potential entry points for interventions targeting the right population, at the right time in children's lives and in the right settings (Ames et al. 2018). This kind of analysis also reinforces how gender, much like childhood, is socially constructed and is surrounded by norms and ideologies which determine behaviours and actions of adults and children (Norozi and Moen 2016; Lorber and Farrell 1991; Richardson and May 1999).

In both cases, the Integrated Child-Centred Framework and the age, gender and power framework successfully translated fundamental childhood studies concepts into practical tools for learning and planning. By plotting data onto these tools, the concepts were activated, interrogated and, ultimately, helped policymakers think through the implications of violence prevention implementation.

Using data to translate these important concepts is critical for practitioners as well – such as teachers and social workers. It provides an important space for **reflexivity**, especially among front line providers who are often the first point of contact for vulnerable children. These outcomes of this process are testimony to how a theory applied in a human-centred and pragmatic way can indeed directly improve children's lives. On a national policy level, these include the engagement of government ministries not typically involved in debates around children's wellbeing, as well as contributing to legal reforms and budget reallocations that, in some cases for the first time ever, directed government funding to nationally led violence prevention research (Boyden et al. 2018).

> Participating in the study helped me, as a policymaker, to rethink the importance of generating evidence-based prevention strategies. It also evidenced how important it is to apply the intersectional approach to understand the complexity of VAC. For example, I understood that variables like age, gender and culture have a key role in the drivers of violence against children. Further, the study influenced my decision to study for a PhD to improve my research skills to prevent violence.
>
> *Dr Karina Padilla, Social Policy, Peru*

Age and Gender: Violent Discipline in the Home, Peru

BOYS

	PRE-ADOLESCENCE		EARLY ADOLESCENCE		MIDDLE ADOLESCENCE		LATE ADOLESCENCE	YOUTH				YOUNG ADULTHOOD	

Age | 9 | 10 | 11 | 12 | 13 | 14 | 15 | 16 | 17 | 18 | 19 | 20 | 21 | 22 | 23 | 24

GIRLS

PRE-ADOLESCENCE	EARLY ADOLESCENCE	MIDDLE ADOLESCENCE	LATE ADOLESCENCE	YOUTH	YOUNG ADULTHOOD

Boys say they first experience physical violence **at home** at a younger age than girls.

Boys 9-11 are more likely than girls to say someone who lives with them **at home** had kicked, beaten or punched them.

Boys 12-17 are more likely than girls to say someone they live with **at home** has beaten them up or tried to beat them up with objects like a belt or rope.

Girls 9-11 are more likely than boys to say someone had or tried to attack them with a knife, firearm or weapon **at home.**

Most **girls 10-11** say this is when they first experienced physical violence **at home.**

Girls 12-17 are more likely than boys to say someone who lives **at home** has spanked or slapped them.

Girls 15-17 are more likely to have experienced physical violence **at home,** in the past year, than boys.

Figure 6.5 How age and gender affect vulnerability to violence: An example on children's experiences of violent discipline in Peru. *Source:* Maternowska and Potts 2017, copyright United Nations Children's Fund (UNICEF).

Conclusion

Drawing on case studies from a multi-country study addressing the drivers of violence affecting children, this Chapter demonstrates how concepts from the field of childhood studies can be applied in real-world settings where policymakers and practitioners of child protection are making important decisions around children's safety. Placing interdisciplinary practice-based knowledge alongside research-based knowledge helps close the theory–practice gap, in this case challenging abstract, static notions of childhood. Framing the domains of socio-ecological framework *around* the child and disaggregating data by age and gender *across* the life course opened a space for data and evidence take on national meaning and purpose.

As research practitioners, we framed the study in this Chapter as a traditional **social constructionist** approach, building on aspects of the **'new' sociology of childhood** as argued (in all its complexity) in Chapter 2. Our mixed-methods approach was also decidedly humanistic, acknowledging the diversity of experiences, as we worked with diverse types of professionals and across different national settings. By creating a space for dialogue and debate, notions around globally accepted definitions of violence and the meaning of different data points exploded, forcing us to reconsider our own positions of power and our own assumptions about data and evidence. By challenging data sovereignty, governments felt empowered and, at the same time, became more accountable to children.

Throughout this book, the idea of children's social space is paramount. That space is, as the drivers of violence work clearly demonstrates, defined by law, politics, religion, economics, social class, gender, ethnicity and other factors. At the same time, scholars in the field rightly warn that to have an overly deterministic view of childhood is limiting. Children and their evolving identities are more than the combined effect of such social structural forces. Children constantly also exercise agency: they make deliberate decisions and choices as independent social actors.

Chapter 3 celebrates the interdisciplinary nature of childhood studies. The Chapter highlights the synergies of a more traditional public health approach to prevention and the ways that a life course analysis can be applied to more meaningful understandings of childhood as children grow and mature from infancy through to young adults. Typically, public health **paradigms** offer narrow socio-biological explanations (e.g. age and stage or a risk factor/deficit model of childhood). Using expanded definition of childhood at each stage from infancy to the older adolescent provides useful direction and a grid upon which a more holistic understanding of childhood can be explored. Moving beyond simplistic **dichotomies** between structure and the individual, accounting for a more fluid understanding of 'what causes violence', can create a more enabling environment to produce innovative ideas about prevention, ethics and **social justice** (Corker and Shakespeare 2002).

As both scholars and practitioners in the field of childhood studies would argue, children's vulnerability and their ability to protect themselves from violence change over time with their evolving capacities. In this way, both the fields of public health – as well as theoretical studies of children's rights, gender and intersectionality – can contribute to build a more robust theory. From a practice perspective, the field of child protection and the system in which it is embedded are interdisciplinary. It relies on collaborative interagency working which lends itself to what Burman calls the **'child as method'** approach or centring the category of child across disciplines. The frameworks presented in this Chapter, through collaborative working across sectors, can serve as a starting point for interdisciplinary perspectives for violence prevention (see Chapter 4).

An interdisciplinary practice also highlights how to engage children in research not as bystanders but as active analysts alongside adults. The centrality of children in all aspects of life – including research about them – is prominently featured throughout the field of childhood studies. By blurring disciplinary boundaries and establishing interdisciplinary thinking, childhood study theorists argue that we can better question institutional dynamics, knowledge production and information control as is evidenced through the multi-country study examples in this Chapter (Corker and Shakespeare 2002).

In Chapter 4, the all-important issue of children's rights is explored in detail. The protection of children from all forms of violence is a fundamental right enshrined in the UN Convention on the Rights of the Child. Likewise, the inclusion of a specific target (SDG 16.2) in the 2030 Agenda for Sustainable Development to end all forms of violence against children highlights, on a global platform, a renewed impetus towards the realization of the right of every child to live free from fear, neglect, abuse and exploitation. Several other SDG targets address specific forms of violence and harm towards children, such as child marriage and female genital mutilation (target 5.3), and the eradication of child labour, including the recruitment and use of child soldiers (target 8.7).

The comprehensive approach taken to addressing the drivers of violence, across all child-service sectors – health, police, education and social welfare – presents opportunities to deliver on children's rights so that children themselves are heard and participate in the decision-making processes that affect their lives (Article 12, UNCRC). Documenting how these rights are exercised by children and young people, through research and practice uptake, is an important future consideration (Tisdall and Cuevas-Parra 2021).

Central to childhood studies is understanding and locating intersectionality – where multiple grounds of discrimination operate at the same time – discussed in Chapter 5. Understanding the many and again complex ways in which children are denied the equal enjoyment of their rights and freedoms because of discrimination against them based on their age in combination with gender, ethnicity, disability, national status, economic status and other grounds was an important aspect of the multi-country study. Admittedly, the data analysis around intersectionality in the four countries under study was binary – with an over-focus on boys and girls. Issues of LGBTQI were raised during national analyses but as a data-driven study, there was little, if any, published evidence on this topic. Increasingly, research on non-binary gender identities is gaining traction and, as a result, research practitioners can move this critical issue to the centre of debates on recognizing children's rights and ensuring that prevention and response services meet their needs.

The field of childhood studies, as surveyed across the Chapters of this book, is an exciting and complex interdisciplinary field. *Studying* childhood offers a broad approach to *understanding* childhood, but equally important is the ability to translate these ideas into practical and forward-thinking changes for children in their day-to-day lives. The multi-country study on the drivers of violence, in one small way and through a pragmatic public health research approach, offers some insights on how to build informed political will to protect children, though much more needs to be done to understand how to fully protect children from violence. The child-centred approach helped frame and explain how the all-too frequent experience of violence affecting children is not just a brutal violation of rights against children but in fact a complicated issue that requires the triangulation of data and debate from a variety of child-service fields such as teaching, social work, child and family law, police services and health care. Importantly, the work identifies the importance of different national and regional models for child protection that include the political, cultural and sociological influences that have shaped violence against children (Parton 2020). By moving from simplistic, dichotomous thinking to embracing more complex approaches that include the structural and institutional drivers allows for more holistic approaches to preventing violence against children. As this Chapter has illustrated, no policy or programme is neutral and all approaches need to be reviewed, evaluated, adapted through reflexive processes that consider simultaneously notions of power and agency.

This Chapter and this book offer perspectives on childhood studies which as a discipline has now been shaped by thinkers for several centuries. Today, much like Descartes in the seventeenth century and others who followed, we are still asking: What is childhood? Because the nature of childhood is never static, we may never know the full answer to this age-old question, but by applying a context-driven **multidisciplinary** lens to our work and keeping our approach human-centred, child-centred and fully attuned to national perspectives, we can indeed commit – as researchers and practitioners – to constantly building more relevant theory and practice at the same time.

References

Ames, P., Anderson, J., Martin, A., Rodriguez, R., and Potts, A. (2018), 'The Multi-Country Study on the Drivers of Violence Affecting Children in Peru: The Process and Its Outcomes', *Vulnerable Children and Youth Studies*, 13 (Suppl 1): 52–64.

Belsky, J. (1980), 'Child Maltreatment: An Ecological Integration', *American Psychologist*, 35 (4): 320–35.

Bennett, S., Hart, S. N., and Ann Svevo-Cianci, K. (2009), 'The Need for a General Comment for Article 19 of the UN Convention on the Rights of the Child: Toward Enlightenment and Progress for Child Protection', *Child Abuse Negl.*, 33 (11):783–90.

Blaise, M. (2005), *Playing It Straight: Uncovering Gender Discourses in the Early Childhood Classroom*, New York and London: Routledge.

Boyden, J., Jewkes, R., Ligiero, D., Subrahmanian, R., and Taylor, H. (2018), 'Situating the Drivers of Violence: Building a Global Movement Through National Engagement, Evidence and Action', *Vulnerable Children and Youth Studies*, 13 (Suppl 1): 1–11.

Bronfenbrenner, U. (1979), *The Ecology of Human Development: Experiments by Nature and Design*, Cambridge, MA: Harvard University Press.

Brown, T. N. and Herman, J. (2015), *Intimate Partner Violence and Sexual Abuse Among LGBT People*, eScholarship, University of California.

Cappa, C. and Petrowski, N. (2020), 'Thirty Years After the Adoption of the Convention on the Rights of the Child: Progress and Challenges in Building Statistical Evidence on Violence Against Children', *Child Abuse & Neglect*, 110 (1): 104460.

Centers for Disease Control and Prevention (n.d.), 'Violence Prevention: The Social-Ecological Model'. Available online: https://www.cdc.gov/violenceprevention/about/social-ecologicalmodel.html (accessed 21 May 2022).

Child Frontiers (2011), 'Mapping and Assessing Child Protection Systems in West and Central Africa. A Five-country Analysis Paper', *Child Frontiers Ltd*, June. Available online: https://resourcecentre.savethechildren.net/document/mapping-and-assessing-child-protection-systems-west-and-central-africa-five-country-analysis/ (accessed 24 May 2022).

Corker, M. and Shakespeare T., (eds) (2002), *Disability/Postmodernity: Embodying Disability Theory*, London: Continuum..

Crane, J. (2018), 'Chapter 1, Introduction', in *Child Protection in England, 1960–2000: Expertise, Experience, and Emotion*, Cham, CH: Palgrave Macmillan. Available online: https://www.ncbi.nlm.nih.gov/books/NBK535576/ (accessed 24 March 2023).

Elder, G. H. (1998), 'The Life Course as Developmental Theory', *Child Development*, 69 (1): 1–12.

Elliott, S. and Davis, J. (2018), 'Challenging Taken-for-Granted Ideas in Early Childhood Education: A Critique of Bronfenbrenner's Ecological Systems Theory in the age of Post-humanism', in K. Malone, E. Barratt Hacking, and A. Cutter-Mackenzie (eds), *Research Handbook on Childhood Nature: Assemblages of Childhood and Nature Research, Springer International Handbooks of Education*, 1–36, Cham: Springer.

Finkelhor, D. (1984), *Child Sexual Abuse: New Theory and Research*, New York: Free Press.

Fulu, E. and Miedema, S. (2015), 'Violence Against Women: Globalizing the Integrated Ecological Model', *Violence Against Women*, 21 (12): 1431–55.

Gender Identity and Research Society (2022), 'Terminology'. Available online: https://www.gires.org.uk/resources/terminology/ (accessed 1 June 2022).

Hart, J. (2015), 'The (Anti-)politics of "Child Protection"', *Open Democracy: Beyond Trafficking and Slavery*, 23 July. Available online: https://www.opendemocracy.net/en/beyond-trafficking-and-slavery/antipolitics-of-child-protection/ (accessed 21 May 2022).

Hart, J. and Boyden, J. (2018), 'Childhood (Re)materialized: Bringing Political-Economy into the Field', in S. Spyrou, R. Rosen, and D. T. Cook (eds), *Reimagining Childhood Studies*, 75–91, London: Bloomsbury Academic.

Heise, L. L. (1998), 'Violence Against Women: An Integrated, Ecological Framework', *Violence Against Women*, 4 (3): 262–90.

Heise, L. L., Moore, K., and Toubia, N. (1995), *Sexual Coercion and Reproductive Health: A Focus on Research*, New York: Population Council.

Houston, S. (2017), 'Towards a Critical Ecology of Child Development: Aligning the Theories of Bronfenbrenner and Bourdieu', *Families, Relationships and Societies*, 6 (1): 53–69.

Hyman, I., Vahabi, M., Bailey, A., Patel, S., Guruge, S., Wilson-Mitchell, K., and Wong, J. P. H. (2016), 'Taking Action on Violence Through Research, Policy, and Practice', *Global Health Research and Policy*, 1: 6.

Izumi, N. and Baago Rasmussen, L. (2018), 'The Multi-Country Study on the Drivers of Violence Affecting Children in Zimbabwe: Using a Mixed Methods, Multi-stakeholder Approach to Discover What Drives Violence', *Vulnerable Children and Youth Studies*, 13 (Suppl 1): 65–74.

Jabeen, T. (2013), 'A History of Contemporary Child Protection in the Global South (with a Special Focus on South Asia and Pakistan)', *Journal of the Research Society of Pakistan*, 50 (1): 138–59.

Jamieson, L., Feinstein, C., Kapell, A., and Dulieu, N. (2021), *Working Together: Including Children in Research on Violence Against Children. A Resource Pack for Research Practitioners*. Edinburgh: End Violence Partnership Knowledge Network, End Violence Lab and Save the Children.

Jones, L. M., Mitchell, K. J., and Finkelhor, D. (2013), 'Online Harassment in Context: Trends from Three Youth Internet Safety Surveys (2000, 2005, 2010)', *Psychology of Violence*, 3 (1): 53–69.

Kardefelt-Winther, D. and Maternowska, C. (2020), 'Addressing Violence Against Children Online and Offline', *Nature Human Behaviour*, 4: 227–30.

Keshavarzian, G. and Canavera, M. (2021), 'Conversation #2: Confronting Colonialism, Racism and Patriarchy in Child Welfare and Child Rights Programming', *Reconstructing Children's Rights, Reconstructing Children's Rights Institute, CPC Learning Network / Columbia Mailman School of Public Health*. Available online: http://www.cpcnetwork.org/wp-content/uploads /2021/05/Reconstructing-Childrens-Rights-2_v04.pdf (accessed 21 May 2022).

Khuzwayo, N. and Taylor, M. (2018), 'Exploring the Socio-ecological Levels for Prevention of Sexual Risk Behaviours of the Youth in uMgungundlovu District Municipality, KwaZulu-Natal', *African Journal of Primary Health Care & Family Medicine*, 10 (1): e1–e8.

Kiss, L., Quinlan-Davidson, M., Pasquero, L., Olle Tejero, P., Hogg, C., Theis, J., and Hossain, M. (2020), 'Male and LGBT Survivors of Sexual Violence in Conflict Situations: A Realist Review of Health Interventions in low- and Middle-income Countries', *Conflict and Health*, 14: Article number 11.

Konstantoni, K. (2012), 'Children's Peer Relationships and Social Identities: Exploring Cases of Young Children's Agency and Complex Interdependencies from the Minority World', *Children's Geographies*, 10: 337–46.

Konstantoni, K., Kustatscher, M., and Emejulu, A. (2017), 'Travelling with Intersectionality Across Time, Place and Space', *Children's Geographies*, 15 (1): 1–5.

Kustatscher, M., (2015), *Exploring Young Children's Social Identities: Performing Social Class, Gender and Ethnicity in Primary School*, Edinburgh: The University of Edinburgh.

Lansdown, G. (2005), 'The Evolving Capacities of the Child', *Innocenti Insights*, 11: 1–62. Available online: https://www.unicef-irc.org/publications/384-the -evolving-capacities-of-the-child.html.

Lansdown, G. and O'Kane, C. (2014), *A Toolkit for Monitoring and Evaluating Children's Participation: Introduction. Booklet 1*, London: The Save the Children Fund.

Le Hong, L., Vu Thi, L. T., and Maternowska, M. (2018), 'Applying the Child-centred and Integrated Framework for Violence Prevention: A Case Study on Physical Violence in Viet Nam', *Vulnerable Children and Youth Studies*, 13 (Suppl 1): 36–51.

Lobe, B., Velicu, A., Staksrud, E., Chaudron, S., and Di Gioia, R. (2020), *How Children (10–18) Experienced Online Risks During the Covid-19 Lockdown – Spring 2020*, Luxembourg: Publications Office of the European Union.

Lorber, J. E. and Farrell, S. A. (1991), *The Social Construction of Gender*, Newbury Park: Sage Publications, Inc.

Love, C. (2002), 'Maori Perspectives on Collaboration and Colonization in Contemporary Aotearoa/New Zealand Child and Family Welfare Policies and Practices', Paper presented at the Positive Systems of Child Welfare Conference, Waterloo, ON, June.

Macnaughton, G. (2000), *Rethinking Gender in Early Childhood Education*, London: Paul Chapman Pub.

Macnaughton, G. (2006), *Respect for Diversity: An International Overview: Working Paper 40*, The Hague: Bernard Van Leer Foundation.

Maternowska, M. C. and Fry, D. (2018), 'The Multi-Country Study on the Drivers of Violence Affecting Children: An Overview', *Vulnerable Children and Youth Studies*, 13 (Suppl 1): 12–25.

Maternowska, M. C. and Potts, A. (2017), *The Multi-Country Study on the Drivers of Violence Affecting Children: A Child-centred and Integrated Framework for Violence Prevention*, Florence: UNICEF Office of Research – Innocenti. Available online: https://www.unicef-irc.org/research/pdf/448 -child-centered-brief.pdf.

Maternowska, M. C., Potts, A., Fry, D., and Casey, T. (2018), 'Research That Drives Change: Conceptualizing and Conducting Nationally Led Violence

Prevention Research', Innocenti Research Reports, UNICEF Office of Research – Innocenti, Florence. Available online: https://www.unicefirc.org/publications/991-drivers-of-violence-national-research.html.

Mause, L. D. (1994), 'The History of Child Abuse', *Sexual Addiction & Compulsivity: The Journal of Treatment and Prevention*, 1 (1): 77–91.

Metzler, M., Merrick, M. T., Klevens, J., Ports, K. A., and Ford, D. C. (2017), 'Adverse Childhood Experiences and Life Opportunities: Shifting the Narrative', *Children and Youth Services Review*, 72: 141–9.

Nace, A., Maternowska, C., Fernandez, B., and Cravero, K. (2021), 'The Violence Against Children Surveys (VACS): Using VACS Data to Drive Programmes and Policies', *Global Public Health*, 1–19. Available online: https://www.tandfonline.com/doi/full/10.1080/17441692.2021.2010116.

Norozi, S. A. and Moen, T. (2016), 'Childhood as a Social Construction', *Journal of Educational and Social Research,* 6 (2): 75.

Oswell, D. (2012), 'Introduction', in *The Agency of Children: From Family to Global Human Rights*, 3–8, Cambridge: Cambridge University Press.

Parton, N. (2020), 'Addressing the Relatively Autonomous Relationship Between Child Maltreatment and Child Protection Policies and Practices', *International Journal on Child Maltreatment*, 3: 19–34.

Pells, K., Morrow, V., Maternowska, M. C., and Potts, A. (2018), 'A Socioecological Approach to Children's Experiences of Violence: Evidence from Young Lives', *Vulnerable Children and Youth Studies*, 13 (Suppl 1): 26–35.

Prout, A. and James, A. (1997), 'A New Paradigm for the Sociology of Childhood? Provenance, Promise and Problems', in A. James and A. Prout (eds), *Constructing and Reconstructing Childhood. Contemporary Issues in the Sociological Study of Childhood*, 2nd edn, 6–28, London and Philadelphia: Routledge/Falmer.

Qvortrup, J., Bardy, M., Sgritta, G., and Wintersberger, H. (1994), *Childhood Matters: Social Theory, Practice and Politics*, Avebury: Aldershot.

Richardson, D. and May, H. (1999), 'Deserving Victims?: Sexual Status and the Social Construction of Violence', *The Sociological Review*, 47 (2): 308–31.

Rubin, K. H., Bukowski, W., and Parker, J. G. (1998), 'Peer Interactions, Relationships, and Groups', in W. Damon and N. Eisenberg (eds), *Handbook of Child Psychology: Social, Emotional, and Personality Development*, 619–700, Hoboken, NJ: John Wiley & Sons, Inc.

Sampson, Y. and Daniel, M. (2020), 'Towards a Sustainable NGO Intervention on Child Protection: Taking Indigenous Knowledge Seriously', *Development in Practice*, 31: 2.

Taft, J. K. (2015), '"Adults Talk too Much": Intergenerational Dialogue and Power in the Peruvian Movement of Working Children', *Childhood*, 22 (4): 460–73. https://doi.org/10.1177/0907568214555148.

Tekkas Kerman, K. and Betrus, P. (2020), 'Violence Against Women in Turkey: A Social Ecological Framework of Determinants and Prevention Strategies', *Trauma, Violence, & Abuse*, 21 (3): 510–26.

Tesar, M. (2016), 'Children's Power Relations, Resistance, and Subject Positions', in *Encyclopedia of Educational Philosophy and Theory*, 978–81, New York: Springer.

Tisdall, E. K. M and Cuevas-Parra, P. (2021), 'Beyond the Familiar Challenges for Children and Young People's Participation Rights: The Potential of Activism', *The International Journal of Human Rights*, 26 (5): 792–810.

Tisdall, E. K. M. and Punch, S. (2012), 'Not So 'New'? Looking Critically at Childhood Studies', *Children's Geographies*, 10: 249–64.

Tolland, L and Evans, J. (2019), *What Is the Difference Between Sex and Gender? Exploring the Difference Between Sex and Gender, Looking at Concepts That Are Important to the Sustainable Development Goals*, London: UK Census. Available online: https://www.ons.gov.uk/economy/environmentalaccounts /articles/whatisthedifferencebetweensexandgender/2019-02-21 (accessed 1 June 2022).

UNICEF (2016), 'Children on the Move', 31 August. Available online: https:// www.unicef-irc.org/article/1390-age-gender-and-policymaking-on -migration-what-are-the-links.html (accessed 21 May 2022).

United Nations Economic and Social Council (2008), *UNICEF Child Protection Strategy*, E/ICEF/2008/5/Rev.1, par. 12–13.

Vu, T. T. H. (2016), 'Understanding Children's Experiences of Violence in Viet Nam: Evidence from Young Lives', Innocenti Working Paper 2016–26, Florence: UNICEF Office of Research.

Wilson, S. (2016), 'Digital Technologies, Children and Young People's Relationships and Self-care', *Children's Geographies*, 14 (3): 282–94.

World Health Organization, (2016), *INSPIRE: Seven Strategies for Ending Violence Against Children*, Geneva: World Health Organization.

World Health Organization, (2020), *Global Status Report on Preventing Violence Against Children 2020: Executive Summary*, Geneva: World Health Organization.

World Health Organization, (n.d.), *INSPIRE: Seven Strategies for Ending Violence Against Children*, Geneva: World Health Organization. Available online: https://www.who.int/teams/social-determinants-of-health/violence -prevention/inspire-technical-package (accessed 21 May 2022).

Young Scot (n.d.). *Understanding Gender Identity*. Available online: https:// young.scot/get-informed/national/understanding-gender-identity (accessed 26 May 2022).

Commentary on Childhood Studies in Practice

Amanda Third

The challenge of ending violence against children

Alongside phenomena like climate change, **gender** inequality and poverty, the challenge of ending **violence against children** (VAC) – both online and offline – constitutes one of the 'wicked problems'[1] of our times: it is a highly complex and multifaceted challenge that resists simple solutions.

Despite decades of investment, unwavering commitment and sustained action by hosts of organizations working locally, nationally and internationally, significant gains have been few, very hard won and difficult to evidence and sustain. As Maternowksa and Fry stress, violence prevention efforts struggle to build the political will and the social change mechanisms that are necessary to address the macro social, cultural, economic and political **drivers** of VAC. Consequently, in many countries, children are no better protected from violence than previously; and, in some places, rates of VAC are alarmingly high and, as a consequence of the COVID-19 pandemic, possibly escalating (Bourgault et al. 2021).

Acknowledging the systemic nature of VAC and the need to scale up efforts to combat it, ambitious and powerful coalitions have formed around

Sustainable Development Goal 16.2, which calls for an end to VAC (see End Violence Against Children, n.d.). The international violence prevention community recognizes that future success will be dependent on: catalysing leadership to drive political and financial commitments; building cross-sector partnerships to amplify the impacts of interventions; and coordinating efforts to minimize duplication, use resources efficiently and sustain initiatives over time. But, so too, there is a need: to ground advocacy, prevention and interventions in robust evidence; to monitor progress systematically; and to facilitate knowledge sharing within and between national **child protection** communities of practice (End Violence Against Children, n.d.). That is, high-quality data and evidence are critical to ensuring the success of child protection efforts.

In this volume, Maternowska and Fry engage with the question of how to best enable evidence-based practice and, thereby, strengthen child protection systems. Their Chapter reflects on a project to work closely with those who are in a position to champion or enact change to synthesize and to channel the key insights from qualitative and quantitative research on VAC in four countries into national decision-making processes. They raise an important set of questions about what constitutes robust data and how such data and evidence can be mobilized to advance prevention efforts addressing VAC online and offline.

In doing so, Maternowska and Fry insist on the interconnection of theory and practice. Further, they argue that more theoretically informed fields, such as **childhood studies**, can inform the ways that data are collected and interpreted in so-called 'real world' settings, but also highlight how policy and practitioner interpretations of data can challenge and help to refine, for example, how **childhood** is theorized.

Evidencing VAC

Among other things, Maternowska and Fry call for more and better-quality data and evidence to drive systemic change to prevent VAC. But what kind of data and evidence are needed to level up child protection efforts?

Maternowska and Fry make a case for data and evidence that can be activated in advocacy, policy, programming and professional practice. They argue that enabling 'end-users' – which here refers to representatives of government, practitioners and others with decision-making power or the capacity to lead change at the implementation level – to participate in the collation and analysis of data can prompt powerful evidence-based prevention and response to VAC.

Maternowska and Fry recognize the power of staging opportunities for end-users to grapple with both qualitative and quantitative evidence. While quantitative evidence can map the prevalence of VAC and indicate broad trends shaping incidence and response, qualitative evidence can help to unpack the issues in further detail and to identify ground-level triggers for behaviour change. Both kinds of evidence are important to tackle VAC. But Maternowska and Fry show that in the hands of end-users, qualitative and quantitative evidence are most powerful in combination.

Further, they demonstrate that there is great potential for the smaller-scale, in-depth and highly contextualized work that is characteristic of childhood studies to influence policy, programming and professional practice. But activating this potential is dependent on forging pathways and opportunities for childhood studies to encounter 'the field', and vice versa. Crucially, such encounters should not smooth over the tensions and disjunctures that emerge when more theoretically oriented fields play in the space of **praxis**. Instead, they must 'enable competing perspectives to bump up against one another, colliding, contesting and shaping one another in unexpected and fruitful ways' (Third 2016: 95).

Engaging stakeholders in the generation and interpretation of data and evidence certainly ensures that it 'comes to life' in spaces where change can be enacted. But, in the domain of evidence, what of the idea, which has been so foundational to childhood studies, of the *child as a social agent* (Qvortrup et al. 2009)?

While **child participation** has influenced many areas of child rights-focused policy, practice and programming for some time, it has been relatively slower to infiltrate ways of doing in the field of child protection, not least because the imperative to protect *highly vulnerable children* does not always sit comfortably with the vision of *the agentic child* that drives child participation **discourse**. Children increasingly participate in the co-design of VAC prevention initiatives, yielding some significant success (see, for example, OSRSGVC, 2020). But children are very rarely considered as agents in the systems and processes of evidence generation. Evidence, it would seem, is the dominion of adults.

How might children themselves participate in generating, interpreting and wielding evidence to support the achievement of SDG 16.2? To briefly explore this question, I discuss a project to develop child-centred indicators for violence prevention (CCI project), led by the Young and Resilient Research Centre at Western Sydney, in partnership with the City Social Welfare and Development Office (CSWDO) of the City of Valenzuela (Philippines) and End Violence Against Children. We chose to work in the Philippines because VAC is an entrenched challenge there: three in five Filipino children experience physical and/or psychological violence, and one in four children experiences sexual violence (CPNF and UNICEF Philippines 2017). At the same time, the Philippines has a significant history of evidence-based intervention and prevention, and there is momentum building around a national plan of action (CPNF and UNICEF Philippines 2017).

Child-centred indicators for violence prevention

By way of background to the CCI project, in 2016, ten agencies joined forces to develop the INSPIRE framework to create a step change in prevention and response to VAC internationally (UNICEF 2018a: 22). They developed seven INSPIRE strategies for ending VAC, laid out in an implementation guide, guidance on scaling and adapting the strategies; and an *INSPIRE Indicator Guidance and Results Framework* (IGRF) to foster robust data collection to evidence the impacts of the INSPIRE strategies (UNICEF 2018b).

The IGRF recommends periodically measuring results such as changes in laws and policies, social norms, and professionals' awareness and skills. It privileges quantitative measures and also often recommends evaluating the impacts of the INSPIRE strategies on VAC using proxy measures, such as: partner rates of violence against women; acceptability of wife beating; attitudes about women's right to refuse sex; and women's/girls' empowerment (INSPIRE indicators 1.10; 4.3; 4.4; 7.3 respectively; see UNICEF 2018b).

Recognizing that children's own lived experiences are marginalized within the IGRF, the CCI project set out to develop a complementary set of child-centred indicators. Using an open-innovation process, we ran a series of creative and participatory workshops (fourteen total) separately with fifty-four diverse children[2] and eighty individuals and organizations who support them to generate child-centred definitions and indicators of violence and safety. The process culminated with an intergenerational workshop in which child and adult stakeholders worked together to devise ways of measuring against the child-centred indicators (for a discussion of the methodology, see Third et al. 2020). Through this process, we sought to explore the value of qualitative data that documents children's experiences for the process of monitoring and reporting against the INSPIRE strategies. Further, acknowledging that the INSPIRE strategies target *national* action, we aimed to unpack how the process of developing and implementing child-centred indicators might support effective *localization* of violence prevention efforts.

In workshops, children expressed sophisticated understandings of violence as both a physical and psychological phenomenon that can play out institutionally, in social groups or in interpersonal relationships. Importantly, while they could identify them, children were less likely to highlight structural and institutional drivers of violence. Instead, their narration of violence tended to focus on localized conditions and the relationships they encounter in their everyday lives. Children reported worrying about an array of forms of violence, with their most immediate concerns centring on 'child abuse, theft, murder, kidnapping, bashing, gang violence, domestic violence, violence associated with drugs/alcohol, and discrimination' (Third et al. 2020: 27). Children living in institutional care, on the streets or with disability reported more direct experiences of violence and a heightened sense of fear. Children across the project identified navigating a constant threat of violence in their immediate environments, which makes them feel unsafe, regardless of whether they are at risk of being a direct victim. This included threats to their safety stemming from the pollution of their environments and the intensifying impacts of climate change.

In response to these experiences, children believe all places in their communities should be safe for them. They called, in particular, for institutional responses to VAC – laws, policies, dedicated agencies, programmes and professional support – in their communities. They also noted that strong positive relationships with family, peers and other community members are critical to enhancing their safety.

The workshop series generated a preliminary set of child-centred indicators and measures, which the research team then mapped to the IGRF to ascertain alignment and/or complementarity. This process revealed that the majority of factors that matter to children (86 per cent) aligned with the IGRF at the indicator level, suggesting that the IGRF is measuring against the key themes children identify as important to reducing violence in their everyday lives. However, children's contributions raised a range of new indicators not captured by the IGRF and, perhaps most importantly, highlighted that different measures from those identified in the IGRF are required to evaluate the impact of child protection initiatives on their lived experiences of violence and safety.

The intergenerational, open-innovation approach in this project enabled children to explore their ideas and express their views about how to prevent VAC in their communities, and to realize that, alongside adults, they can take action. Adult stakeholders reported that, through this process, they learned the value of working with children to guide decision-making and to frame up action plans that are aligned to personal and institutional goals, capacities and resources.

Post workshops, the Child Social Welfare Office has drawn on children's insights about the specificities of VAC in the City to localize the INSPIRE strategies and the national plan of action and to develop bespoke initiatives for the City of Valenzuela. So too, they have established a City Data and Evidence Committee to establish routine processes of data collection and analysis, which integrate the child-centred indicators and measures developed in this project, to document the impacts of the City's violence prevention efforts. In doing so, they are attempting to bring a child-centred lens to monitoring and reporting efforts and thereby prioritize direct impacts on children themselves.

There is still much work to be done to refine and to scale up the use of the child-centred indicators and measures generated in the CCI project. However, as with the project elaborated in Maternowska and Fry's Chapter, the CCI project clearly demonstrates the value of translating childhood studies principles and methods into policy, programming and professional practice in the field of child protection.

As Maternowska and Fry point out, impacting the challenge of VAC requires that the global community commits to a long-term and systematic programme of action to address the structural drivers of VAC. Such a process must proceed in a reflexive manner, generating and routinely reflecting on high-quality data to track how specific interventions impact the dynamics of complex systems and to determine how to address emergent needs. The work of generating evidence must engage the full range of stakeholders in the production, analysis and activation of data and evidence, including children themselves. The road ahead is challenging but if we resist the temptation to revert to orthodoxies and make room for the necessary dialogues between theory and practice, between qualitative and quantitative data, and between adults and children, we will surely find ways to support more children to live violence-free while simultaneously advancing the field of knowledge. The value of concept and methods drawn from childhood studies in this trajectory cannot be underestimated.

Notes

1. See Rittel and Webber 1973.
2. Participants included residents of the Bahay Kalinga (temporary accommodation for child survivors of sexual violence: 12 per cent) and the Bahay Pag-asa (short-term residential centre for male children defined as in conflict with the law: 12 per cent), street children (12 per cent) and children living with a disability (12 per cent).

References

Bourgault, S., Peterman, A., and O'Donnell, M. (2021), *Violence Against Women and Children During COVID-19— One Year On and 100 Papers in a Fourth Research Round Up*, Center for Global Development. Available online: https://prevention-collaborative.org/wp-content/uploads/2021/08/CGD_2021_VAWC-Covid-19-Fourth-Research-Round-Up.pdf.

Council for the Welfare of Children (CPNF) and UNICEF Philippines (2017), *Philippine Plan of Action to End Violence against Children (PPAEVAC)*, Manila: Council for the Welfare of Children and UNICEF Philippines.

End Violence Against Children (n.d.). Available online: https://www.end-violence.org (accessed 27 June 2022).

Office of the Special Representative of the Secretary-General on Violence against Children 2020 (OSRSGVC) (2020), *When Children Take the Lead: 10 Child Participation Approaches to Tackle Violence*. Available online: https://violenceagainstchildren.un.org/sites/violenceagainstchildren.un.org/files/documents/publications/10_cases_of_child_participation_report.pdf.

Qvortrup, J., Corsaro, W.A., and Honig, M. (2009), *The Palgrave Handbook of Childhood Studies*. Edited by Basingstoke, Hampshire: Palgrave Macmillan.

Rittel, H. and Webber, M. (1973). 'Dilemmas in a General Theory of Planning', *Policy Sciences*, 4: 155–169.

Third, A. (2016), 'The Tactical Researcher: Rethinking Cultural Studies Research as Pedagogy', in A. Hickey (ed.), *The Pedagogies of Cultural Studies*, 93–115, London and New York: Routledge.

Third, A. et al. (2020), *Child-centred Indicators for Violence Prevention: Summary Report on a Living Lab in the City of Valenzuela, Philippines*, Sydney: Western Sydney University.

UNICEF (2018a), *INSPIRE Handbook: Action for Implementing the Seven Strategies*, Geneva: World Health Organization.

UNICEF (2018b), *INSPIRE Indicator Guidance and Results Framework*, New York: UNICEF.

Wenger, E. (2000), 'Communities of Practice and Social Learning Systems', *Organisation Articles*, 7 (2): 225–46.

7

Conclusion

Using Childhood Studies Concepts to Further Emancipatory Praxis

Laura Weiner and John M. Davis

Introduction

Throughout the book, we have presented **childhood studies** from its broadest theoretical points to its more specific applications in research, policy and **childhood** practice. Across the five main Chapters of the book, common ideas and debates surface around the diverse understandings of childhoods. In this conclusion, we draw together the overarching questions across Chapters and synthesize the key gaps and arguments.

We do so from our standpoint as authors and the intersecting crises impacting children and young people today (Moore et al. 2021). From John's experience as a researcher, teacher and practitioner, we utilize **early childhood** and disability studies examples to unpack the key concepts that may inform your practice going forward. From Laura's experience as a postgraduate student grappling with her PhD research with young activists in informal learning spaces, we reflect on how 'advanced level' research can benefit from engaging with critical childhood studies. We turn to contemporary examples – the COVID-19 pandemic, Black Lives Matter, LGBTQ+ legislation and the climate crisis – affecting children today. In so doing we draw out why childhood studies topics, and the negotiation process involving them, matter. We hope this discussion offers a template of self-questioning and for engaging with these themes in relation to your own identities and work.

The conclusion is organized into three main themes. First, we review the fundamental idea that childhood is **socially constructed**, which has implications for policy and practice, and how those constructions and **knowledge production** in turn need to be challenged by **decolonization**. Second, we consider the implications of children's rights and **intersectionality**, particularly in light of contemporary examples. Third, we suggest the value of multi-level analysis to address complex problems such as violence against children. Such analysis can move beyond fixed concepts, theories and **disciplines**, as the last section concludes, to embrace the dynamism of our field and to be continuously reviewing, critiquing and debating.

Constructions of children and childhoods

An enduring theme in the book is how childhood studies sees children as social actors in their families, communities and society (see Chapter 2). In answering the question 'What is childhood studies?', Chapter 2 analyses emergent ideas that challenged the way 'mainstream' disciplines approached childhood. The Chapter interrogates the idea that childhood is **socially constructed** and connects that notion to debates around **materialism**, **agency**, **generational orders** and **childism/adultism**. In particular, the Chapter considers the implications of understanding childhood as a relational concept, variable to context, history, time and space. Specifically, it turns to decolonizing theory to problematize the imposition of developmentalism on children. Further, it critiques **global North** preoccupations with humans as the central defining category, hierarchically superior to other species and perceiving the non-human as inanimate material to be exploited.

Understanding childhood as socially constructed opens space to critique representations of childhood as potentially 'evil', 'innocents' and/or homogenous cultural groupings (James et al. 1998). Childhood studies allows us to examine the practical implications of these **discourses** for areas involving and impacting children. For example, such understandings are used to question the institutionalization processes around childhood. Prout (2000) challenges the explosion of early childhood centres, which can impose rigid control of early childhood time and space. Informal learning spaces for older children and **young people** have also faced constraints, with youth policies and funding directing these spaces towards evidencing academic and employability outcomes and control of antisocial behaviour – often replacing more informal, youth-led/designed or relational practices (Fusco et al. 2013; Denmead 2019). Both examples show how time and space for children are controlled by policies and practices, which in turn are propelled by particular constructions of and concerns for childhood.

Early childhood studies has flourished as a field in itself, drawing heavily from childhood studies; for example, early childhood studies builds on notions of children's agency and eschews processes of adultism when seeking to promote 'child-led', 'free flow', 'creative' and 'outdoor' play (Bruce et al. 2020). In turn, youth studies shares a symbiotic relationship with childhood studies, benefiting from the breaking down of the child–adult binary (Johansson and Herz 2019), discussions of time/space (Woodman and Leccardi 2015) and generationality (Woodman and Wyn 2015). These ideas help to expand on how younger and older children are discussed in relation to their learning spaces.

Applying these concepts, we see in both early childhood education and youth informal education that there is nothing natural to generational orders, as both involve pedagogies that can be very adult-led, very child-led or something quite different to this binary (Larson et al. 2005; Waters and Maynard 2010). In both spaces children are involved in collaborative meaning-making that balances the power relations between adults and children in ways that characterize all human beings involved in a setting/situation as learners. Yet, the Chapter 2 Commentary points out that traditionally children are subjected to greater regulation than adults and that regulation impacts on specific children in disproportionate ways. In fostering discussion on decolonization and **social justice** in childhood studies, our book invites you to question **universality** and to reflect critically on what modes we put forth as dominant. From this perspective, we understand that childhood studies approaches which reify and homogenize children's agency may be just as debilitating as adultist notions from psychology that perceive children's identities to be derived solely from parental or teacher-led **socialization**.

Similarly, in discussions concerning the funding of early years childcare and learning services, the 'materialist' idea that childhood is a crucial time in human life when productive 'future adults' are generated often trumps other ideas and here sociological concepts can be just as limiting as psychological ones (e.g. when children are confined to early years centres for 4.5 days a week or young people are subjected to normative values in community out-of-school provision that lack flexibility and awareness of anti-discriminatory practice (Davis and Milarvie Quarrell 2020; Prout 2000)). We should be concerned when investment in children's services becomes unchallengeable because it is believed to reap benefits at both the individual level (e.g. educationally) and the societal level (e.g. as 'an equalizer' to address poverty, malnutrition, morbidity, mortality, **gender** rights and inequality) (Davis and Hancock 2007, McNair et al. 2021). From this rigidity, early childhood curriculum and informal learning pedagogies become problematic when they are based in culturally **hegemonic** values, parachute in individualistic values from other countries and are imposed in a predefined and predetermined manner that overemphasize technical discourses and iron out childhood difference (see also Dahlberg et al. 1999; MacNaughton 2003). For example, the focus of 'quality indicators' based on culturally biased or ideologically laden discourse within early childhood education in India or youth development spaces in the United States reflects these concerns (Blaisdell et al. 2019; Davis and Milarvie Quarrell 2020; Fusco et al. 2013; McNair et al. 2021; Weiner 2019).

Chapter 2 concludes by questioning how Indigenous **ontologies** can be brought into our thinking with care and respect to different world views: for example, adopting **post-humanist** understandings of agency not as something to be possessed but as something that arises from the intra-connections between bodies as they make themselves known to each other (Myers 2019). The critique of global North preoccupations has recently been employed to challenge the imposition of child-development models of early years in nursery settings in India (Blaisdell et al. 2019), where dominant global North childhood discourses were parachuted into Indian early years provision in a manner that specifically set out to reject Indigenous knowledge (Aruldos and Davis 2015; Viruru 2001). Such prejudiced approaches to policy and practice raise questions concerning whose childhoods count? How can we counteract discrimination concerning Indigenous knowledge, history and pedagogy?

Chapter 3's consideration of how childhood studies fits with claims to **multi**-, **inter**- and **transdisciplinary** approaches furthers discussion on how we understand childhoods. The Chapter asks readers to consider the emotionality of debates between disciplines around childhood constructions in a manner that recognizes how the ambiguous nature of childhood studies leaves it open to exploitation when exported. We see this, for example, where reified notions of children's agency result in early years professionals becoming fearful of leading learning activities even when children request their involvement (Bruce et al. 2020) or when **young people's** activist goals are put at odds with the standardized youth development goals (Kwon 2013). These kinds of tensions help us question if concepts remain true to their founding positions during the exportation process. At the same time, these examples demonstrate our aim to encourage exploration of false **dichotomies** and to re-focus 'old' theory – it is not a nil sum game where the sociology of childhood wins and psychology loses, but rather a tricky balancing act where different theories have different usefulness in different contexts (see Chapter 6, for example, on the benefits of multi-level childhood psychology).

The takeaway is that theories, like us and like children, are not fixed entities. Theory adapts, develops and may be useful in one context and not so in another. We see several examples in this book of what can be lost if we stick to 'fixed' positions and perspectives. For instance, Chapter 3 helps to focus on what is gained/lost and held back/advanced in thinking through disciplinary lenses. Questioning whether childhood studies is a **paradigm** (with its own debates/conventions, ways of producing knowledge), a field (a looser connection of ideas and theories) or a discipline (which encapsulates different paradigms) promotes more flexible thinking in how those in childhood studies can utilize theory and disciplinary conventions in their work.

Interdisciplinary approaches are continually debated in respect to childhood studies (see Commentary Chapter 3), but reflecting on these ideas may help centre children in research and work (Burman 2019), carve opportunities for more **inclusive** childhood narratives to be created (Watson 2012) and enhance the flow of multiple **knowledges** from previously compartmentalized disciplines (Ramadier 2004). As discussed in Chapter 3, 'Working *across* and *with* multiple disciplines can open new perspectives and insights and is much needed in times of complex global problems' (89). Inevitable debate between fields can provide much-needed wisdom on contemporary childhoods and their challenges (see Chapter 3), and serious efforts to fully understand children's lives across the globe require living with and parsing out these tensions. Particularly in such contexts, it is important to recognize the intersectionality of the children involved – beyond the simplicity of providing a check box.

Children's rights, intersectionality and praxis

Chapter 4 addresses topics within children's rights including enforceability, universality and alternatives (e.g. **wellbeing** and **vulnerability**). The Chapter charts arguments for (and against) children's **human rights**, critiques their expression through international and regional human rights instruments and challenges the concepts and practices of children's rights. Questions arise on whether children's rights and childhood studies are seen as separate entities or synergistic fields.

A similar argument occurred between the 'disability movement' and disability studies in the 1990s; academics who recognized different types of social models of disability were criticized for watering down the 'materialist' usefulness of the 'traditional' social model. We can explain this in terms of disabled children's involvement in an early years setting. A materialist rights-based model of early childhood can be useful if it stimulates governments to provide universal early years services. However, once the funding is available for buildings and staff, disabled children will only benefit from accessing the service if the architect uses inclusive design that listens to children during the design process. Similarly, once in the building, more fluid and complex models of disability and childhood may be usefully employed when seeking to ensure a flexible enough setting so disabled children are enabled to interact with staff and other children in varied ways. Here we do not have to choose between different theories; rather, we seek to explore how different theories have different benefits in different contexts and in relation to different staff and pupils. Corker and Shakespeare (2002) suggest that context is everything when arguing that straightforward political narratives (e.g. the social/material model of disability) can act as a more readily available springboard for activism and that the skill is to introduce more questioning approaches without losing your non-academic audience. We have tried for a similar approach in this book.

Rights discourses have been challenged for failing to encompass all that is important for children and childhood (such as relationships, love and friendships), for being part of the neo-colonial project and for failing specific groups (e.g. Gypsy, Traveller and other communities that are 'on the move'). The translation of international legal standards into lived realities is a complex endeavour (Hanson and Nieuwenhuys 2012). Claims that the rights to education, protection, healthy development and non-discrimination have been fulfilled tell us little about *how* they have (supposedly) been fulfilled (Blaisdell et al. 2019). Having national policies on children's rights does not prevent local variation in outcomes and conceptual thinking (Davis et al. 2014; Meegan and MacPhail 2006). While international legislation and domestic policies have their place in terms of instilling standards, inspiring social norms and requiring change and accountability, rights equally must be realized in practice and, most importantly for our book, in the lives of children.

Later Chapters in our book pose questions about how we engender improved systems of inclusive, socially just and **anti-discriminatory** education (Chapter 5) and how we develop capacity building for coherent rights-based systems for local partners involved in interdisciplinary work (Chapter 6). At the centre of such developments is the quandary of balancing collective versus individual rights, especially given the tendency to individualism in the global North and more collective **cultures** in the **global South**. A transdisciplinary, decolonizing, inclusive and anti-discriminatory rights-based focus challenges top-down and **deficits-based** approaches and questions what transformative processes are required to enable change (Mitchell and Moore 2012). Such problems in context require you to develop a critical view of whether or not rights exist and their utility in practice.

Tensions arise when considering the universal claims of human rights. For instance, how participation rights might interfere/interact with protection sparks a potentially uneasy balance between **children's participation**, their best interests and their ability to exercise their rights even when at odds with their parents' rights. In the US context, contemporary examples around children's vaccination decisions, access to gender-affirming healthcare and education for LGBTQ+ children and the use of Critical Race Theory in schools highlight possible tensions between parents and children (Conner 2021; Hendrix et al. 2016; Temkin 2021). Indeed, attention to these topics has been condemned by select media and government outlets as a 'war on parents' (House GOP 2022; Shapiro 2022) and framed with language around 'parental rights' (Parental Rights in Education (CS/CS/HB 1557) 2022), with such rhetoric polarizing children's versus parents' rights in some contexts. Ensuring protection has also been placed at odds with young people's rights, with local governments instituting curfews in the name of defending them from (gun) violence (Rushing 2022; Wilson et al. 2016). In contrast, children's rights to participate are intricately tied with a concern for a 'right to life' in varied student organizing campaigns; for example, in young activists defending LGBTQ+ recognition in schools, utilizing Critical Race Theory in the context of Black Lives Matter and racial justice, calling for improved COVID-19 safety measures, and protesting for gun control (Conner 2021; Gomez 2022; Ruiz 2022; Siemaszko 2022).

Children's rights have also been critiqued on **post-structural** grounds for, at times, appearing inflexible when other concepts may have value due to their portability or cultural verisimilitude. Here we see the nature of current childhood social theory – every theory and approach is dependent on context and no approach will always work in the same way. When carrying out your work, you could pose questions about who is included in constructions, policies and practices of childhood – and who is not.

In this book there are several points in which we draw out alternatives to the founding theories and frameworks of the **'new' sociology of childhood**, with the Commentaries further broadening how we apply ideas from and across childhood studies. Chapter 5 and its accompanying Commentary detail the continued effects of the colonial past on the present childhood studies field. By illuminating the historical, colonial, sexist and discriminatory processes that have become commonplace when it comes to children (e.g. age and developmental stages), we can begin to reframe the 'foundations' of childhood studies less as canonical knowledge and more as produced knowledge that shows the traces of time and context.

The COVID-19 pandemic, both traumatic and catastrophic, has demonstrated that rights in the global North are often taken for granted (e.g. to education and/or play). Universally, children experienced school closures, reduced interactions with friends or more distant family members and severely limited access to public spaces. These are experiences that disabled and disadvantaged children were all too familiar with pre-pandemic. While divisions between groups in society have never been more obvious (Mude et al. 2021; Public Health England 2020; Yaya et al. 2020), this moment offers the potential to bring people together to foster complex, **integrated working** and thoughtful solutions that draw on intersectionality.

The book also highlights that many of the questions addressed by childhood studies are inherently interdisciplinary; for example, the entanglement of social and biological aspects in children's lives. In writing this book we could not have guessed how important this would become. The cultural, socio-economic, legal and environmental characteristics of climate change and global health challenges (e.g. the COVID-19 pandemic) require thinking across disciplines.

Drawing on decolonization arguments (see Chapter 2), Chapter 5 further raises questions about the global community and our positions in it. We are currently standing at a crossroads with choices to make concerning the societies we want to 'live' and 'be' in, and the extent to which we wish to build societies that:

- Recognize all people's capabilities.
- Appreciate our natural environment.
- Seek to eradicate poverty.
- Value equal access to land.
- Appreciate the things we (children and adults) can make with our hands.
- Challenge **neoliberal** ideas concerning sedentary living, individual ownership, wealth and status.
- Utilize the wisdom of all people.

As we go forward, post-COVID-19 pandemic, you will have opportunities in your own practices and work to ask: How do we enable an empathetic society? How do we avoid division, distrust and dissolution? Chapter 5 may serve as a guide by suggesting that intersectionality sits between critical analysis and social action. However, the Chapter also poses questions about how radical the concept becomes when it is 'whitened' during travel. The Chapter draws from **anti-racist** work that requires critical reflection on whiteness and its impact, including white privilege and how knowledge is understood, produced and communicated. The Chapter specifically asks you to consider the concept of **radical praxis**, which explores who is being included or excluded (see also Cologon et al. 2019). In so doing, it asks whether you are committed to processes of positive change while exploring the positional relationships between **hegemonic whiteness** research, policy and activism.

As a concept, intersectionality asks you to consider how societal barriers, discrimination and injustice stem from more than one single issue. The term 'intersectionality' covers examples where people's identities are not given credence in established thinking and writing. Racism, homophobia, class-based discrimination, sectarianism, exploitation of the poor and disability-discrimination can all stem from processes of institutional silencing.

When thinking about intersectionality in practical contexts, we find that discrimination is not always overt (Davis and Hancock 2007; Konstantoni and Emejulu 2017). For example, underlying inequalities might remain hidden in early years settings and resulting disadvantages of underlying inequalities may be both intentional and unintentional (Siraj-Blatchford 2010). Educational settings may assume celebratory discourses around 'diversity', which, if implemented without critical reflection, mute those differences and inequalities that should be challenged rather than celebrated (Kustatscher 2015). In turn, not all members of 'structurally oppressed groups' experience the same types of oppression in the same way because identities are multifaceted (Siraj-Blatchford 2010). Chapter 2 considers Pace-Crosschild's (2018) research on Indigenous child and family centres (Opokaa'sin), located in traditional Blackfoot country in present-day Western Canada, to discuss the rejection of imposed colonial values (such as patriarchy, women's labour, the nuclear family and capitalist ideas about children) to culturally reconnect with traditional Blackfoot language instruction, storytelling, music and elders' teaching. And, Chapter 5 argues that intersectionality can provide the tools to support a process of critical attention to, yet also **deconstruction** of, the various categories that come to constitute children and childhoods (Konstantoni and Emejulu 2017).

Although childhood studies is no different to other disciplines that have failed to challenge hegemonic whiteness, intersectionality and childhood studies share a commitment to deconstructing categories. To be true to intersectionality's origins and potential, childhood scholars who want to take intersectionality seriously need to go beyond using it as a theoretical or analytical framework and ensure that their work is aligned with emancipatory praxis and alliances that challenge intersectional inequalities in children's everyday lives.

Multi-level analysis: Embracing dynamism and the 'hidden' in your work

In the 1990s, childhood studies scholars were keen to critique rigid notions in sociology and anthropology that characterized childhood agency, culture and identity as only deriving from parental influences. In this book, we have built on these earlier criticisms to explore how children as themselves are situated in our practices and research. Ideas like materialism, rights, wellbeing and protection variably arise in the Chapters to speak to this. We see these ideas more generally as connected to childhood studies debates about agency, **embodiment** and change, which are undercurrents in every context.

Chapter 6 draws these themes to the forefront by posing questions about how conceptual and methodological resources from childhood studies support and challenge practice with children in a range of settings. The Chapter traces a multi-country research project addressing the **drivers** of violence (i.e. patterns of interpersonal violence) using **socio-ecological** systems theory of **child development** from psychology and the intersections of age, gender and power in childhood from sociology. The Chapter explains that drivers of violence – or the conditions in which violence occurs – are connected to larger structural and institutional factors and that most violence affecting children occurs in families, communities and schools. This suggests that a child's vulnerability and ability to protect themselves from violence changes over time with their evolving capacities. This notion, derived from child development, combines with the understanding that **risk and protective factors** for violence affecting children can be measured at individual, interpersonal and community levels.

The Chapter highlights that children's capacity changes over time and space. And yet, the Chapter moves beyond simplistic age/stage categories by illustrating that children are more than the combined effects of social structure and highlighting the embodied nature of violence and protection. We need to pay attention to children – rather than only adults/families – if we are to confront the violence to which children are subjected.

Children are products of external structural and institutional forces as much as individual, biological and cultural traits. Childhood exists in social spaces and places that are defined by law, politics, religion, economics and so on; further, the nature of childhood is further influenced by social class, generation, gender, **ethnicity** and so on. Yet, within such structures and institutes, simple acts of kindness, listening and understanding can offer children the biggest of all protection (the protection of sense of self) without huge expenditures. Throughout the book we have encouraged you to consider yourself as an active reader who can use this book to make a difference in your own practice and in the lives of others.

Chapter 6 raises a fascinating possibility. Working from a multi-layered, multi-discipline and multi-stakeholder approach, we can question modernist ideas about enlightenment, truth and economic imperatives that create a false dichotomy between structure and the individual. While there are exceptions, **child protection** systems overall face significant challenges protecting children from violence, exploitation, abuse and neglect. In its approach, the Chapter encourages using a balanced methodological approach that does not privilege a single method or perspective. Through its findings, Chapter 6 demonstrates that the structural determinants of violence – such as poverty, gender inequity or migration – are not as distant as they may appear from children's everyday existence. Combined, the Chapter encourages us to understand the tensions between individual, structural and cultural approaches to child protection and how to interpret them.

Just as Chapter 2 argues that there is no simple divide between the social and biological aspects of childhood, Chapter 6 encourages you to think about attempts to develop sophisticated child protection practice. The Chapter critiques rigid, socio-biological (e.g. age and stage of vulnerability) and material/structural concepts of child protection (e.g. in terms of explaining the local of vulnerability). It celebrates complexity when the analysis becomes more dynamic considering issues of gender, identity and power in ways that question binary assumptions. Studies in disability and childhood have critiqued the lack of a power, political and intersectional understanding of inclusion in ecological/Bronfenbrenner-type thinking. Ravenscroft and colleagues (2019), developing ideas from post-structural childhood studies and disability studies (see Davis and Watson 2002), argue that disabled children are often excluded from planning around inclusion. Such writing questions the power politics of structures around children that are often designed by adult/male 'expert' professionals (Davis et al. 2014; Ravenscroft et al. 2019).

In practice, intersectionality can also draw this critique to the foreground. Within the Te Whāriki-Early-Childhood-Curriculum in New Zealand – which seeks to give voice to and enshrine the place of Māori culture in early education – the concept 'whakamana' (translated in English as 'empowerment') requires that children's capacities are supported through listening, guiding and respecting (My ECE n.d.). This concept contrasts with notions of hierarchical control in which those above (e.g. adults) grant capacity on those below (e.g. children). The Te Whāriki curriculum's intersectional goals are that children's lives are understood holistically (e.g. the whole child; mind, emotions, creativity, history and social identity);

children's experiences are interconnected with the environment (e.g. outdoor play valued as meaningful learning); spontaneous play is recognized as important; children gain confidence in and control of their bodies; children learn strategies for active exploration, thinking and reasoning; and children develop working theories for making sense of the natural, social, physical and material worlds. These goals seem full of wisdom. Yet, no one approach is perfect – and barriers remain. For example, discrimination against Māori folk has not disappeared simply because New Zealand has a more culturally sensitive curriculum (Lee et al. 2013; Smith and May 2018). Not all aspects of the Te Whāriki curriculum were introduced in the manner originally agreed, and many teachers lack the necessary cultural or linguistic knowledge to promote the curriculum's key cultural meanings (Education Review Office 2018, Murata 2014). Emancipatory praxis requires us to grapple with the imperfections of the systems and contexts within which we find ourselves. With this book, we hope to encourage you to relate your and others' experiences and geographies when applying theory in policy, practice and research towards engaging in emancipatory praxis.

Conclusion

Here we have outlined how the Chapters in this book, as a whole, situate theory in both policy and practice, and how your experiences within and beyond academic scholarship can impact this process. We (the authors) have sought to introduce you to childhood studies as an academic field that has implications for change both in and beyond academia while recognizing that childhood studies can never be separated from the societies, times, contexts and spaces within which it is studied.

Throughout the textbook we ask readers to see dynamism embedded in what and how we study, research and practice, always acknowledging that children are each unique and ever-changing and that conceptions of childhood develop across temporal, geographical and other spheres. We recognize that disciplines appear fixed as we critique them and yet often produce new and varied ideas. As practitioners and researchers, we conclude that theory must be continuously reviewed, critiqued, built upon and debated. Doing so enables us to relocate children as the focal point of practice, theory and analysis within childhood studies and understand them as partners, collaborators and co-constructors.

Now that you are here, we welcome you to join us and push further. This book provides some of the preliminary steps: posing questions that draw contentions in childhood studies to the forefront; asking you to engage reflexively with what these debates mean to you, your practice and research; and considering how your **positionality** colours the theories and concepts you engage with. From here, we pose the need to reflect on these debates and take action in your own work – be that your practice, research, teaching, activism or policymaking. We wish you well in your journey as you continue to learn and explore in this space.

References

Aruldos, A. and Davis, J. M. (2015), 'Children's Rights and Early Years Provision in India', in A. B. Smith (ed.), *Enhancing Children's Rights: Connecting Research, Policy and Practice*, 95–107, Basingstoke: Palgrave Macmillan.

Blaisdell, C., Davis, J. M., Aruldoss, V., and McNair, L. (2019), 'Towards a More Participatory Fulfilment of Young Children's Rights in Early Learning Settings: Unpacking Universalist Ideals in India, Scotland and the EU', in J. Murray, B. Blue Swadener, and K. Smith (eds), *The Routledge International Handbook of Young Children's Rights*, 395–405, London: Routledge.

Bruce, T., McNair, L., and Whinnett, J. (eds) (2020), *Putting Storytelling at the Heart of Early Childhood Practice: A Reflective Guide for Early Years Practitioners*, London: Routledge.

Burman, E. (2019), 'Child as Method: Implications for Decolonising Educational Research', *International Studies in Sociology of Education*, 28 (1): 4–26.

Cologon, K., Cologon, T., Mevawalla, Z., and Niland, A. (2019), 'Generative Listening: Using Arts-based Inquiry to Investigate Young Children's Perspectives of Inclusion, Exclusion and Disability', *Journal of Early Childhood Research*, 17 (1): 54–69.

Conner, J. O. (2021), 'Critical Race Theory Sparks Activism in Students', *The Conversation*. Available online: http://theconversation.com/critical-race -theory-sparks-activism-in-students-162649 (accessed 20 June 2022).

Corker, M. and Shakespeare, T. (eds) (2002), *Disability/Postmodernity: Embodying Disability Theory*, London: Continuum.

Dahlberg, G., Moss, P., and Pence, A. (1999), *Beyond Quality in Early Childhood Education and Care: Languages of Evaluation*, London: Routledge.

Davis, J. and Hancock, A. (2007), *Early Years Services for Black and Ethnic Minority Families: A Strategy for the Children and Families Department*, Edinburgh: University of Edinburgh/City of Edinburgh Council.

Davis, J., Hill, L., Tisdall, K., Cairns, L., and McCausland, S. (2014), *Social Justice, the Common Weal and Children and Young People in Scotland*, The Jimmy Reid Foundation. Available online: http://reidfoundation.org/wpcontent/uploads/2014/03/Childhood1. pdf (accessed 15 May 2017).

Davis, J. and Milarvie Quarrell, C. (2020), 'Irish Diaspora and Sporting Cultures of Conflict, Stability, and Unity: Analysing the Power Politics of Community Development, Resistance, and Disempowerment Through a Case Study Comparison of Benny Lynch and "The Glasgow Effect"', in R. Phillips, M. Brennan, and T. Li (eds), *Culture, Community, and Development*, 124–46, New York: Routledge.

Davis, J. and Watson, N. (2002), 'Countering Stereotypes of Disability: Disabled Children and Resistance', in M. Corker and T. Shakespeare (eds), *Disability/Postmodernity: Embodying Disability Theory*, 159–74, London: Continuum.

Denmead, T. (2019), *The Creative Underclass: Youth, Race, and the Gentrifying City*, Durham and London: Duke University Press.

Education Review Office (2018), 'Awareness and Confidence to Work with Te Whāriki', 12 July. Available online: https://ero.govt.nz/our-research/awareness-and-confidence-to-work-with-te-whariki-2017 (accessed 13 June 2022).

Fusco, D., Lawrence, A., Matloff-Nieves, S., and Ramos, E. (2013), 'The Accordion Effect: Is Quality in Afterschool Getting the Squeeze?', *Journal of Youth Development*, 8 (2): 4–14.

Gomez, M. (2022), 'As Student Activists Fight for COVID Safety Measures at Schools, Some Face Criticism', *Los Angeles Times*, 27 January. Available online: https://www.latimes.com/california/story/2022-01-27/students-are-organizing-for-increased-safety-measures (accessed 30 June 2022).

Hanson, K. and Nieuwenhuys, O. (2012), 'Living Rights, Social Justice, Translations', in K. Hanson and O. Nieuwenhuys (eds), *Reconceptualizing Children's Rights in International Development: Living Rights, Social Justice, translations*, 3–26, Cambridge: Cambridge University Press.

Hendrix, K. S., Sturm, L. A., Zimet, G. D., and Meslin, E. M. (2016), 'Ethics and Childhood Vaccination Policy in the United States', *American Journal of Public Health*, 106 (2): 273–8.

House GOP (2022), 'Biden's War on Parents', *House Republicans*, 18 January. Available online: https://www.gop.gov/bidens-war-on-parents/ (accessed 14 June 2022).

James, A., Jenks, C., and Prout, A. (1998), *Theorizing Childhood*, Cambridge: Polity Press.

Johansson, T. and Herz, M. (2019), 'The Theoretical Landscape of Youth Studies', in T. Johansson and M. Herz (eds), *Youth Studies in Transition: Culture, Generation and New Learning Processes*, 11–28, Cham: Springer International Publishing.

Konstantoni, K. and Emejulu, A. (2017), 'When Intersectionality Met Childhood Studies: The Dilemmas of a Travelling Concept', *Children's Geographies*, 15 (1): 6–22.

Kustatscher, M. (2015), *Exploring Young Children's Social Identities: Performing Social Class, Gender and Ethnicity in Primary School*, Edinburgh: The University of Edinburgh.

Kwon, S. A. (2013), *Uncivil Youth: Race, Activism, and Affirmative Governmentality*, Durham and London: Duke University Press.

Larson, R., Walker, K., and Pearce, N. (2005), 'A Comparison of Youth-driven and Adult-driven Youth Programs: Balancing Inputs from Youth and Adults', *Journal of Community Psychology*, 33 (1): 57–74.

Lee, W., Carr, M., Soutar, B., and Mitchell, L. (2013), *Understanding the Te Whariki Approach: Early Years Education in Practice*, London: Routledge.

MacNaughton, G. (2003), 'Eclipsing Voice in Research with Young Children', *Australasian Journal of Early Childhood*, 28 (1): 36–43.

McNair, L. J., Blaisdell, C., Davis, J. M., and Addison, L. J. (2021), 'Acts of Pedagogical Resistance: Marking out an Ethical Boundary Against Human Technologies', *Policy Futures in Education*, 19 (4): 478–92.

Meegan, S. and Macphail, A. (2006), 'Inclusive Education: Ireland's Education Provision for Children with Special Educational Needs', *Irish Educational Studies*, 25: 53–62.

Mitchell and Moore (eds) (2012), *Politics, Participation & Power Relations: Transdisciplinary Approaches to Critical Citizenship in the Classroom and Community*, Leiden: Brill.

Moore, K., Hanckel, B., Nunn, C., and Atherton, S. (2021), 'Making Sense of Intersecting Crises: Promises, Challenges, and Possibilities of Intersectional Perspectives in Youth Research', *Journal of Applied Youth Studies*, 4 (5): 423–8.

Mude, W., Oguoma, V. M., Nyanhanda, T., Mwanri, L., and Njue, C. (2021), 'Racial Disparities in COVID-19 Pandemic Cases, Hospitalisations, and Deaths: A Systematic Review and Meta-analysis', *Journal of Global Health*, 11: 05015.

Murata (2014), '[New Zealand] Overview and Recent Issues of New Zealand Early Childhood Education Curriculum (Te Whāriki)', July 18. Available online: https://www.childresearch.net/projects/ecec/2014_04.html (accessed 13 June 2022).

My ECE (n.d.), 'Te Whariki – What Is This Early Childhood "Curriculum" That ECE Services Are Required by the Ministry of Education to Follow?', *My*

ECE. Available online: https://www.myece.org.nz/educational-curriculum
-aspects/106-te-whariki-curriculum (accessed 13 June 2022).

Myers, C. (2019), *Children and Materialities: The Force of the More-than-
Human in Children's Classroom Lives*, Singapore: Springer Nature Singapore.

Pace-Crosschild, T. (2018), 'Decolonising Childrearing and Challenging the
Patriarchal Nuclear Family Through Indigenous Knowledges', in R. Rosen
and K. Twamley, (eds), *Feminism and the Politics of Childhood: Friends or
Foes?*, 191–200, London: UCL Press.

Parental Rights in Education, CS/CS/HB 1557 (2022), Available online: https://
www.myfloridahouse.gov/Sections/Bills/billsdetail.aspx?BillId=76545.

Prout, A. (2000), 'Childhood Bodies: Construction, Agency and Hybridity',
in A. Prout and J. Campling (eds), *The Body, Childhood and Society*, 1–19,
London: Palgrave Macmillan.

Public Health England (2020), 'Disparities in the Risk and Outcomes of
COVID-19', 2 June. Available online: https://www.gov.uk/government
/publications/covid-19-review-of-disparities-in-risks-and-outcomes
(accessed 12 June 2022).

Ramadier, T. (2004), 'Transdisciplinarity and Its Challenges: The Case of Urban
Studies', *Futures*, 36: 423–39.

Ravenscroft, J., Davis, J., Bilgin, M., and Wazni, K. (2019), 'Factors That
Influence Elementary School Teachers' Attitudes Towards Inclusion of
Visually Impaired Children in Turkey', *Disability & Society*, 34 (4): 629–56.

Ruiz, R. (2022), 'How Florida's "Don't Say Gay" Bill Turned Students Into
Activists', *Mashable*, 30 June. Available online: https://mashable.com/article/
dont-say-gay-florida-young-lgbtq-activists (accessed 30 June 2022).

Rushing, E. (2022), 'Philly Likely to Set a 10 p.m. Curfew for Minors This
Summer Under New Council Bill. Experts Say It's "Pointless"', 16 June.
Available online: https://www.inquirer.com/news/philadelphia/philadelphia
-curfew-summer-2022-minors-20220616.html (accessed 17 June 2022).

Shapiro, B. (2022), 'The War on Parents Continues', *The Daily Signal*,
23 February. Available online: https://www.dailysignal.com/2022/02/23/the
-war-on-parents-continues/ (accessed 14 June 2022).

Siemaszko, C. (2022), 'Students Stage Walkouts Across U.S. to Protest Texas
School Massacre', *NBC News*, 26 May. Available online: https://www
.nbcnews.com/news/us-news/students-stage-walkouts-us-protest-texas
-school-massacre-rcna30735 (accessed 30 June 2022).

Siraj-Blatchford, I. (2010), 'Learning in the Home and at School: How Working
Class Children "Succeed Against the Odds"', *British Educational Research
Journal*, 36 (3): 463–82.

Smith, A. and May, H. (2018), 'Connections Between Early Childhood Policy
and Research in Aotearoa New Zealand: 1970s–2010s', in M. Fleer and
B. van Oers (eds), *International Handbook of Early Childhood Education*,

Springer International Handbooks of Education, 531–49, Dordrecht: Springer.

Temkin, D. (2021), 'Policies That Discriminate Against LGBTQ Students Are Not Aligned with Child Development Research', *Child Trends*, 28 April. Available online: https://www.childtrends.org/blog/policies-that-discriminate-against-lgbtq-students-are-not-aligned-with-child-development-research (accessed 14 June 2022).

Viruru, R. (2001), 'Colonized Through Language: The Case of Early Childhood Education', *Contemporary Issues in Early Childhood*, 2 (1): 31–47.

Waters, J. and Maynard, T. (2010), 'What's so Interesting Outside? A Study of Child-initiated Interaction with Teachers in the Natural Outdoor Environment', *European Early Childhood Education Research Journal*, 18 (4): 473–83.

Watson, N. (2012), 'Theorising the Lives of Disabled Children: How Can Disability Theory Help?', *Children and Society*, 26: 192–202.

Weiner, L. (2019), 'Invisible Alternatives: The Shaping Effect of Quality Discourse in Philadelphia's Afterschool Youth Development Sector', MPhil diss., University of Cambridge.

Wilson, D. B., Gill, C., Olaghere, A., and McClure, D. (2016), 'Juvenile Curfew Effects on Criminal Behavior and Victimization: A Systematic Review', *Campbell Systematic Reviews*, 12: 1–97.

Woodman, D. and Leccardi, C. (2015), 'Time and Space in Youth Studies', in J. Wyn and H. Cahill (eds), *Handbook of Children and Youth Studies*, 1–14, Singapore: Springer.

Woodman, D. and Wyn, J. (2015), *Youth and Generation: Rethinking Change and Inequality in the Lives of Young People*, London: SAGE Publications Ltd.

Yaya, S., Yeboah, H., Charles, C. H., et al. (2020), 'Ethnic and Racial Disparities in COVID-19-related Deaths: Counting the Trees, Hiding the Forest', *BMJ Global Health*, 5 (6): 1–5.

Glossary

To note that certain of these concepts are contested in the literature and these contentions are discussed further in the relevant Chapters. If a concept is contested, here we provide a working definition for this book.

Term	Definition
adultism	societal negative prejudice against children (akin to sexism, racism or anti-Semitism)
agency	the capacity to choose, act and influence matters; to 'make a difference'
anti-discriminatory	an approach to prevent discrimination for personal characteristics (e.g. age, gender, marital status, pregnancy, disability, race, religion or belief, sex, sexual orientation)
anti-racism	the practice or policy of identifying, addressing and opposing racism
assemblages	a concept developed by Deleuze and Guattari, highlighting how the connectivity between different entities creates complex new meanings
autonomy (autonomous)	the liberty to follow one's own will and to make choices, often considered a component of self-determination
biopolitics	politics relating to the administration of the population, often associated with the work of Foucault
Black feminist thought	a critical social theory based in knowledge and perspectives of Black women, building on Hill Collins' and other seminal scholars' thinking to resist intersectional oppression
Bronfenbrenner's ecological systems theory	a socio-ecological theory which draws on the premise that an individual's social environment influences their development
child as method	an analytical and methodological framework developed by Burman, which centres and simultaneously deconstructs children and childhoods in research, policy and practice

(*Continued*)

Term	Definition
child development	drawing from developmental psychology, an age and stage-based way of thinking about childhood; critiqued in childhood studies for inherent assumptions which may universalize or colonize particular constructions of childhood
child protection	systems to assess and treat cases of violence against children and establish procedures towards prevention and reduction of violence against children
childhood	generally accepted to be the first period in the human lifespan, understood differently depending on geographical, cultural and historical contexts
childhood studies	an interdisciplinary scholarly field dedicated to the critical interrogation of childhoods and children's lives in research, policy and practice
childism	deconstructs adultism and reconstructs social norms to be inclusive of children
children's geographies	a sub-discipline of human geography, closely related to childhood studies, with a focus on place and space in children's lives
children's participation	ongoing processes between children and adults, based on mutual respect and in which children learn how their views and those of adults have been considered in decision-making (according to the UN Committee on the Rights of the Child)
children's rights commissioners	a children's rights institution – ideally with statutory standing, powers and independent from government – that monitors, promotes and protects children's human rights
commodification of knowledges	the process of turning knowledges, for instance, Indigenous knowledges, into commodities for profit
counter-hegemonic praxis	a practice that involves identifying, addressing and opposing power imbalances through collective action
critical realism	a pool of philosophical theories that distinguish between the 'real' world (which cannot be observed and exists independently from human perceptions, theories and constructions) and the 'observable world' (which can be understood if people consider the structures that generate events in the observable world)

Term	Definition
culture	socially, contextually and historically situated beliefs, norms, customs, identities and habits
decolonization	a practice that aims to challenge and undo historical and ongoing processes of colonialism, with a focus on intellectual, emotional, economic and political reversal of colonial injustices; in childhood studies, can additionally refer to deconstructing dominant models of childhood and promoting exploration of children's varied positionalities with the ongoing influences of colonialism and racism
deconstructionism (deconstructionist)	in childhood studies, a philosophical stance which argues that childhood/children are only formed through discourse and thus do not have a material existence
deficits-based approach	an approach which emphasizes children and young people as risks or problems requiring intervention; in opposition to strengths-based, an approach which emphasizes children and young people's strengths and the ability to build on these characteristics
developmental life course	how children grow and change as they move through childhood and into adolescence
dichotomy (dichotomies)	a set or assumed contrast between two things (i.e. binary categories); in childhood studies, examples include 'human beings' versus 'human becomings', and childhood versus adulthood
discipline	broadly, a field of study or shared branch of knowledge which is constituted by ongoing processes of discourse and boundary making
discourse	refers to how, through language, knowledge is thought about, communicated and constituted
drivers (in relation to violence)	institutional and structural factors that create conditions in which violence is more or less likely to happen
duty-bearer	all those who must respect, promote and fulfil human rights and abstain from human rights violations
early childhood	the first period of children's lives, often described from birth until five (and sometimes eight) years of age
early intervention	addressing a perceived problem (such as health or educational inequalities) at an early stage of the issue and/or the life course

(Continued)

Term	Definition
embodied (embodiment)	a recognition that bodies are not only biological entities but also socially and culturally constructed, and sites of discipline and differentiation
epistemic (or cognitive) justice	a kind of justice that explores how knowledge is understood, produced and communicated in relation to power, and accordingly assumes that knowledge is value-laden and not neutral
epistemology (epistemological)	the philosophical study of the nature of knowledge; for instance, an epistemology of childhood asks, 'What is childhood? How can we know about childhood?'
feminist post-structuralist theory	a branch of feminist theory drawing on post-structuralist thought, particularly interested in discursive constructions of (gender) identity, subjectivities and power
genealogy	the tracing of a concept's histories and meanings, from its origins to changing understandings in different locations and times
gender	commonly understood to describe the socially constructed roles that men and women inhabit in society; biological and socialization theories emphasize binary understandings of gender (female/male) while post-structuralist and queer theories challenge binaries and gender norms
General Comments (from the UN Committee on the Rights of the Child)	authoritative interpretations of the UNCRC, which can elaborate on particular UNCRC articles or children's rights issues
generational order (generationing)	social ordering through age-based social categories (e.g. children as a social category)
global North (or Global North)/global South (or Global South)	denotes how different countries in the Northern and Southern hemisphere are commonly grouped together in terms of their socio-economic and political histories and contexts; critiqued as a euphemism for previous, more value-laden terms (e.g. 'developing/developed countries') and for obscuring colonial legacies
hegemonic (hegemony)	the dominance or authority of some groups or ideas over others, often legitimized through particular social and cultural norms
hegemonic whiteness (white hegemony)	a system in which 'whiteness' is reflected in dominant (often unnamed) social practices and is unexplored or not challenged, thus impacting individual and societal power to benefit 'whiteness'

Term	Definition
human becomings versus human beings	theoretical debate around how children are constructed; as 'human becomings', children are predominantly understood as future adults, whereas as 'human beings' children are seen as social actors in their present
human rights	rights that are inherent to all human beings, recognizing and protecting their human dignity; such rights apply to how people live in society and with each other, often enshrined in international human rights law
immanent	something that is existing within; inherently part of something
informed assent	process of ethically informing and gaining permission of research participants who are not able to provide legal consent (e.g. based on age)
informed consent	process of ethically informing and gaining permission of people to be research participants
inclusion (inclusive)	an environment in which everyone, regardless of identities, abilities and differences, is valued, respected and able to participate
integrated working (integration; integrated approach)	in childhood studies, refers to different supports for a child working in tandem to positively impact the child
interdisciplinary (cross-disciplinary, multidisciplinary, transdisciplinary)	the drawing on knowledge and views of diverse disciplinary fields, such as childhood studies foundations in sociology, anthropology, human geography, children's rights studies, philosophy, cultural studies and history; debates around these terms are not settled but explore how different disciplines can work alongside or with each other with differing degrees of synthesis of approaches and knowledge
intergeneragency (inter-generational relations)	a term which emphasizes both generational and agency aspects in the relations between children and adults
interest theories of rights	rights exist because people have interests, and these interests are necessary for human survival and flourishing; often contrasted to will theories of rights
intersectional (intersectionality)	critical theoretical framework and praxis connoting the impact of interrelated social categories (e.g. gender, race, class) in relation to marginalization and power

(Continued)

Term	Definition
intra-generagency (intra-generational relations)	a term which emphasizes the interplay within generations in relations between members within the same generation (e.g. between children)
knowledges	the plural form of 'knowledge' recognizes that there is more than one type of knowledge; typically used in pluralist, feminist, post-structuralist and decolonial perspectives
knowledge production	the ways in which knowledge(s) are produced: that is, created and understood by individuals and society
legal rights	rights that are stated in law; in contrast to moral or natural rights, which are not always stated in law
liberal theory of rights	argues for individuals to have rights, typically on the basis of individuals being autonomous and rational
living rights	rights that people have, shape and experience in their daily lives, which give them meaning in context
Majority/Minority World	a way of grouping countries (similar to global North/South), which recognizes that the 'majority' of population and landmass is located in Africa, Asia and Latin America; aims to move away from the privileging of minority/global North perspectives in global research
maltreatment (violence against children)	physical, sexual, emotional abuse and neglect against children
materialism (or materiality)/ new materialism	a philosophical approach which recognizes that relationships and meanings are grounded in physical 'matter' and which rejects dichotomies such as nature/culture
moral (or natural) rights	rights that are asserted but are not necessarily stated in law nor always legally enforceable; in contrast to legal rights which are stated in law
multiple childhoods	the idea that there is not a singular concept of childhood
negative (or libertarian) rights	rights not to be interfered with by the state or others, unless for exceptional and justifiable reasons: for example, civil and political rights, such as liberty, the right to own property and freedom of expression
neoliberal (neoliberalism)	an ideology based on free markets, privatization and laissez-faire policies

Term	Definition
'new' sociology of childhood	an area of social sciences that grew in the 1990s, that emphasized childhood as a social construction, children as social actors and that childhood and children were worthy of research study
normative	deriving from or establishing particular social standards or norms (e.g. behaviours)
ontology (ontological)	theory on nature of being; for instance, an ontology of childhood asks, 'How do we know what childhood is?'
Optional Protocols of the UNCRC	additions to the UNCRC, which are separately ratified by Member States
paradigm	a set of truths/practices which are accepted as 'normal' within a discipline; in methodological literature, associated particularly with debates on qualitative versus quantitative approaches to knowledge production
positionality	the impact of an individual's subjectivities (e.g. field, geography, identities, epistemology) upon their perspective
positive (or protection) rights	rights that require the state or others to act or provide something: for example, the right to an adequate standard of living or the right to education
post-humanism	a theoretical position that aims to decentre the human and rejects dualisms (e.g. mind/body, nature/culture) (see also materialism/new materialism)
post-structuralism	a philosophical approach emphasizing how relations of power come to construct what is seen as truth, identity or structures
praxis (radical praxis)	refers to the enactment of theories and ideas, with a focus on action and process
protagonismo or protagonism (English)	a prominent concept in Latin American childhood studies literature, recognizing children as proactive social actors in their communities and societies and having competence and a sense of autonomy
psychoanalytical	a theory and therapeutic practice, originating in the work of Freud, which places importance on unconscious mental processes
Queer theory	a critical social theory that deconstructs gender binaries and norms and challenges inequalities associated with them

(*Continued*)

Term	Definition
race/ethnicity	terms often used to describe people's identities based on histories, culture, language, nationality or religion; the concept of race derives from long disproved theories around biological or physical traits but retains a close link with skin colour, whereas ethnicity is often seen as self-identified and emphasizes social and cultural belonging
racialization	the process of ascribing racial identities to individuals or groups of people which oftentimes leads to stereotyping, discrimination and social exclusion and bringing ideas around different races into existence
ratification (of UNCRC)	when a United Nations' Member State ratifies a Convention and becomes a 'State Party' committed to protecting, respecting and fulfilling the rights contained within that Convention and to holding themselves accountable before the international community
reconceptualist movement	childhood studies movement emerging in the 1990s with a focus on challenging regulatory discourses, particularly about early childhood; drew on feminist, decolonial and post-structuralist perspectives
reflexivity	a theoretical and methodological approach in social research that recognizes and makes transparent the researcher's impact on their research focus, design and findings
risk and protective factors (of violence)	factors that reflect the likelihood of violence occurring due to individual, interpersonal and community level characteristics
safeguarding	to protect a child's health, wellbeing and rights, enabling them to live free from harm, abuse and neglect
social actor	an individual who undertakes a social action, thus expressing agency and competence
social construction of childhood	a theoretical approach to understanding how children and childhood are seen; particularly emphasizing childhood as a relational concept, variable to context, history, time and space
social constructionism	theoretical paradigm which sees reality and knowledge as constructed through discourse
social constructivism	theoretical paradigm which sees reality and knowledge as constructed within individuals

Term	Definition
social justice	as conceptualized by Honneth, a person's right to be treated with regard/care, to be entitled to legal rights and to be recognized as having attributes and strengths
socialization	theory of development which articulates how individuals internalize societal norms and ideologies
socio-ecological framework	a critical tool for understanding how environmental factors influencing an individual interact within and between a number of physical, social, political and economic levels
structural (or systemic) inequalities	inequalities which disadvantage groups of people and are created and replicated through institutions and societal structures
Sustainable Development Goals (SDGs)	seventeen goals which form the core of the 2030 Agenda for Sustainable Development
United Nations Convention on the Rights of the Child (UNCRC)	international law passed by the United Nations Assembly in 1989, which addresses the economic, social, cultural, civil and political rights of children
universalize (universality)	to assume that particular ideas apply across different contexts
vulnerability	according to Fineman, a universal and inevitable condition of being human because beings are embodied and dependent on others
wellbeing	the combination of feeling good and functioning well, for individuals or societies, involving both objective and subjective judgements
will theories of rights	rights exist to protect individual will (i.e. individual freedoms, liberties and autonomy) as long as such rights do not violate others' rights; often contrasted to interest theories of rights
young people/youth	a later period in the life of children, often associated with ages 12–18 or 12–25

Index